FOR KING & COUNTRY AT LOOS

2nd Lieutenant Charles Francis Burgoyne Hodgins (1895–1915).

FOR KING & COUNTRY AT LOOS

THE TALE OF 2/LT CHARLIE HODGINS IN WORLD WAR I

PETER JACOBS

Greenhill Books

For King & Country at Loos
First published in 2025 by
Greenhill Books,
c/o Pen & Sword Books Ltd,
George House, Unit 12 & 13,
Beevor Street, Off Pontefract Road,
Barnsley, South Yorkshire S71 1HN

www.greenhillbooks.com
contact@greenhillbooks.com

Print ISBN: 978–1–78438–952–9
ePub: 978–1–78438–953–6
Kindle: 978–1–78438–954–3
PDF: 978–1–78438–955–0

CIP data records for this title are available from the British Library

The Publisher's authorised representative in the EU for product safety is Authorised Rep Compliance Ltd, Ground Floor, 71 Lower Baggot Street, Dublin D02 P593, Ireland.
www.arccompliance.com

Edited and designed by Donald Sommerville
Typeset in 11/13.5 pt. Adobe Caslon Pro

Printed and bound in the UK by CPI Group (UK) Ltd,
Croydon, CR0 4YY

Contents

Acknowledgements

Books such as this would not be possible without the help of others. First, I would like to thank my friend Richard Black for making me aware of Charlie's archive. Without that first connection this story would have remained untold. I would also like to thank the staff at The National Archives for their help and cooperation over many years. Thank you, too, to Tony Fields, the Manager at the Rifles (Berkshire and Wiltshire) Museum in Salisbury, for his help with my early enquiries, and Lesley Koulouris, the Archivist at Berkhamsted School, for her help and hospitality during my visit to the school. From that visit I was able to contact Janice Boakes and Jenny Sherwood at the Berkhamsted Local History & Museum Society who helped me find out where Charlie had lived during his time at the school, and so I would like to say, 'Thank you ladies for your help.' And thank you also to Francy Puthussery for his continuous interest in the book.

I am also grateful to the Commonwealth War Graves Commission, particularly Paul Davis who was able to tell me where Charlie's remains were eventually found. It was like putting the final piece of a jigsaw in place. And I would like to thank my colleagues at the Western Front Association in Lincoln for sharing their knowledge with me during the past couple of years. Without the help of all these people, and many others during my visits to France, this book would not have been possible. And while mentioning my visits to France, I would like to thank my daughter, Rebecca, for accompanying me on my travels over the years and for sharing my enthusiasm for military history, as well as taking many photographs, some of which are included in this book. I must also thank my wife, Claire, for putting up with losing me to my study for hours on end, days at a time, over many, many years.

Finally, I would like to thank Michael Leventhal and all at Greenhill Books for giving me the opportunity to tell Charlie's story.

Introduction

As an author and keen military historian, I am always looking for a previously undiscovered story. And so, when my good friend Richard Black, a leading dealer of specialist British military items, showed me the First World War medals of 2nd Lieutenant Charlie Hodgins and the associated archive of letters, photographs, telegrams, and other bits and pieces, I was instantly drawn to what had been put in front of me. I could see the collection included a bronze memorial plaque named to Charlie, which meant, sadly, that he had died, but other than that I knew nothing about him.

Having purchased the collection, I set about finding out more. At first, I simply wanted to research Charlie's time on the Western Front, but the more I read the many letters he had sent home, and the telegrams and newspaper articles following his death, the more there was to find out. There was a story to tell, but it was unfortunately one that was typical of so many tales of the First World War.

My research took me to the former battlefield in northern France where Charlie had died. Once one of the most important coal-mining regions in France, the natural chalk landscape and industrial wasteland defines this region like no other, but I was sad at the thought of just how much slaughter took place in this small parcel of land. For the Loos battlefield on its opening day, which is where this story takes us, is mostly contained within an area now bounded by the D166 and D943 roads in the west, to the D947 to the east, while the D941, which runs parallel to the Canal d'Aire (known to the British in 1915 as the La Bassée Canal), effectively marks the northern-most part of the British advance, and Loos-en-Gohelle[1] the south. A circular route connecting Vermelles–Loos-en-Gohelle–Hulluch–

1. Not to be confused with the nearby commune of Loos (a suburb of Lille). The battle gets its name from Loos-en-Gohelle.

Auchy-les-Mines–Vermelles, is about fifteen miles and today takes only around half an hour to drive. Within this small space, a great many people died.

Piecing together the last moments of someone's life can be an emotional experience: even now, more than a hundred years later. Charlie's short life came to a tragic end many miles from his family and home. Fortunately for us, though, to help piece Charlie's story together, his father had kept everything relating to his son during the First World War – his medals, his letters, photographs, the telegrams, and the newspaper articles following Charlie's death. Collectively, these all help to tell the story. And with access to war diaries, other official records and personal accounts, I have been able to put Charlie's letters into context. We can now better understand what he was doing at the time and what was happening elsewhere. But please note, when quoting from an original source, whether it is from one of Charlie's letters or elsewhere, I have left the wording, spelling and grammar as written at the time. Charlie naturally uses imperial units of measurement in his writings and I follow his example in my text.

So, this is the story of Charlie Hodgins. It is not only a story of personal courage, but it is symbolic of what so many families suffered during the First World War. And that is the point. It is not a tale of someone who went on to become a national hero. This is a young man, still in his teens, who has volunteered to do his bit, who has left his home, his family, and the surroundings familiar to him and gone off to fight in a war in a country he has never seen. And, like many others, he never returned. Charlie Hodgins is just one of many thousands who lie in cemeteries along what was once the Western Front.

Chapter One

Made of the Right Stuff

Eight miles to the north of Arras in northern France is Souchez, a small commune in the Pas-de-Calais department in the Hauts-de-France. A small river, the Souchez, a tributary of the Deûle, flows peacefully through its centre and, with an expanding population now of around 2,500, things have changed in the 100-plus years since the guns fell silent on the Western Front. The church of Saint-Nicolas was soon rebuilt, as was most of the area, and then in 1932 the Basilica de Notre-Dame-de-Lorette, designed by the renowned French architect Louis Marie Cordonnier, was built overlooking Souchez. In the wake of the widespread destruction in this part of France, it was Cordonnier who took the lead in rebuilding civic buildings and local churches in the traditional style.

Just to the south of Souchez, alongside the D937 leading to Arras, is the Cabaret Rouge British Cemetery. Immaculately maintained by the Commonwealth War Graves Commission, the cemetery takes its name from a small, red-bricked, red-tiled café that stood close to the site in the early days of the First World War. After the café was destroyed by shellfire, Commonwealth troops began burying their dead there. Then, with the war over, the cemetery was enlarged, and for much of the twentieth century it remained an open cemetery, meaning that any newly discovered remains of fallen servicemen in that region were taken there for burial. Today, Cabaret Rouge contains over 7,650 burials of the First World War, over half of which remain unidentified. Many headstones have the words 'A Soldier of the Great War' and 'Known Unto God' above and below a Christian cross. And even when there is a name, a regiment, a rank or a date of death on a headstone it can be all too easy to glance briefly and move on. There are simply too many headstones to take in the details of each one. But behind each name there is a story to tell.

More than a century has now passed since the cemetery's early days, but Cabaret Rouge looks as peaceful and tranquil now as it surely always has. And Cabaret Rouge is important for this story because amongst the endless rows of headstones is one marking the burial plot of 2nd Lieutenant C. F. B. Hodgins of the Wiltshire Regiment, shown as having died on 25 September 1915. So, who was he and why is he buried in the Cabaret Rouge British Cemetery in northern France? What happened on 25 September 1915 that resulted in him losing his life? How old was he and where was he from? What did he look like and what was the impact on his family when they found out he had been killed? There were so many questions to ask, and the answers took some finding out, but just like all those to have fallen in the First World War his story deserves to be told. For, as it turned out, Charlie Hodgins was one of a lost generation who died for King and Country at Loos.

* * *

In life and death, timing is everything and no date is more fundamental than the era of one's birth. For example, those born in the early years of

Charlie Hodgins was born into an Army family. His father, Charles (*standing far right behind his men*) was an officer in the Royal Artillery and had served with the Hazara Field Force in the Black Mountain Expedition during 1891.

the twentieth century were fortunate enough to be too young for service in the First World War. They would spend their early adult years in the roaring 1920s. But for those born even five years earlier fate offered a much different prospect. Their generation was called upon, quite literally, to serve King and Country during the horrors of war. One of that generation was Charles Francis Burgoyne Hodgins, known as Charlie, who was born in Dover on 12 June 1895.

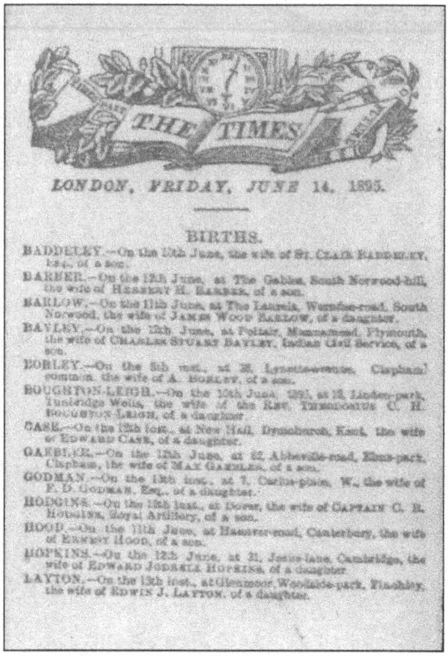

THE TIMES

LONDON, FRIDAY, JUNE 14, 1895.

BIRTHS.

BADDELEY.—On the 12th June, the wife of St. Clair Baddeley, Esq., of a son.

BARBER.—On the 12th June, at The Gables, South Norwood-hill, the wife of Herbert H. Barber, of a son.

BARLOW.—On the 11th June, at The Laurels, [illegible]-road, South Norwood, the wife of James Wood Barlow, of a daughter.

BAYLEY.—On the 12th June, at [illegible], [illegible]-road, Plymouth, the wife of Charles Stuart Bayley, Indian Civil Service, of a son.

BORLEY.—On the 8th inst., at [illegible], [illegible], Clapham-common, the wife of A. Borley, of a son.

BOUGHTON-LEIGH.—On the 10th June, [illegible], at [illegible], Linden-park, Tunbridge Wells, the wife of the Rev. Theodosius C. H. Boughton-Leigh, of a daughter.

CASE.—On the 12th inst., at New Hall, Dymchurch, Kent, the wife of Edward Case, of a daughter.

GAMBLES.—On the 12th June, at 62, Abbeville-road, Elms-park, Clapham, the wife of Max Gambles, of a son.

GODMAN.—On the 13th inst., at 7, Carlos-place, W., the wife of F. D. Godman, Esq., of a daughter.

HODGINS.—On the 12th inst., at Dover, the wife of Captain C. R. Hodgins, Royal Artillery, of a son.

HOOD.—On the 11th June, at Hanover-road, Canterbury, the wife of Ernest Hood, of a son.

HOPKINS.—On the 12th June, at 21, Jesus-lane, Cambridge, the wife of Edward Jodrell Hopkins, of a daughter.

LAYTON.—On the 13th inst., at Glenmoor, Woodside-park, Finchley, the wife of Edwin J. Layton, of a daughter.

The Times, dated 14 June 1895, announcing the birth of Charlie at Dover on the 12th. (*Cantuar Photo Co., Bromley, Kent*)

With its roots in Ireland, the Hodgins family had since become a well-connected one in Canadian social and professional circles. Charlie's father, Charles Richard Hodgins, was born in Toronto in 1863. He was the third son of Thomas Hodgins, a leading Anglo-Irish lawyer, Master in Chancery and a Judge of the Admiralty Division of the Supreme Court of Toronto, and Millicent Burgoyne (née Scoble), who was English and the daughter of John Scoble, who had been an anti-slavery campaigner and politician in Canada West. Rather than choose a career in law or politics, Charles would instead opt for the military. He attended the Upper Canada College in Toronto and then entered the Royal Military College of Canada at Kingston, Ontario, in September 1881 at the age of eighteen. Four years later Charles was commissioned into the British Army, as a lieutenant in the Royal Artillery.

After qualifying as an instructor at the School of Army Signals in Aldershot, Charles served in India with the 9th Mountain Battery and while he was in India he met and married Aimée Gertrude Burgess, the eldest daughter of an army colonel. The couple were married in Bengal in January 1891 and their first son, Richard Douglas Scoble Hodgins, was born in Khadki (then known as Kirkee), Bombay, at the end of the year, when Charles was the assistant superintendent of Ordnance Factories at Khadki and Kanpur (Cawnpore). During 1891 Charles also served with the Hazara Field Force in the second Black Mountain Expedition, conducting operations against the Hussanzais and Akazais.

Charlie's parents, Charles and Aimée, pictured in 1894 at their home in Sunderland where their second son, Arthur, was born.

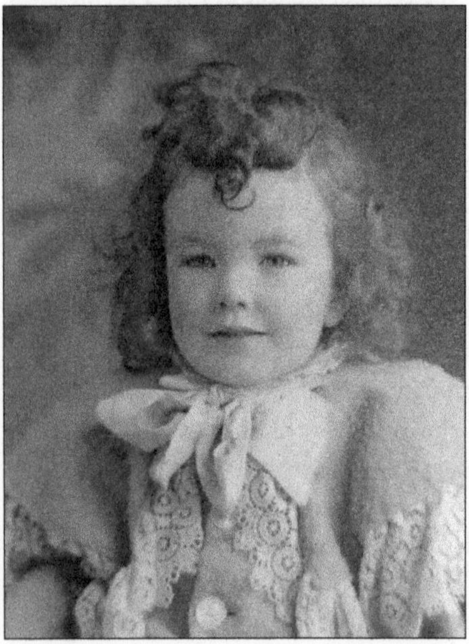

The earliest photograph of Charlie in the archive, probably taken in early 1897.

After returning to Britain, the couple's second son, Arthur, was born in Sunderland in 1894. By the time Charlie was born the following year, Charles was a captain and the adjutant of the Cinque Ports Artillery Volunteers based in Dover. The threat of a French invasion in 1859 raised the enthusiasm for part-time army volunteers, and to augment the Royal Artillery several coastal artillery corps formed along the Kent and Sussex coast – the ancient Cinque Ports – and soon brought together as the Cinque Ports Artillery Volunteers. Two years later came John, also born in Dover and known to the family as Jack. There was a fifth son, Horatio, also born in Kent, who sadly died within a year of birth at the turn of the century, and finally came Patrick, born in 1903, who would be too young to serve in the First World War.

By the time Patrick was born, Charles had spent three more years overseas, this time in Sierra Leone where he raised and commanded a battery of West African Field Artillery. He then returned to Britain once more, for further training at the Army Ordnance College before being appointed to a position with the Royal Arsenal at Woolwich.

The Hodgins boys had been born into the itinerant army way of life. The family were now living in Hyde Vale near Woolwich and were able to stay there the following year when Charles became the chief ordnance officer at the Royal Dockyard, Woolwich, on promotion to the rank of major. His next posting was to be overseas, this time to the Straits

Settlement at Singapore. Charles and Aimée, however, decided that their boys needed stability and an education in England, so rather than the whole family moving out east, Aimée and the boys set up home in Berkhamsted, Hertfordshire, so that the four older boys could attend the school there.

Three generations of the family pictured in 1903. *From left to right:* Charles, Richard (his oldest son, also known as Dick), and Charles's mother, Millicent.

Berkhamsted School was founded in the mid-sixteenth century by John Incent, Dean of St Paul's Cathedral, at a time when senior clergy often established and supported schools. When the Hodgins boys arrived there in 1906 the school had expanded significantly since its early days though, for more than 300 years, the Old School House had been its only building. Now the school included a new chapel, a bursar's block, boarding houses, and a swimming pool, all in the centre of the town between Castle Street and Mill Street. But the school was far from finished. The Headmaster, the Reverend Thomas Fry, now in his seventeenth year at the helm, had more elaborate plans for the development of the school, which included the building of more boarding houses and classrooms.

The South African War at the turn of the century had also provided a boost to the already flourishing national institution of army volunteers. Officers' Training Corps and Cadet Corps were being introduced into universities, public schools and grammar schools (all of these being male-only at this time), to attract and train pupils to become future army officers; the belief was that because the boys were from the upper classes, they had been born to lead. Not only that, but the so-called 'better schools' possessed the three top ingredients needed to cultivate the English warrior-gentleman – sport, a patriotic curriculum and chapel. Many Old Berkhamstedians had fought against the Boers and the school now had a link with a company of the Hertfordshire Rifle Volunteers, which led to a Cadet Corps being set up at the school. The school roll had now passed 400, nearly three times the size of the school when Fry had taken over. The town of Berkhamsted was growing and more was being done to increase the number of day boys at

By the time the Hodgins boys arrived at Berkhamsted in 1906, the Headmaster, Thomas Fry, was in his seventeenth year in charge. Fry (*seated centre*) is pictured with his staff. (*Berkhamsted School*)

A science laboratory at Berkhamsted School, around the time the four Hodgins brothers were pupils. Boys – and masters – in this photo were of a generation that would soon be called upon by their country in war. (*Berkhamsted School*)

the school, which included the Hodgins brothers.

And so, it was against this backdrop that the four Hodgins boys arrived at Berkhamsted School with their father on 21 March 1906. The four were the only admissions on that date. As to how long they might be there, none of them knew. It might be one year or maybe two, but probably no longer than that.

With their father having gone overseas, the Hodgins boys lived with their mother in a house called Bryntirion on Cross Oak Road, less than a mile's walk from the school. As day boys they were under similar rules to the boarders. The younger boys were put into the Juniors. They were allowed to meet their older siblings during school hours, but they were taught separately. Subjects included English composition, English literature, elementary science, mathematics, history, geography, modern languages and Latin. Outside the classroom there was sport – football, cricket and athletics – whilst away from the playing fields there was also swimming, gymnastics and tennis. There was also the school chapel, with the day boys encouraged to join the school choir and attend morning and afternoon service. The Bible was taught to all.

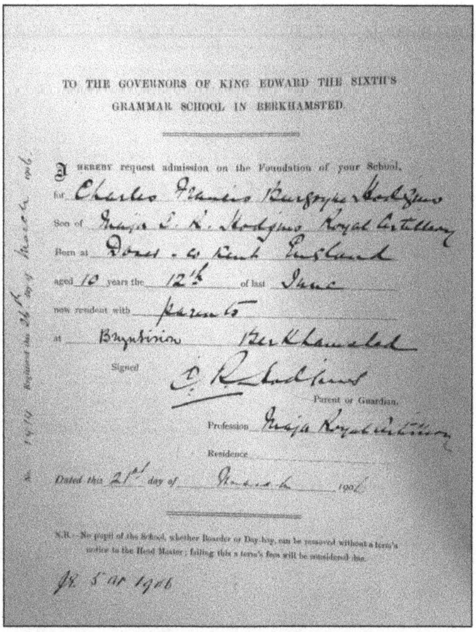

TO THE GOVERNORS OF KING EDWARD THE SIXTH'S
GRAMMAR SCHOOL IN BERKHAMSTED.

I HEREBY request admission on the Foundation of your School,
for Charles Francis Burgoyne Hodgins
Son of Major C. R. Hodgins Royal Artillery
Born at Dover ... Kent England
aged 10 years the 12th of last June
now resident with parents
at Bryntirion Berkhamsted
Signed
Parent or Guardian.
Profession Major Royal Artillery
Residence
Dated this 21st day of March 1906

N.B.—No pupil of the School, whether Boarder or Day-boy, can be removed without a term's notice to the Head Master; failing this a term's fees will be considered due.

School Register dated 21 March 1906, showing Charlie's admission. There are similar entries for Richard, Arthur and John. (*Berkhamsted School*)

For all young boys growing up in the early twentieth century, school days would shape and even influence their future life. Boys grew up quickly; they had to. Fry had resuscitated Berkhamsted, and the Hodgins brothers were fortunate to be amongst the generation of boys who were to benefit from his vision, personal drive, and utter dedication to the school. Europe would soon be at war and young boys like the Hodgins brothers would soon be joining their school masters when called upon to serve King and Country.

The four oldest Hodgins boys left Berkhamsted in the summer of 1908. Interestingly, the school records show nothing against their names, suggesting that none of them excelled at sport nor were part of the Cadet Corps during their time at the school, which is surprising when their father

While Charlie continued his education in England, his father was sent to serve overseas. Charles (*seated centre*) is shown here in Ceylon in 1910 while commanding a detachment of the Army Ordnance Corps. Charles and his fellow officers wear black armbands, probably mourning the death of Edward VII.

was an army officer. Although Charlie and John were too young to join the cadets, Richard was fourteen when he arrived at the school and sixteen when he left, and Arthur was just a couple of years younger than that. It might have been because they knew they were not to be at the school for long that neither of the older boys became part of the cadets.

With their father to remain overseas, having now been posted to a detachment of the Army Ordnance Corps in Ceylon and India, it was decided that Aimée and the youngest boy, Patrick, would join him. This would leave Arthur, Charlie, and John to complete their education in Britain, while Richard sailed for Canada to live with Charles's oldest brother, Percy, in Toronto, first to attend college there after which Richard would accept a position in a bank.

One of the earliest letters to have survived in the Hodgins archive is from Percy to Charles senior. It is addressed to Major C. R. Hodgins at the Ordnance Office in Ceylon and dated 17 December 1909. In addition to the brotherly and general family chat, the letter includes a few lines about Richard, who by now was known to the family as Dick:

> I suppose Dick has kept you posted in the family news, though I know he does not write as often as he should. He has settled down at home and says he isn't a bit homesick, which is a comfort. He seems to like his work at the bank and is very conscientious about it. I only wish he wrote a bit more. I have advised him to take some writing lessons. He is also not exactly slow, but very deliberate and you cannot hustle him, which is rather a drawback in a bank, but he will probably get over that in time. He ought to make up his mind within the next year as to what he intends finally to do. I would not recommend any boy to stay in a bank longer than a few years just to get a business training. He is a very bright and intelligent lad and ought to do well, but he is like the Hodgins in that he is young for his age. All the Hodgins develop late in life. If there is anything you would like Dick to take up you might let me know as he ought to have plenty of time to study up in the evenings.

A poor-quality image from 1910 but it shows Charlie (*right*) with his younger brother John.

Arthur, Charlie, and John, meanwhile, had become boarders at the United Services College, which had moved from its original location at Westward Ho! to St Mark's in Windsor a few years before. The college had been founded some forty years earlier to prepare sons of military officers for careers in the armed forces. With the rest of their family overseas, the college and Windsor thus became home for the three brothers. The 1911 Census shows all three boys boarding there at the ages of seventeen, fifteen, and fourteen.

With his time overseas finally up, Charles returned to England with Aimée and Patrick. He had not long left to serve and so he decided to see out his army career in Britain, while his family settled in Canada ahead of him returning to his homeland on retiring from the army. On 7 September 1912, the Hodgins family – Charles, Aimée, and the four boys – sailed from Liverpool on the passenger steam ship SS *Canada* of the British Dominion Line, their destination Montreal. Charlie, then aged seventeen, was off to live in Canada.

Even if the First World War had not come along, Charlie might well have followed in his father's footsteps and gone into the army. Not only was his father in the army, but his uncle, Arthur Edward Hodgins (Charles's older brother), was also a graduate of the Royal Military College in Canada and an artillery officer. The army was in the Hodgins' blood and having been educated at Berkhamsted and the United Services College, and with his father a major, Charlie was certainly made of the right stuff. Then the assassination of Archduke Franz Ferdinand, the heir to the Austro-Hungarian throne, in Sarajevo on 28 June 1914, triggered a catastrophic chain of events. A series of mobilisations and declarations of war followed, with Germany invading neutral Belgium. Britain then issued an ultimatum to Germany to withdraw or face war, and when the Germans failed to comply Britain declared war on Germany.

When Europe went to war in August 1914, Charlie, having just turned nineteen, was thousands of miles away in Canada, living with his mother and brothers on the family farm in Granville Ferry in Nova Scotia. Charles, now in his early fifties and still in England, was soon to retire from the army and was due to join them. That, however, would have to wait.

Chapter Two

For King and Country

Granville Ferry is situated in Annapolis County, on the northern bank of the Annapolis River, in the Canadian Province of Nova Scotia. Once a major shipbuilding centre in the golden age of sail and the northern terminus for ferries crossing the river, this small community has little more than a hundred people in the present day. Back in 1914, though, Granville Ferry was Charlie's home, and it was on the family's remote farm called Pembroke that he spent the early days of the First World War.

Life on the farm brought arduous work. The weather turned in mid-August that year and there followed three weeks of heavy rain, delaying the hay-making and cutting of the barley. Charlie was not entirely happy with how things were turning out on the farm, as he explained in a letter dated 9 September 1914 to his father, then living in Woolwich Common, just a short walk from Woolwich Arsenal:

> My Dear Father
>
> Still no news of you except that vague telegram to begin packing. None of us understood it or to who it was referred. We all supposed it was to mother. I suppose you have got a good billet in London, and is the London Arsenal the same thing as Woolwich Arsenal?
>
> I have quite found out now the impossibility of working this farm with the present hands, and I have fully made up my mind that if I am to stay on here in your place some change must be made as I find out more and more. With Arthur it is a case of he looks on me as a younger brother and it is beneath his dignity to do as I ask. [With] the weather being too dull to hay I said to the boys we will go through the roots and pull up by hand all the weeds (which are tolerably thick and commencing to seed) such as skunk tail grass, cadlock, cooch and several others. I then

got on to culling some cabbages and seeing Jack I called him to get a bath of water and some salt. Arthur was seen going down to the garden. My job took me an hour and when I had done at about 10.30, I looked around. No Arthur so I walked around to find him. This went on till 11. Then I saw him furiously hacking with a hoe between the mangels. Down I come, no Jack so off I go and find him in the workshop sharpening a hoe. I told him he would not want one. 'Oh, Arthur's using one', so I convinced him Arthur was of no account and at 11.30 I assembled all hands on the field. 'Arthur' say I. 'I said to hand weed thus, it is not safe to use a hoe.' No notice. 'Arthur, get to the end of a row and start hand weeding!' No notice. My request was repeated. He turned round and looks at me. Again, my request. "Which row?' says he. 'Any row' say I. 'Which row?' again. 'Any row, the third row now if you like.' All this time he goes on hacking with his hoe to the utmost peril of the root crops around him. 'Stop that, will you Arthur and hand weed.' No answer. 'If you don't stop, I will tell you to go away because I consider a hoe dangerous to the roots!' Still no response but continues hacking. 'Arthur, go away. I would rather do without you. A hoe is more dangerous and not so thorough as hand weeding or come to the end of a row and start to weed.' Here he again stops. 'Which row?' says he. 'Any row!' say I. 'Which row?' again, 'any row!' By this time, I was getting angry. He returned to his hoeing. So, I was furious. I said to him 'I will get mother to order you off.' But mother was in her bedroom and heard the latter part of it. She told Arthur to hand weed as I said. He then pretended he did not understand me and said to mother 'If you will ask that cursed young fool to explain.' But mother made him hand weed. Now this is as near as I can remember an honest account, and the only reason I tell is to let you know how I am getting on and mind you this is not the first occurrence of this kind, there are lots, in fact, daily occurrences. With Jack, he thinks himself too big to be told what to do. Mother thinks that I could get along with Arthur but not with Jack, but I would take two Jacks to one Arthur and that's saying a good deal.

Charlie's letter goes on to update his father on the rest of the farm – about the apples, barley, cows, and chickens, and how bad the weather had been, which meant the hay was not yet in. The letter ends:

> I could write a lot more, but it has gone ten. I am afraid this is a rather complaining letter, but I must let you know. I have put up with quite a lot lately. I must say goodbye now and good luck. We hope to hear from you soon.
>
> Ever your loving son, Charlie
>
> P.S. Mother is having some trouble with the servants lately and Clara is giving herself tremendous airs. There will be an earthquake here if it goes on, or I won't be here!

It is the earliest letter in the Hodgins archive written by Charlie. The letter refers to a telegram from his father telling them to begin packing, but as the letter says they were confused about who the instruction was for. Charles was expecting to remain in Britain for as long as the war lasted, but who was he saying should leave Canada to be with him? The boys assumed it was their mother, but what about them? The letter otherwise seems to be little more than a sibling spat, although why Charlie felt he could boss Arthur around is not known, but Charlie clearly wanted to share with his father what was happening on the farm, not that there was much his father could do about it! What is surprising, though, is the letter makes no mention of the war. It does not even refer to what extent his father might become involved, nor is there any mention of the recruiting hype that was going on in Canada at that time.

It was not as if there was nothing happening, far from it. In Europe, the British Expeditionary Force, the BEF, had already crossed the Channel and had fought at Mons before having to retreat towards Paris, fighting rear-guard actions along the way. At the time Charlie was writing his letter the British were holding the Germans at the River Marne and would soon be advancing towards the Aisne.

It would take time, of course, for news to reach remote parts of Canada, such as Glanville Ferry, but clearly, as far as Charlie was concerned, the war in Europe seemed a million miles away. However, as part of the British Empire, Canada was also at war with Germany, though Canada had no real military forces – only an army of around 3,000 men and a small navy. There were also part-time militia units and many English-speaking Canadians had strong ties with Britain. Since there was therefore plenty of support for the war, the Canadian Government offered Britain a Canadian Expeditionary Force of 25,000 men to serve as a division under British command. The response across Canada was as it was in Britain at that time. Some 33,000 volunteers came forward, more would follow, many of them members of the militia and veterans of the South African War, with the

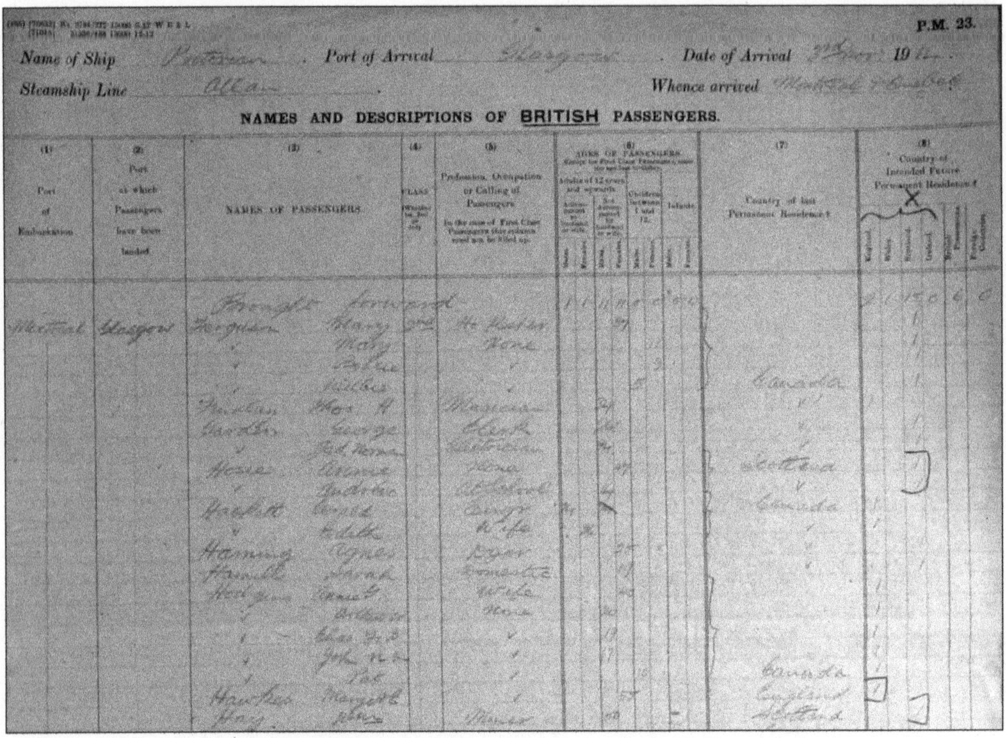

P.M. 23.

Name of Ship Pretorian . Port of Arrival Glasgow . Date of Arrival 191

Steamship Line Allan . Whence arrived Montreal & Quebec

NAMES AND DESCRIPTIONS OF BRITISH PASSENGERS.

The passenger list for the SS *Pretorian* taking the four Hodgins boys and their mother to Glasgow in November 1914.

first contingent, the 1st Canadian Expeditionary Force, sailing for Britain in late September on board thirty-two troop-carrying ships, escorted by seven warships of the Royal Navy, and landing at Plymouth on 16 October.

With Charles still in England and Europe at war, the Hodgins family decided they should be together. It was what Charles had meant in his telegram. Not only that, but Charlie had become frustrated with life on the farm, so too his brothers. They wanted to do their bit for King and Country. They might have volunteered for the CEF, but with connections to the British Army through their father, they decided to respond to Britain's call for young men of 'good general education' between the ages of seventeen and thirty, and who were former cadets of the universities, colleges, and schools, to whom a temporary commission in the Army might be given. And so, Aimée was to sail to Britain with the four boys. She would look after Patrick, while the older boys went off to war. Dick, meanwhile, was already in England. After living with his uncle in Canada, he had left the bank and travelled out east to join his parents where he joined the Ceylon

Planters Rifle Corps at the age of eighteen and then the South India Mounted Rifles. When the rest of the family sailed for Canada in 1912, Dick stayed in the east. Then, following the outbreak of war in Europe, he returned to Britain and went straight to the Royal Military Academy at Woolwich from where he would soon be commissioned into the Royal Field Artillery.

In late October 1914, Aimée and her four sons sailed for Britain on board the SS *Pretorian* of the Allan Shipping Line, arriving in Glasgow on 3 November. For Charlie Hodgins, it was his first step to war.

Chapter Three

The Wiltshires

When Britain went to war in 1914 its regular army was small by European standards of the time, a mere 250,000 strong, but highly trained. Even with the Territorials and other reserves that could be called upon, the army could muster fewer than 750,000 men. The German Army was five times larger, and so Britain's Secretary of State for War, Lord Kitchener, called for volunteers.

Kitchener had set his sights on expanding the British Army by 500,000 men. For the infantry regiments these volunteers would make up new battalions, called Service Battalions, raised from the tens of thousands of volunteers streaming into the recruiting offices across the country in response to the call to arms. The first 100,000 volunteers recruited into these Service Battalions were to form the First New Army, known as K.1, which was to consist of six divisions. But because of the overwhelming number of volunteers, a second New Army, K.2, also of six divisions, was raised and then a third, K.3, of the same size. Initially, there was a shortage of uniforms and equipment and there were no military barracks for the men to use, and so the volunteers trained for war wearing whatever clothes they had and practised with whatever they could find. Tweed suits, flat caps and broom handles were seen on parade in every city and town.

By the end of 1914, the optimistic idea that the war would be over by Christmas had been shown to be nonsense. The BEF was in effect no more, having suffered around 90 per cent casualties. Towns such as Mons and Ypres, and rivers such as the Marne and the Aisne, had already been cemented into the history of the British Army. A Christmas truce was about as good as it got on the Western Front, when soldiers on both sides sang traditional festive songs, played mouth organs, and shouted seasonal greetings across what had become known as no-man's land. Men stood up, walked around. Some socialised their enemies while others helped bury their dead. In many places not a shot was fired. Some even played football.

It was cold, and misty along large sectors of the front, and the ground was hard, but it was Christmas. And there was not much activity in the days that followed. The mobile war seen during the early weeks of conflict had now stalled into something of a stalemate as both sides settled down to static trench warfare. New officers were needed as soon as possible to replace those killed, wounded or taken as prisoners of war.

For a young man with the right background, like Charlie, it was not overly difficult to secure a commission in the British Army at that early stage of the war. An officer was a gentleman in those days and comparatively few men were commissioned from within the army ranks. Those volunteering from the lower classes would usually go straight into the lower ranks. This imbalance changed dramatically during the war to the point that almost half of newly commissioned officers in 1918 were from working- or lower middle-class backgrounds. But, for now, most new commissions during the early months of the war went to those young men with a 'good general education' who had come from what was considered to be the right family background.

By January 1915, Charlie was at the Royal Military College, Sandhurst, in Berkshire. For more than a hundred years the college had been responsible for training infantry and cavalry officers for the British and Indian Armies. During the First World War, officers either graduated with a regular commission, for those who saw the army as a career, or a temporary commission for those who intended to be officers only for the duration of the war. There was also the Special Reserve for those who were to be full-time officers for the duration of the war, but who would then go on to the Reserve list once hostilities were over from which they could be called upon in the future should they ever be required. Officers for the Royal Artillery and the Royal Engineers, meanwhile, were trained at the Royal Military Academy, Woolwich, and it would not be until after the Second World War that the two training establishments would merge at Sandhurst to provide officer training for all arms across the service. And so Charlie's enrolment at Sandhurst meant that he was to take a different path into the army than the rest of his family who were commissioned into the artillery. Whether it was his personal choice not to join the artillery or whether it was in response to the army's needs at the time is not known, but Charlie was destined for the infantry instead.

By the time Charlie arrived at Sandhurst the training course had been reduced from the eighteen months it had been before the war to just three months, simply because of the high casualty rate on the Western Front. The high demand for officers meant there were several intakes going through

Sandhurst at the same time. These were spread across different companies for the purpose of training. Charlie was put into 'F' Company. He was accommodated in the room next to one of his physical fitness instructors, 33-year-old Basil Maclear, a former Irish rugby international who had been capped eleven times before the war. Now he was a captain in the Royal Dublin Fusiliers and on the staff at Sandhurst.

The drastic reduction in training time meant that all the academic content of the pre-war course had been taken out. The cadets were, however, taught the reasons for how the war had come about. This was to give them a better understanding of the current political situation in the world and the international relations between the different nations. Cadets needed to understand why they were fighting, and if they understood why they were fighting then they could, as officers, pass on their knowledge and wisdom to the men under their command. But just about all the time at Sandhurst was dedicated to practical military training. This included drill, musketry, horsemanship, digging trenches, and practising combat manoeuvres in the surrounding countryside, with practice trench raids often taking place at night. One cadet company would attack a position as another defended, with flares and fake bombs used to add a touch of realism. At the end of the exercise everyone would stand up, brush themselves down and go back to camp, although the cadets would find out all too soon that the reality of war was quite different.

It was important for the training at Sandhurst to be based on the enemy's strategies and tactics that had been witnessed so far during the early months of the war, some of which was documented in the training manuals for the cadets to read. In a manual titled *Notes From the Front*, collated by the General Staff and dated 1914, it states:

> The following points are particularly emphasized in all reports received from the front:-
>
> 1. The importance of constant practice in digging at night. It is considered that actual practice in supplying food and ammunition to men in the trenches at night would be very useful training.
> 2. The necessity for scrupulous care of rifles in order to ensure their smooth working during rapid fire.
> 3. The need for impressing upon young officers the fact that one of their first and most important duties is to look after the comfort and well-being of their men at all times, and that it

must be a point of honour to do so before thinking of their own needs.

4. The importance of inculcating the doctrine that the temporary exposure of a flank owing to a local success on the part of the enemy should be looked upon as an occasion for counter-attack and not for withdrawal. Proper measures to watch the flanks should be taken and men should be held ready to counter-attack if a flank is threatened, but the idea that a withdrawal is always justified merely because a flank is temporarily turned should never be permitted to take root. It should be a point of honour with all officers to carry through any task confided to them without asking for reinforcements.
5. The necessity for careful training in wood and village fighting, especially the latter; attention is directed to Sections 141–146, Infantry Training, 1914.

The manual goes on to include sections on Cavalry, Artillery, Divisional Signal Companies, Infantry, Entrenched Positions, Army Service Corps, and Billeting. In the Infantry section, when reporting on German infantry, it states:

> Our infantry has proved itself superior in every respect to that of the enemy. The shooting of the German infantry is poor, and the men will not face the bayonet. Unless they are supported by a superior artillery fire, they have no chance against British infantry either in attack or defence.

The section also includes a paragraph on German machine guns:

> The German guns are usually posted singly or in pairs and frequently wait for an opportunity for surprise by opening fire with great effect at close range. The enemy display great skill in posting machine guns on a flank so as to bring enfilade fire to bear on the attacking troops [. . .] Machine guns are easily put out of action by artillery fire; great care is therefore necessary in selecting positions for our own machine guns, and in occupying them without attracting attention.

The manual also features comments from a staff officer at the front, which include:

1. The Germans usually attack about 3 p.m. or at dusk, and then entrench during the night within 200 yards of our lines; they

also take advantage of fog in the early morning. They make a little progress occasionally in this way, but it is slow work and they have lost enormously. They shoot badly with the rifle, and nearly all the damage is done by artillery fire and machine guns.

2. As far as our infantry is concerned, there is never any difficulty about seeing the target. Fire is seldom opened at greater ranges than 500 yards, and when the Germans come on in close formation rapid fire at 200 and 300 yards causes enormous casualties in their ranks. Fire direction and control has been, therefore, a simple matter and the value of elaborate training in these matters has not been apparent.
3. Cover from view has become more important than field of fire. It is better to have a field of fire of 100 yards and to be invisible, than to have one of 600 yards and to be an easy target for artillery.
4. Owing to the enemy's artillery fire by day, digging is nearly always done at night, and this requires much practice. Some sort of rough cover from shrapnel and head cover are added if time allows, and also if they can be made without making the trench conspicuous.
5. The principal subjects of training required by infantry are, in order of importance:
    a. Entrenching, especially in the dark.
    b. Rapid fire.
    c. Cover from view of artillery for the trenches.
    d. Bringing enfilade fire to bear on the enemy's trenches wherever possible.
    e. Skilful use of machine guns. Infantry must be careful when advancing that an enemy's machine gun is not hidden on the flank ready to open enfilade fire. Some regiments have lost very heavily from being caught in this way.

About a third of Charlie's training at Sandhurst was dedicated to trench warfare. The war might have been in its early months, but it had already become apparent that trench warfare was there to stay. The general line of an entrenched position was determined by the strategical or tactical situation with the exact line of defence to be occupied determined by a detailed reconnaissance of the ground. The teaching was that whenever possible,

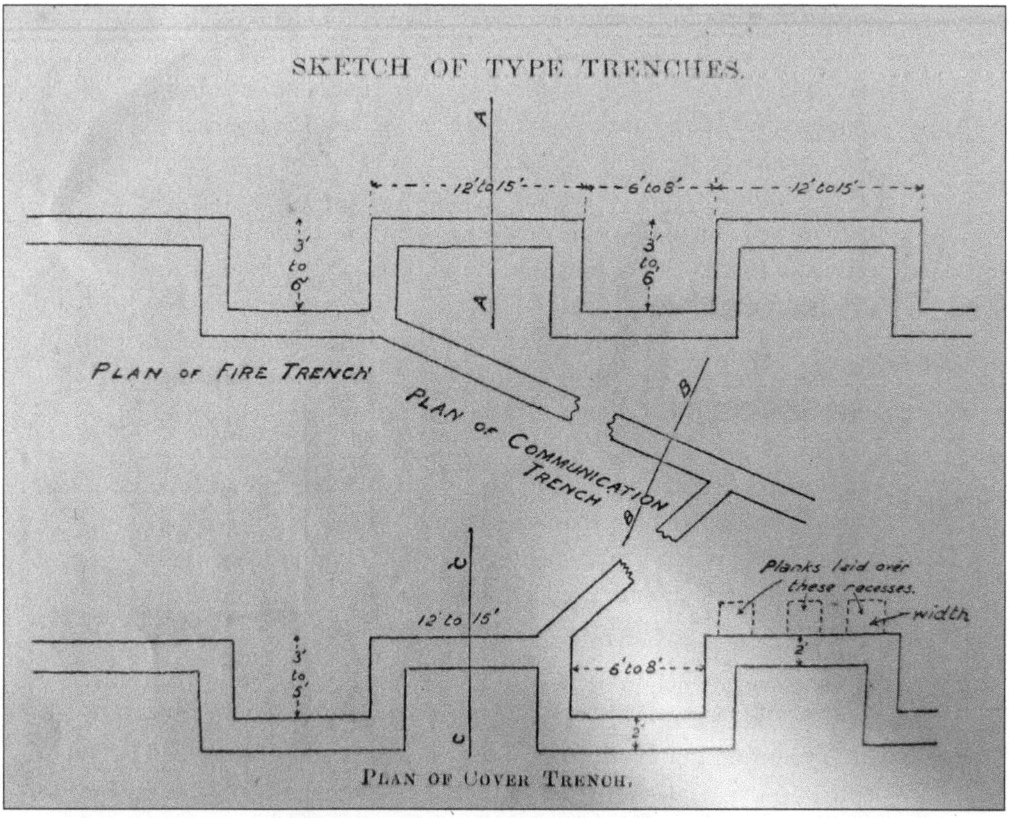

By January 1915, Charlie was at the Royal Military College, Sandhurst. Around one-third of his training there was dedicated to trench warfare. Shown here is a page from the training manual.

trenches were sited so that they were not under artillery observation with having an extensive field of fire being a secondary consideration. In the case of open country, it was considered better to select a 'back position', say behind the crest of a hill, with a field of fire of between 300 or 400 yards. This compelled the enemy to expose his infantry to British rifle and shrapnel fire. *Notes From The Front* claims that 'Such positions were held on the Aisne with slight loss to our troops and heavy loss to the enemy' and under a paragraph heading 'Design of Trenches', it states:

> Fire trenches should be of the recessed and traversed type whenever time permits. They must be deep, narrow, and with low command. The rifle when resting on the parapet, must sweep the ground immediately in front. Strong traverses should be

> provided every 6 or 8 yards to localize the effect of high explosive shell falling into the trench, and also to give protection against enfilade fire. All excavated earth must be concealed. Earth not required for the parapet should be placed behind the trenches to afford protection against the back blast of high explosive shells, provided the trenches are not rendered conspicuous thereby. Elbow rests should be either dispensed with or made as narrow as possible. Most men, however, prefer making their own niches for the forearm to rest against. Recesses under parapets must be shored up. The bottom of the recess should be above the level of the bottom of the trench so that in wet weather the seat so formed will remain dry. Headcover and overhead cover may be provided when trenches are not in positions liable to be rushed. They must in no case restrict the free use of the rifle. With overhead cover a continuous loophole is the best form. When other types of loopholes have been used, the tendency has been to make them too small and, more especially, too narrow. Drainage must be provided.

The cadets were taught that a second row of trenches, called cover trenches, should be dug to the rear of the fire trenches, to which the men could retire during bombardment, with the fire trenches being held by as few men as possible. These trenches should be of a similar design to the fire trenches and should be connected to them by zig-zag or concealed approaches, and could be quite close to the fire trenches, typically around 25 yards. Latrines and dressing stations should also be provided in these trenches and the use of overhead cover would make it difficult to ascertain from the air whether the trenches were occupied or not. Dummy trenches were also encouraged, especially if they could be made to appear occupied to any observation from the air.

There was also a paragraph in the manual about obstacles:

> Barbed wire entanglements or other obstacles should be from 20 to 50 yards in front of the trench. In positions where there is a liability of the trench being rushed sentries may be placed in rifle pits in the entanglements. Where woods run into the position they should be entangled on the near side as much as possible and the undergrowth cleared.

Training manuals were all well and good, but the problem remained that much of what the cadets were meant to learn at Sandhurst in early 1915 was being taught by instructors who had no experience of the Western Front. Not only that but the supply demands of the front meant that training was less of a priority: training often had to be carried out using obsolete equipment.

In the later stages of the war, important tactical lessons would be taught by officers who had served at the front and had gained valuable experience of major offensives, but when Charlie was at Sandhurst the art of trench warfare was still relatively new and there had yet to be any major offensives carried out. The unfortunate fact was that despite the best intentions of the instructors and staff at the time, who all did what they could to prepare the cadets for what was to come, there was little time to learn. The reality was that for a new young subaltern like Charlie, who was still only nineteen years old, there was barely the time, or the expertise, to teach him what he would need to know to get him through the early weeks on the Western Front. He would have to learn that for himself.

While he was at Sandhurst Charlie formed a close friendship with a cadet called John Cortis. Cortis had been born in Worthing, Sussex, and was six months older than Charlie having celebrated his twentieth birthday just four days before Christmas 1914. Their similar age presumably helped the two young men get on well together. They talked at length about their families. Cortis had a younger brother, Walter, who was still at school. His father, Arthur, was a chemist and his mother, Lilian, a secretary. She had been born in Russia to British parents. His parents now lived in Beaconsfield. Cortis had also attended the United Services College, after which he had completed his education at Christ's Hospital in Horsham, representing the latter at Bisley because he was such a good shot. He had then worked at the Hungerford branch of the Capital and Counties Bank and was a keen sportsman in various outdoor games, and was already a member of the local golf, tennis, and hockey clubs. Cortis was in the process of studying for his final examination of the Bankers' Institute when war was declared and, like so many young men of his generation, he had dropped everything to volunteer to serve King and Country. He had initially enlisted as a private in the Royal Fusiliers, but was immediately identified as a potential officer. Now he was at Sandhurst.

Charlie and John Cortis talked of going off to war together. They wanted to join the same regiment and could hardly wait to get going. Amongst their group there was also 21-year-old Gerald Stamford from Newbury. He was the grandson of a colonel in the Bombay Light Horse and had been educated at Lancing College. And there was 19-year-old Guy Holman from Eastbourne, 20-year-old Frank Verran from Camberley, and 19-year-

Charlie relaxing at Sandhurst, probably in his own room.

old Reginald Palmer, the only son of a clergyman in Nottingham. The list went on. None of them wanted to miss the 'Big Show'. There would be so much to tell their parents when they got back home after it was all over. It was very exciting.

With their time at Sandhurst coming to an end, the cadets were given a form to complete to express their preferences for posting. A few would go to the cavalry, but they would be drawn from 'K' Company, which meant that for most cadets there were two main options – the Army Service Corps or the infantry. In the case of the infantry, the cadets could put down their choice of regiments, listed in their order of preference. Then, without any prior notification, Charlie was told he was to graduate early. So, too, John Cortis.

On 8 March 1915, Charlie wrote to his father who by then was working in the Ordnance Office at Bingley Hall in Birmingham:

My Dear Father,

I got an awful surprise this morning, we were just off for a morning's company training on bicycles when I was suddenly called out by our C.O., Major Riddel, and was told to go and get examined to pass out on the 17th. I do not know why this should be as my lot is the next lot after this, and all this morning I have been tearing round to M.O.s, adjutants and other officials signing things.

I was given a preference form and told to fill it in right away, which I did putting down 1) A.S.C., 2) West Kents, and 3) Royal Irish Regiment. I am trying for A.S.C. as it is your advice, but it does not seem what I would like, but all the same I am only prejudiced against it, I may like it very much after all.

I am afraid this is very scrawly and hurried but I am also hurried. I hope you are quite well and fixed up OK, also mother is well. How does she like her new house?

I have had my revolver issued to me two days ago. It is a ripping little Webley Mark V, about the same size and weight as yours. I have decided to keep the Magnapole compass; it works very well. I have no more lines now and must go, so goodbye.

Ever your loving son, Charlie.

P.S. Have just had my preference form returned as A.S.C. is now drawn from the Cavalry Company (K), there being no time to teach riding etc. May be able to get transferred into A.S.C. sometime. Put down West Kents first, Wiltshire's second and Royal Irish Regiment. How's that?

The sudden rush to bring Sandhurst graduations forward could only have been because of the urgent need for officers on the Western Front. Not that the cadets would have known it at that time, but the BEF was about to launch an attack against German defences at the village of Neuve Chapelle in the Artois region of France. It was to be the first British-initiated offensive and prompted by French doubts about Britain's commitment to the war. The hope was for the British to break through the German lines and advance towards Aubers Ridge, beyond which was a wide flat plateau ideal for open warfare, and, perhaps, on towards the big prize of the German-occupied city of Lille. This would coincide with a French assault at Vimy Ridge, which would then threaten La Bassée from the south.

Charlie had clearly done well enough at Sandhurst to be considered ready for early graduation. His initial preference to join the Army Service Corps appears to have been down to his father's influence, presumably because his father wanted to keep Charlie out of the infantry in the hope of keeping his son safe for as long as possible. Not that being in the ASC would guarantee a safe passage through the war, far from it, but losses amongst young infantry officers were already mounting on an unimaginable scale. It would later be said that the average life expectancy of a subaltern on the Western Front could be counted in weeks rather than in months, and the sad fact was that a junior officer was five times more likely to be killed than a private. The statistics were never in the subaltern's favour.

As for Charlie's choice of infantry regiments, he might well have selected the West Kents because of his place of birth and the Royal Irish because of the Hodgins family's origins in Ireland. But when he had to remove the Army Service Corps from his preferences, he decided to add the Wiltshire Regiment instead, although he does not explain in his letter his reason why. He might have been influenced by others at Sandhurst at that time, who knows? But it was the Wiltshire Regiment that Charlie was going to join.

Like all regiments of the British Army, the Wiltshire Regiment boasted a long and proud history under various names. Raised in the south-west of England in the mid-eighteenth century, the 62nd Foot – as it was called then – fought in nearly all the campaigns that were to become landmarks in the foundation of the British Empire before, in 1881, the 62nd merged with the 99th Foot to become the 1st and 2nd Battalions, The Duke of Edinburgh's Wiltshire Regiment.

Much has changed since then, of course, and after a series of post-Second World War amalgamations of other fine infantry regiments, the Wiltshire name faded into history to be replaced by a more modern title, The Rifles. Back in the summer of 1914, though, the Wiltshire Regiment was like most other infantry regiments of the day, with two regular battalions. The 1st Battalion had just returned home to Tidworth after eighteen years' overseas service, much of which had been spent in India, while the 2nd Battalion was serving as part of the Gibraltar Garrison having earlier seen action in the South African War. But all that quickly changed following the outbreak of the First World War. The 1st Battalion went straight to France as part of the 3rd Division and within days was in action with the BEF at Mons, after which it took part in the epic retreat to the Marne, fighting heroic rear-guard actions along the way.

The 2nd Battalion, meanwhile, had sailed for Britain at the end of August 1914. After arriving in Southampton, it marched to Lyndhurst in the New Forest to join the 21st Infantry Brigade, part of the newly formed 7th Division. The battalion's strength was then 24 officers and 876 other ranks, but by the end of September new arrivals had brought its strength up to its war establishment of 30 officers and around a thousand men. Then, in October, the battalion crossed the Channel and was soon embroiled in the bloody, and costly, First Battle of Ypres; within three weeks of arriving at the front the 2nd Wiltshires had been reduced to a fraction of its original strength after many had been killed, wounded, or overrun and captured by the Germans.

By early 1915, both of Wiltshires' regular battalions had settled down to trench warfare and the stalemate of the Western Front. The regiment had also mobilised its Territorials, as the 4th Battalion, and for each of Kitchener's New Armies a Service Battalion had been raised; and so, the 5th, 6th, and 7th Wiltshires were born.

It was clear the war would not be over soon. The Germans were fighting a holding war in the west, where they occupied strong positions, while in the east they were forcing the Russians back. The next phase of the war in the west would see the BEF launch a handful of small offensives in support of the French.

On 17 March 1915, Charlie Hodgins was one of 100 new officers graduating from Sandhurst, all commissioned with the rank of 2nd lieutenant, effective from the following day. All but 18 were off to the infantry, spread across 35 different regiments, the remainder being destined for the cavalry or the Army Service Corps, with two officers placed on the unattached list with a view to being appointed to the Indian Army.

Charlie was one of nine graduating officers given a temporary commission and posted to the Wiltshire Regiment. Along with nine others destined for the Worcestershire Regiment, this was the highest number allocated to any unit. For the record, the nine gazetted officers posted to the Wiltshire Regiment were: O. Emanuel; E. H. Hill; J. H. Cortis; G. H. W. Holman; G. M. Stamford; C. F. B. Hodgins; G. Bryer-Ash; F. N. Verran; and R. J. A. Palmer. With the Service Battalions still under training and not yet ready to go to the front, the nine new graduating officers were split between the Wiltshires' two regular battalions, with four going to the 1st Battalion and five – George Bryer-Ash, John Cortis, Charlie Hodgins, Gerald Stamford, and Frank Verran – posted to the 2nd Battalion.

The reason for so many young subalterns being sent to join the Wiltshires and Worcesters is almost certainly because both regiments had suffered heavily at Neuve Chapelle the week before. In the case of the 1st Worcesters, the battalion had gone into action on 10 March with 26 officers and 870 other ranks, but three days later could only muster 7 officers and 450 men. Nineteen officers had been killed or wounded. It was a similar story for the 2nd Wiltshires, which had also lost 19 officers killed, wounded or missing, to add to the 276 other ranks lost during the battle. When the battalion retired to its billets to lick its wounds, it had been reduced to 7 officers and 600 men.

The immediate demand for replacements meant that some of the Sandhurst graduates went straight to France. Verran and Bryer-Ash, for example, were given just a few days' embarkation leave before going off to France to join the 2nd Battalion at the beginning of April, just two weeks after finishing their training. Stamford would not be far behind them, but Charlie and John Cortis did not go to the front immediately. They were instead sent to the 3rd Battalion at Bincombe Camps near Weymouth. The battalion had been mobilised on the outbreak of war under Lieutenant-Colonel Lord Heytesbury and moved to Dorset to protect Portland Harbour from attack, but the 3rd Battalion was also tasked with training and despatching drafts to the fighting battalions to replace the wastage of war.

And so, Charlie and John Cortis were off to Dorset. They would have to be patient and wait for their turn to go to France.

Chapter Four

'Sailing France Tonight Cheeroh!'

After leaving Sandhurst, Charlie enjoyed a few days of leave. He stayed with his parents who were now living in Edgbaston, Birmingham; his father had been promoted to the rank of lieutenant-colonel and was working as a staff officer at Bingley Hall.

Spring was just around the corner and the weather during Charlie's leave was good. By this point, most people seem to have accepted that the early optimists had been wrong; the war clearly was very far from over. The public had become used to being at war. Uniforms were everywhere – in the streets and in the parks – but so too was the sight of those who had returned home wounded.

The initial euphoria and rejoicing of Britain going to war had been tempered by the casualty lists appearing on noticeboards in every village and town. Not only that, but news of Neuve Chapelle was filtering through. Within a few days the Commander-in-Chief of the British Army in France, Field Marshal Sir John French, would write his latest Despatch, which covered the period of Neuve Chapelle, and would include:

> The losses during these three days' fighting were, I regret to say, very severe, numbering –
>
> 190 officers and 2,337 other ranks, killed
> 359 officers and 8,174 other ranks, wounded
> 23 officers and 1,728 other ranks, missing
>
> But the results attained were, in my opinion, wide and far reaching.

The last sentence is a typical optimistic comment from a senior officer designed to cover the harsh reality of the heavy casualties suffered. But what else was Sir John expected to say? French was a former cavalry officer and had been given command of the BEF at the outbreak of war, but his relationship with France's senior generals was fragile and not helped by him being in command of a much weaker subordinate army. But even though the BEF had suffered nearly 13,000 casualties in just three days of fighting at Neuve Chapelle, the public at home seemed to have no intention of turning their backs on the war. Not now. If anything, Neuve Chapelle kindled a new spirit of resolve. Britain had showed its commitment to the war. From now on the British would be seen as more than just an adjunct to the French. Not only that, but the British offensive had set the tone for the months ahead. Artillery barrages to soften up the enemy's defences were to become the norm prior to an attack being made, but both sides were quick to reinforce their defences opposite a point at which an attack seemed imminent. The stalemate that already existed on the Western Front was there to stay.

And so it was against this backdrop that Charlie arrived at Bincombe Camps at the end of March 1915 to prepare to go to war. He was officially posted to the 2nd Battalion Wiltshire Regiment, but attached to the 3rd Battalion, and it seems that he did not expect to stay there for very long, for on 3 April he wrote:

> My Dear Father,
>
> Just a line to say I received your letter this morning enclosing Webb Miles bill. I also asked you what I owed you. I should like to know and it must be something.
>
> I was warned to be ready to go to the Front Tuesday and am consequently very busy getting the necessities of life, i.e. candles, mirrors, matches and numerous things. I may go any time on Tuesday or after with only a few hours notice.
>
> I received from Cox & Co the day before yesterday some papers which I am sure are wrong as they were for officer appointment to service battalions and I am in the second regular battalion attached to the third reserve battalion, but I had them fixed up and signed. But still now, although I wired again to him explaining that I was going to the front to send me a cheque book. I do not expect to hear for some time, certainly after Tuesday, that he has credited my account and I daren't draw a cheque before I hear as one of our Sandhurst chaps did and got his cheque dishonoured. I do not know what I am going to do about paying my mess bill and servant. I think it is a very bad arrangement when chaps are sent to the front without having got their pay or allowances. I get a field allowance of so much a day to cover coal etc but do not get it until the 14th of the month.

I spent the whole of yesterday up in the hills behind Weymouth as O.C. guard. We had to guard the reservoir, the pumping station and the Spring Head. The headquarters was in the Spring Head Hotel in Preston. It was very lonely and having to go round at 12 p.m. was very cheery, my meal was about three miles across country.

The rest of the battalion is coming out here on the 15th, but I do not suppose I will be here. I will send all the kit and my sword up to you as I do not know what to do with it.

There is an awful row going on in here now so I must finish off there, one about four subalterns doing cake walks round the ante room kicking up the hell of a dust. So goodbye with best love to you all. Ever your loving son, CFB Hodgins.

The village of Bincombe and the surrounding hills behind Weymouth that Charlie refers to in his letter are to the north of Littlemore Road, just

The view today from Littlemore Road, Broadwey, near Weymouth, looking towards the South Dorset Ridgeway across what was once the site of Bincombe Camps, home to the 3rd Battalion, Wiltshire Regiment. Charlie arrived here at the end of March 1915.

below the South Dorset Ridgeway and only a mile or so from the historical landmark of the Osmington White Horse. The camp and huts have long gone, but the area remains popular amongst campers and tourists. The Spring Head Hotel, then described by Charlie as the headquarters, is still there. It is now a pub and restaurant called the Springhead and can be found in the village of Sutton Poyntz, just to the north of Preston, while the old pumping station referred to is now a water treatment works and is just yards away, although the reservoir has since been filled in.

As with all of Charlie's letters, there are many interesting points to note when reading them more than a hundred years later. The reference to a servant is one example. Subalterns were given a servant, who would help with the cleaning of uniform and kit and with preparing and cooking food, both in and out of the line, leaving the officer to focus on command. In return, servants were exempt from routine tasks, such as carrying out sentry duty at night. The letter also highlights the issues of finances and equipment, which a young subaltern would face as he was about to go to war. Cox & Co. were army agents helping officers manage their affairs. For some reason Charlie seems a little bothered that he might be joining a service battalion rather than a regular battalion, although this really should not have been a worry at all. At the time Charlie wrote this letter the service battalions were still at home in training, and this might have been his concern. He just wanted to get to the front as quickly as possible. But the reality was the volunteers of the service battalions would prove no less brave than the regular soldiers. Besides, many of the pre-war regulars and Territorials were either dead, wounded or had been taken as prisoners of war, and so the majority of those sent to reinforce the regular battalions during 1915 were young men like Charlie who were far from being experienced soldiers.

With just days to go before he was expecting to leave for the front, Charlie was still trying to gather important items of equipment. Junior officers were given an allowance, typically around £50, to buy their uniform and kit. Some of the regiments had their own approved tailors, but for most it was a case of going to one of the popular tailors in London, in Charlie's case seemingly Webb Miles. The service dress consisted of a tunic with open collar, worn with a shirt and tie, breeches, and a peaked cap, all finished off with a Sam Browne belt (a brown leather belt with a diagonal strap worn over the right shoulder). There was no absolute standard as far as colour was concerned for the above or for other items of clothing, such as shirts, ties, and puttees, which appeared in various tones of green and brown. There was also a range of footwear for the infantry officer, ranging from leather shoes when dressing for a parade to knee-length boots or simple brown ankle boots for the trenches. If spent wisely the officer's personal allowance was enough to buy him a couple of uniforms, a coat or two – such as a greatcoat, a reefer coat, or a trench coat – a revolver, sword, and other accessories such as compasses, binoculars, and a periscope. But everyday items, such as candles, mirrors, and matches, which Charlie was trying to buy prior to going to France, had to come out of his pay. As a new 2nd lieutenant, he was earning a little over 5 shillings a day, paid direct into his London bank account. This would soon rise to 7s 6d a day. There was also a mess allowance of up to 1s 6d a day and an allowance for billeting, which all combined would take a subaltern's pay to around 11s 6d a day. Once overseas, he would also receive a field allowance, which Charlie refers to in his letter, and this would increase his income by a further 2s 6d a day.[1]

Charlie could expect to spend much of his time at the front out in the open, in all weathers and conditions, so it was important to buy the right kit. But with so many young officers now coming out of training, specialist items were in high demand to the point there was a shortage of many essentials. Officers were expected to buy their own side-arms and a revolver, for example, of which there were three common types – by Webley, Colt, and Smith & Wesson, all 0.455-inch calibre weapons – but equipment could be hard to come by. Unofficial kit lists had started to appear, which seemed to grow continuously as more officers experienced time at the front. Those who had gone before were keen to pass on tips and advice for those about to follow. The greatcoat, for example, was considered too bulky and cumbersome for the trenches and so officers would instead purchase a sleeveless leather jerkin for warmth and a cape to provide some protection against the rain.

The truth was that the government suppliers were struggling to meet the demand, and so department stores such as Harrods and Selfridges would help to meet the shortfall. And when stores ran out, officers were left to procure items of equipment in any way they could, even by responding to advertisements in the newspapers. One newspaper ran the following advertisement under the heading 'Comforts For The Trenches':

> Messrs. A.W. Gamage, Limited, of Holborn, announce that they have a large stock of comforts which are especially suitable for men who are recovering from wounds, as well as for those who are still in the fighting line. They call special attention to the cardigan

1. Money conversions: 5s = 25p; 7s 6d = 37½p; 11s 6d = 57½p; etc.

> jackets, scarves, and gloves, which will be most welcome during the coming winter. It is not easy for people at home to form a correct idea of the conditions which prevail in the trenches and aboard the storm-swept ships; but enough is known to enable them to realise that the men will want warm clothing and all the protection possible from the severity of the winter weather. Also, men who are convalescent will require to be well protected, whether they are at home or in base hospitals.

Families of those about to depart for the front would often buy unofficial items of kit, such as rucksacks to carry equipment, anything to help ease the harsh conditions their menfolk would face, or at least to make them feel more closely connected to home. The press also featured appeals to their readers for help, as included in the same 1915 newspaper under the title of 'Knitting Wool':

> Socks, helmets, scarves, mittens, and body belts are all articles which are of undoubted value to the soldier in the trenches or the sailor at sea. An unlimited number of these goods is required for our men, and it behoves all readers to do their very utmost to make as much as possible of this very necessary apparel during the next few months. For the purpose of knitting these goods it is necessary for you to have wool which is most suitable for knitting and which will help you to make a maximum number of garments in the minimum of time. Mr M.D. Wilkinson of Accrington Road, Burnley, announces that he is selling some very fine lines of wool at extremely low prices, and that by buying from him you obtain the wool direct from the manufacturer to your home.

Charlie had initially hoped to be leaving for the front very soon, but his early optimism now disappeared. The following week he was still holding with the 3rd Battalion. His next letter, dated 12 April, reads:

> My Dear Father,
>
> It is a long time since I have had a chance to write to you as I have been very busy and have, with all the other officers warned, been moved into tents. Could you get me a pair of field glasses from store? Let me know what they are or have the chap in charge send me a bill for them as soon as possible.
>
> I am still hanging round here waiting for my orders to quit, which seem a long time turning up. We lost very heavily at Neuve Chapelle, hence the sudden demand for officers but just lately we

have not been so unlucky and so we are evidently being kept on hand. But they might not have warned us if we are not going for so long.

I have not yet heard a word from Cox & Co but take it that all is fixed up as I received a cheque book and nothing else. The adjutant called me up on the phone the other day and asked me about my account as you had wired the Colonel Lord Heytesbury. He seemed rather annoyed. The mess has got into a hole and we all have to pay up a couple of pounds for every month we have been here.

I hope you and mother are quite fit and well, also young Pat. I must end now so goodbye and cheeroh! Ever your loving son, Charles.

In this latest letter, Charlie confirms he has become aware that the sudden demand for officers was because the battalion had lost heavily at Neuve Chapelle. The 2nd Wiltshires had been on the extreme left of the attacking front and the battalion's initial advance had gone well, but progress soon slowed when it came under intense enemy fire. A shortage of ammunition and a German counter-attack prevented a further breakthrough and instead of reinforcing where gains had been made, the British tried to renew the offensive with extremely high losses on both sides.

Four days later, on 16 April, Charlie again wrote to his father:

My Dear Father,

Yours of 13th received and am very sorry about not writing back, but I have been extremely busy lately with the next draught of men. Two of the subalterns have been knocked off the draught work and only three of us left to take 220 men, which necessitates a quantity of work keeping the men fit, what with early morning runs and long marches.

I was told by my company commander to expect to go about 20th inst. I hope you are getting me some glasses x 8 lenses. Also, will you get me a trench periscope from Manchester, made by F. Duerr & Son opticians and periscope makers called the Lifeguard Periscope. I would write for it myself only I do not know when I am going, and it might come down here and lie about here for some time. No one thinks of looking after any poor departed one's kit, letters etc. I will send you a blank cheque, which you can fill up. I think periscopes are about 15 shillings for both. If you think it safe.

When I go, I will wire to you so you will not get anxious. The adjutant was quite ratty about being wired to about me as he is supposed to be over-working and now always casts a steely glance on me now. I have got to pay the company billets now, which means a long trudge round about 30 billets as we have a lot of other men attached from different companies to our company and the unhappy lot of paying billets has come to me. So goodbye and good luck. Hoping you are all well.

Ever your loving son, Charles.

P.S. Had my photo taken at Wheelers. Sending proofs to you so you can choose.

Charlie's letter mentions there being three junior officers to look after 220 men. For a new and young subaltern like Charlie, commanding the respect of his men would always be a challenge. He was off to join a regular battalion and while many of the 'Old Guard' had already become casualties, there were still plenty of wily characters around. They were often full of colourful language, were more worldly than the young subalterns and had far more military experience. Even talking to the men with an air of authority was never going to be easy for a 19-year-old subaltern, let alone leading them into battle. It would be a huge challenge for Charlie and others like him, but the close relationship formed between a subaltern and his platoon would be crucial in the hard times ahead.

With just four days to go until his latest expected date of departure, Charlie was still trying to buy items he thought he would need at the front. It was far from ideal, and this latest letter merely highlights the struggles he faced. The trench periscope he refers to would allow him to look over the top of the trench without putting himself at risk above the parapet. The type he requested was made by the Duerr company, best known for making jam and other preserves, which also used its factories to manufacture other items for the British Army.

As far as the officer's personal kit was concerned, there was a weight limit as to what they could bring with them, typically around 35 pounds. Subalterns would take all sorts of personal equipment with them to the front, such as clothing, a camp bed, a sleeping bag, pipes and cigarettes, matches, food and drink, a primus stove, an electric lamp, toiletries, medicines, first aid kits, and photographs of loved ones at home. Many would also try to arrange for larger items to go with them, beyond their personal allowance, such as a mattress, chairs and tables, washstands, and even portable baths – anything that would make their life better at the front.

These last few days before leaving for France were crucial for Charlie when it came to gathering his kit. There was not a moment to waste. He also writes about the importance of keeping the men fit. The route marches were physically demanding, often in the order of twenty miles or more, and were undertaken in all kinds of weather, carrying heavy kit, the intention being to push the men to their limits. For everyone in the infantry there would be long marches ahead, particularly when moving to and from the front-line trenches. Other forms of transport, such as vehicles and trains, were only used for the longer journeys, such as when the battalion was being moved from one sector to another, and so the men would have to get used to moving around on foot.

There was also the opportunity to develop further the individual skills that had been taught earlier in training. The subaltern had to learn more on many subjects than Sandhurst had taught him – about musketry, bombs and explosives, machine guns, tactics, signalling, trench warfare, and military law. He needed to understand how to handle a working party and how to hand over and relieve another platoon in the trenches, by day or by night. He needed to understand what he would encounter once overseas, such as the topography of the area he was going to and administrative matters, such as billeting. Rather than covering this in any detail at Sandhurst, imparting this knowledge was now specific to the battalion and to the part of the front line that the individual was going to – in Charlie's case the 2nd Wiltshires in France.

Once again, Charlie's expected departure date came and went and on 21 April he was still in Dorset. He wrote to his father:

> My Dear Father,
>
> I received periscope last night and am very pleased with it. Let me know what it cost, and I will send you a cheque. I think it is 15 shillings but am not sure. Concerning field glasses, I think I will carry on with the pair I have if they are not necessary. I sent Webb Miles a cheque for £10 16s 6d and have his receipted bill.
>
> I received a letter from Dick two days ago and enclose it with the others for you to read if you would care to. I do not think there is any risk about going yet, now as officers have been taking draughts over and then returning themselves. It was Neuve Chapelle that caused the sudden rush of officers to France. Those that have gone are only in the base camp, now at Rouen but today a draught left and two more went which shows they are going in driblets. There is absolutely no news and I am extremely bored

having sprained my ankle and had to stay in doing no parades or anything.

I hope mother is still well and young Pat is back at school. Is Arthur still at Dover and Jack at Portsmouth? If not, where have they gone?

With best love and cheeroh. Ever your loving son, Charlie.

Across the Channel, meanwhile, the 2nd Wiltshires had now all but recovered from Neuve Chapelle. After first resting in billets at Estaires the battalion had returned to the trenches east of Laventie and by the beginning of April was nearly back to full strength after receiving further drafts of officers and men. Fourteen junior officers had joined the battalion in the three weeks following Neuve Chapelle, including Frank Verran and George Bryer-Ash, as already described. By the time Charlie had written his latest letter, the battalion had marched the short distance to the Picantin Sector, four miles north of Neuve Chapelle, where the men were in and out of the line between the trenches and billets at La Gorgue.

By this time Charlie had been in Dorset a month and six weeks had passed since he had graduated early from Sandhurst. His next letter is dated 29 April:

My Dear Father,

I have not heard from you since I last wrote, but I suppose you have been busy. I know I have been busier than usual. I have heard nothing else about going to France and do not expect to know until the day I have to go and that will not be until we have a few more casualties.

This really is a most atrocious pen and I cannot find another so you must excuse this atrocious scrawl. I hope you got the two letters I sent you from Dick. One was yours, the other one he sent me. He seems to be having a fairly lively time out there and I wish I was out there taking part. I had a platoon given to me yesterday and we had quite a lively parade then on inspection of the men and all the wounded or unfit were sent to the rear. There were in my company more wounded and unfit than able bodied men. There are two subalterns here who have come home from Ceylon. They do not know you or Dick. One of them was tea planting and knew Coulson.

I started this letter about 4 days ago and then got fed up with the pen so did not finish it but have only just discovered it in my pocket book. With all good luck and cheeroh. Charles.

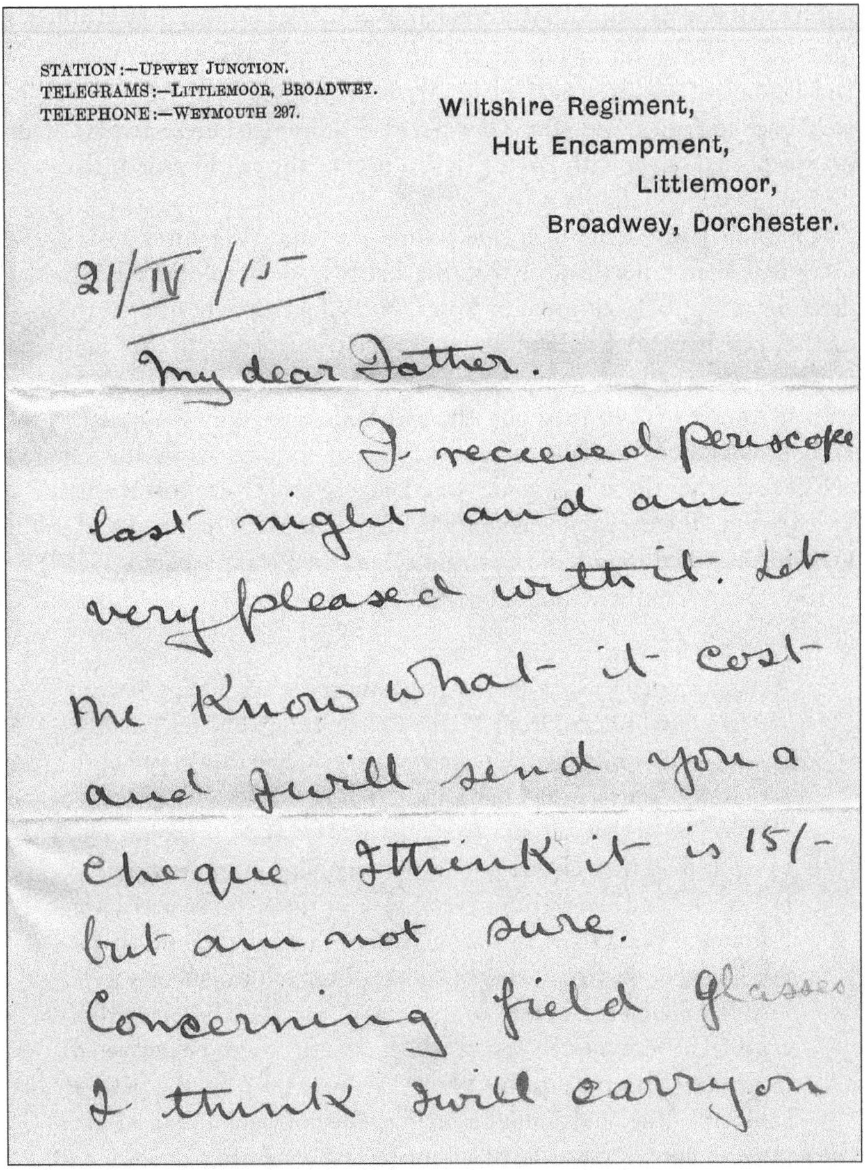
STATION:—UPWEY JUNCTION.
TELEGRAMS:—LITTLEMOOR, BROADWEY.
TELEPHONE:—WEYMOUTH 297.

Wiltshire Regiment,
Hut Encampment,
Littlemoor,
Broadwey, Dorchester.

21/IV/15

My dear Father.

I recieved periscope last night and am very pleased with it. Let me know what it cost and I will send you a cheque I think it is 15/- but am not sure. Conserning field glasses I think I will carry on

First page of Charlie's letter of 21 April 1915, quoted in full in the text opposite and on the previous page. Charlie wrote seven letters during this period while he waited to go to France.

In this latest letter, Charlie refers to his oldest brother having a lively time at the front. After finishing his training at Woolwich in November 1914, Dick had taken a draft of replacements across the Channel to France, but he had not been allowed to stay and so he had returned to Woolwich once more where, on 14 December, he was commissioned as a temporary 2nd lieutenant in the Royal Field Artillery. Then, on 10 March 1915, he went back to France and after a few days holding at Le Havre and Harfleur, he was posted to the 12th Battery RFA, part of the 7th Division, the same division in which Charlie was to serve.

Charlie's latest letter coincided with the 2nd Wiltshires leaving La Gorgue to march northwards with the 21st Brigade to reinforce the British defences at the Belgian town of Ypres. News had already filtered through to the men back in England about the first use of gas by the Germans during what was later to become known as the Second Battle of Ypres. But, as things were to turn out, the 2nd Wiltshires only got as far as the French village of Strazeele, where they spent six days while the generals debated whether the 21st Brigade would be required to support the battle at Ypres or not. The decision was that the brigade was not required and so the Wiltshires turned round and headed back to the Picantin Sector.

On 2 May, Charlie wrote to his father:

> My Dear Father,
>
> I have not heard from you for some time, but I suppose you are very busy. I heard from Mollie this morning. She tells me she has been up to Birmingham lately to see you. She thinks you both very well. I am very glad to hear it.
>
> Did you get an account from the RMC? If so, I should like to see it. Did they charge you for my camp kit, if so, how much? (I mean for bed and washstand etc) because if you did I can recover it from the War Office, it is about £7:6:0. Cox & Co claims that it was issued to me free of charge but at the top of the lists they gave us at Sandhurst it said the cost of these articles will be charged to contingent account, the cost of which can afterwards be recovered from W.O. or words to this effect. Will you send me the Savage automatic pistol and ammunition if you do not want it as in a tight place, chaps tell me, a small automatic is quite useful.
>
> They can't keep me much longer here as I have been warned for over a month now, only we do not seem to have many casualties. I hope you are still quite fit. Ever your loving son, Charles.

Time is clearly starting to drag for Charlie. He had now been at Littlemoor for five weeks. Much had happened across the Channel during that time. The 2nd Wiltshires were now back in the Picantin Sector with a reported strength of 22 officers and 810 men. Then, on 8 May, the 7th

Division was told it must be ready to follow up an attack that was going to be made by the 8th Division during the following morning to secure Aubers Ridge, a commanding position held by the Germans, as part of the British contribution to the Second Battle of Artois.

The division's warning came on the same day that Charlie wrote his next letter to his father. It was Charlie's seventh letter from the Dorset camp and reads:

> My Dear Father,
>
> I received this morning a box of nonpareils from a man up at Birmingham. Thank you for them. They are in a very good condition and very nice. We have been revolver practising this morning and I scored the highest number of points. The last time I scored a possible at thirty yards.
>
> I sent you my lot of the proofs Wheeler sent me as you have not had any yet, but I will go down to Wheelers and blow them up for not sending you the proofs, which they said they had done. These are £2:2:0 per dozen and you can choose which you want. They take rather a long time to do them as they are very busy. Will you send me, if you have got them, the photos which you took of the farm, also of myself and the oxen. Re: the Savage Pistol, it is too light for stopping a man but I am told in fact a captain here was shot in the backside while grappling with a German, and he says if he had had another pistol, even a small bored one, he would not have been hit as while he was down and trying to stick a knife into the German, another one rushed up and shot him, the bullet, however, killing the Hun (H)underneath him.
>
> I am glad to hear mother is better and hope you are well yourself. Ever your loving son, Charles.
>
> P.S. Will there be room to take me in next weekend as I am thinking of trying to get leave this next weekend from Friday till Tuesday?

By the time Charlie's letter arrived home another unmitigated disaster had occurred on the Western Front, this time at Aubers Ridge. The 2nd Wiltshires, however, got away unscathed. The attack had been launched as planned, but the 8th Division had been unable to make much progress and suffered badly. No ground had been won and no tactical advantage gained, and so the Wiltshires were not called upon. Attention would instead be directed to Festubert, a new British offensive in the Artois region of France, and so the 2nd Wiltshires marched to a new position to the west of the village in preparation for that attack, which was due to take place the following week.

While the Battle of Festubert raged across the Channel, Charlie was indeed on leave with his parents in Edgbaston. It was the first time he had been home since arriving in Dorset. But what the family would not find out until later was that Dick had been severely wounded during the opening phase of the battle. He had previously been wounded twice, although he sustained only minor injuries on both occasions, but this time it was more serious as he had been knocked out by a German 8-inch high-explosive shell. From his own account later, the next thing Dick was aware of was being in hospital in York. He was at first blind and semi-paralysed in his right side and leg. He was also suffering heart irregularities, which the doctors said were due to shock when he was knocked out by the shell.

The good news was that Dick would survive, although the reality was that his struggles in life were only just beginning.

By the morning of 25 May, Charlie was back at camp in Dorset. He was then given the news that he had so long been waiting for. He was finally off

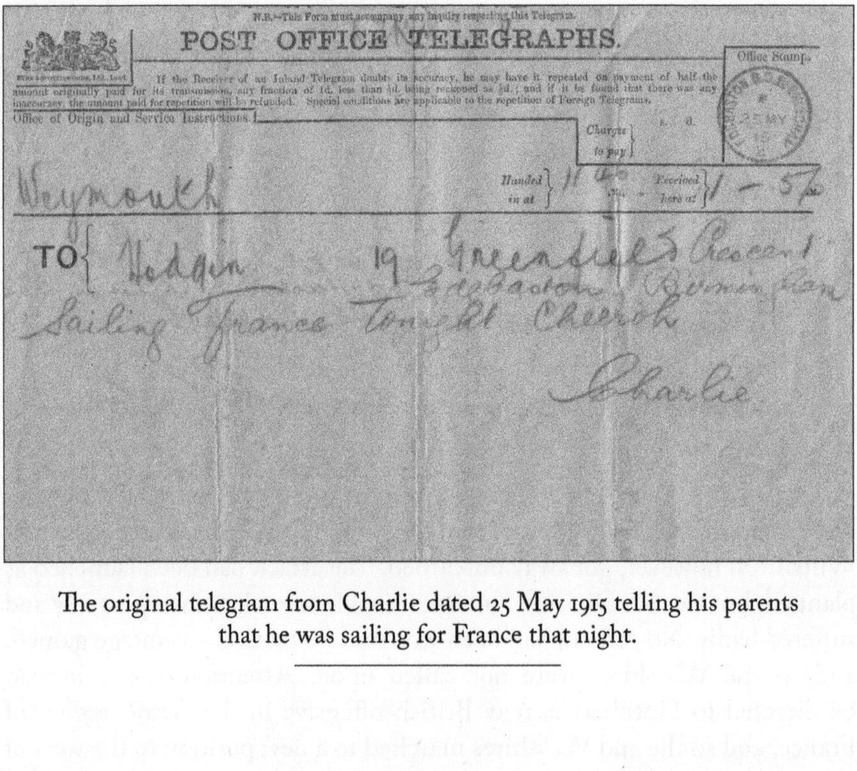

N.B.—This Form must accompany any inquiry respecting this Telegram.

POST OFFICE TELEGRAPHS.

Office Stamp.

If the Receiver of an Inland Telegram doubts its accuracy, he may have it repeated on payment of half the amount originally paid for its transmission, any fraction of 1d. less than ½d. being reckoned as ½d.; and if it be found that there was any inaccuracy, the amount paid for repetition will be refunded. Special conditions are applicable to the repetition of Foreign Telegrams.

Office of Origin and Service Instructions.

Charges to pay s. d.

25 MY 15

Weymouth

Handed in at 11 40 Received here at 1 - 57

TO { Hodgin 19 Greenfield Crescent Edgbaston Birmingham

Sailing France Tonight Cheerioh

Charlie

The original telegram from Charlie dated 25 May 1915 telling his parents that he was sailing for France that night.

to the front. There was just enough time for him to send a telegram to his parents, which read:

> 25/5/15
> *Sent from Weymouth (11.46 a.m.),*
> *Received at Edgbaston, Birmingham (1.05 pm)*
>
> *To Hodgins, 19 Greenfield Crescent, Edgbaston, Birmingham*
>
> Sailing France tonight Cheeroh
> Charlie

At last, Charlie was on his way to war.

Chapter Five

'My Dear Guv'nor'

Just as soon as Britain had gone to war, various large base depots were established in France, notably at the Channel ports of Le Havre, Boulogne, Étaples, Calais and Dieppe, but also inland at Rouen and Abbeville. The depots had several purposes, including serving as transport hubs and as administrative centres for processing the men, horses and equipment going to and from the front. With supplies arriving in large quantities by sea every day, they were first broken down into manageable loads before being sent on by road or rail, whether they were needed at the front or in support.

Le Havre was the main location for infantry base depots, essentially holding camps where men were received from England and kept under training until required by their battalions; this delay could range from just a few days to weeks. IBDs, as they were known, became vast tented cities and temporary home to tens of thousands of men. Each division was allocated its own IBD. No. 1 IBD, for example, provided men for the battalions of the 1st Division. For the 7th Division, which included the 2nd Wiltshires, No. 7 IBD was at Harfleur, situated on the eastern side of Le Havre.

By the time Charlie arrived at Southampton docks at the end of May 1915, laden with his webbing and kit, the departure procedure was running like a well-oiled machine. The troopships sailing back and forth across the Channel were mostly commandeered paddle steamers or cargo ships and varied considerably in their comfort and facilities. But the brass bands and cheering crowds of well-wishers that had earlier lined the streets, platforms and jetties to see off the BEF in 1914 had all but disappeared by the time Charlie set off for war. Yes, there had been people at Weymouth station to see the men of the 2nd Wiltshires off, but they were mostly family and friends rather than strangers waving flags and singing patriotic songs. There would continue to be large-scale movements of battalions across the Channel throughout the war, of course, but these smaller drafts were setting off to replace casualties.

While the departure for war might have now become unremarkable, for those embarking on the troopships to cross the Channel their departure was anything but routine. They were embarking on an adventure. For some it could even be their first time at sea, and most had never been abroad before; foreign travel in those days was mostly for the wealthy. Amongst the hundred men who left Weymouth that day destined for the 2nd Wiltshires in France there would have been a mix of excitement and apprehension. Sadly, the reality was that many of them were about to embark on a one-way journey.

Also travelling with Charlie that day was his friend, John Cortis, and another subaltern they had got to know during their time in Dorset who was off to join the same battalion. This was Edgar Mack who at 21 years old was the oldest of the three, and at 6 feet the tallest. Mack had been born in Lammas, Norfolk, the eldest son of a clergyman, and educated at Bradfield College in Berkshire, where he had been a member of the Officer Training Corps. His parents and two younger brothers now lived in Bishop's Waltham in Hampshire. At the outbreak of war Mack had immediately volunteered to join up and initially attested into the 19th Service Battalion, Royal Fusiliers, but within two months had been considered suitable for a commission. Mack had graduated from Sandhurst before Charlie and Cortis and had also been holding with the 3rd Wiltshire Battalion. Now the three were gallantly off to the front together, like the Three Musketeers.

For the draft, each officer was responsible for ensuring the group of men allocated to him, and their equipment, made it on to the troopship. As each soldier was about to embark he was given a leaflet. It was a copy of Lord Kitchener's message to encourage good relations with Britain's ally, France. It read:

> *[This paper is to be considered by each soldier as confidential, and to be kept in his Active Service Pay Book.]*
>
> You are ordered abroad as a soldier of the King to help our French comrades against the invasion of a common Enemy. You have to perform a task which will need your courage, your energy, your patience. Remember that the honour of the British Army depends on your individual conduct. It will be your duty not only to set an example of discipline and perfect steadiness under fire but also to maintain the most friendly relations with those whom you are helping in this struggle. The operations in which you are engaged will, for the most part, take place in a friendly country, and you can

do your own country no better service than in showing yourself in France and Belgium in the true character of a British soldier.

Be invariably courteous, considerate and kind. Never do anything likely to injure or destroy property, and always look upon looting as a disgraceful act. You are sure to meet a welcome and to be trusted; your conduct must justify that welcome and that trust. Your duty cannot be done unless your health is sound. So keep constantly on your guard against any excesses. In this new experience you may find temptations both in wine and women. You must entirely resist both temptations, and, while treating all women with perfect courtesy, you should avoid any intimacy.

Do your duty bravely.
Fear God.
Honour the King.

KITCHENER,
Field-Marshal

The scale of the operation at Le Havre was an enormous one and so there was a need for clear and concise orders, but there was neither the time nor the resources to brief each unit separately. As one of the officers accompanying the draft of men, Charlie was given two administrative leaflets informing him about what he and his men would need to know during their stay at the base. One was titled 'Special Orders for units passing through Havre Base' and covered matters such as disembarkation procedures, camp accommodation, discipline, and the transport arrangements in place for their onward movement. For camp accommodation, for example, the leaflet states that one tent was to accommodate 'one General or Field Officer; or three Other Officers; or twelve Other Ranks'. And the following paragraph, titled 'Discipline', reads:

> The attention of all Commanding Officers is directed to the urgent necessity of keeping their men in their Camps and not allowing them to stray about the towns or villages in or near which they may be quartered. Unit Commanders in the various Rest Camps must arrange, by means of their regimental police, to watch as far as possible all exits from the camps. No soldier below the rank of SERJEANT will be allowed into HAVRE except on duty. Serjeants, and N.C.O.s above that rank, must be in possession of a pass, signed by their Commanding Officer, up to 8 p.m.

The second leaflet was a medical one, explaining the arrangements in place for the care and welfare of the men while at Havre, and included details of what should be done in the event anyone fell sick.

Once on board the troopship the men were issued with life jackets, and it was soon time to settle down as best they could. Whilst the officers were offered somewhere inside the vessel to rest, many of the men were left in the open on deck.

When the troopship slipped its moorings and eased out of the docks and into the Solent there was no turning back. The war was no longer something they could talk about as being in a faraway place. It was about to arrive. With nothing else to do there was plenty of time to reflect. Many, if not all, must have wondered if they would ever see home again.

Charlie's troopship arrived at Le Havre during the early hours of 26 May 1915. He and the others went straight to Harfleur to be processed. They were told they would have to wait until the call came for them to go to the front, although there was no idea as to how long that would be.

Life at the base depot had a set routine. Breakfast was at 6 a.m. after which the officers and men would gather at one of the training points to get to work. There was more instruction on trench warfare and section attacks, there was physical training on an assault course and, of course, there was drill. Even at the height of the war there was plenty of drill. It was a strange environment, described by some who were there as neither France nor England, but more a large compound run like a training camp.

The 2nd Wiltshires, meanwhile, were 150 miles away in billets at Robecq having left the trenches a week before after suffering further losses at Festubert; the battalion's casualties were listed as 4 officers and 158 men. But, despite licking its wounds, the battalion was still required to march to brigade headquarters at Gonneheim to be inspected by General Joseph Joffre, the Commander-in-Chief of the French Army on the Western Front, before returning to Robecq once more. It was probably the last thing any of the men wanted.

The 2nd Wiltshires were still in the process of replacing those lost at Festubert and so the new arrivals at Harleur were soon on their way. Just two days after they arrived in France, Charlie, John Cortis, and Edgar Mack, were on their way up the line to the front.

At any other time in his life, Charlie's train ride might have seemed a rather peaceful and enjoyable amble through the beautiful French countryside. But this was 1915 and the carriage was far from what he would have been used to travelling in back home, and the journey through Rouen and Abbeville was painfully slow. The train trundled on all day and through the night. At times it moved at little more than walking pace and it would often stop for no apparent reason.

The War Diary for the 2nd Battalion, Wiltshire Regiment, records the date of Charlie's arrival at Robecq as 29 May 1915: Cortis and Mack, too. Charlie was keen to tell his father just as soon as he could get a letter sent home, but from this point on all letters had to be read and censored by an officer before being sent on their way. The letters then passed through a field post office. In the case of the 2nd Wiltshires this was Field Post Office 21 (21 being for 21st Brigade). The postal service was very good considering the many thousands of letters and parcels it had to handle every day, with letters generally arriving at a British destination within a couple of days.

Charlie's first letter from France was written in pencil on small writing paper. He knew it was a Sunday in May, but he was not sure of the date. It was in fact Sunday 30 May. The envelope is equally small and typical of letters sent home from the front. On the envelope, stamped in red, is 'Passed Censor'. It is counter-signed '2nd Lieutenant E. G. Mack' (Edgar Mack) and shows the postmark of Field Post Office 21, dated 2 June 1915. All of Charlie's letters were handled and signed in this way. His first letter from France reads:

2/Wilts,
21st Brigade,
7th Division

Sunday ??. v. 15.

My Dear Guv'nor

Here I am in the train just going up into the trenches to join my Battalion. I hear we have been having it hot lately again but are slowly advancing. This engineer keeps on jamming on his brakes and we get fearful shocks as if we had run into something, but I am getting used to it by now.

I feel extremely dirty as I have had no opportunity to wash or shave for 36 hours and have no prospect of doing so for at least 12 more. Tell mother that the respirators used are the black muslin bag like Miss Lee made, filled with saturated cotton waste in a waterproof bag.

I hope you got my kit o.k. Send me out some toilet paper in a flat package. Tell Major Sheppard that his cigarettes have been most acceptable as I came away in such a hurry that I had no time to bring any if I had wanted to. Send me out also a pair of field boots with canvass tops and leather bottoms as they are just the

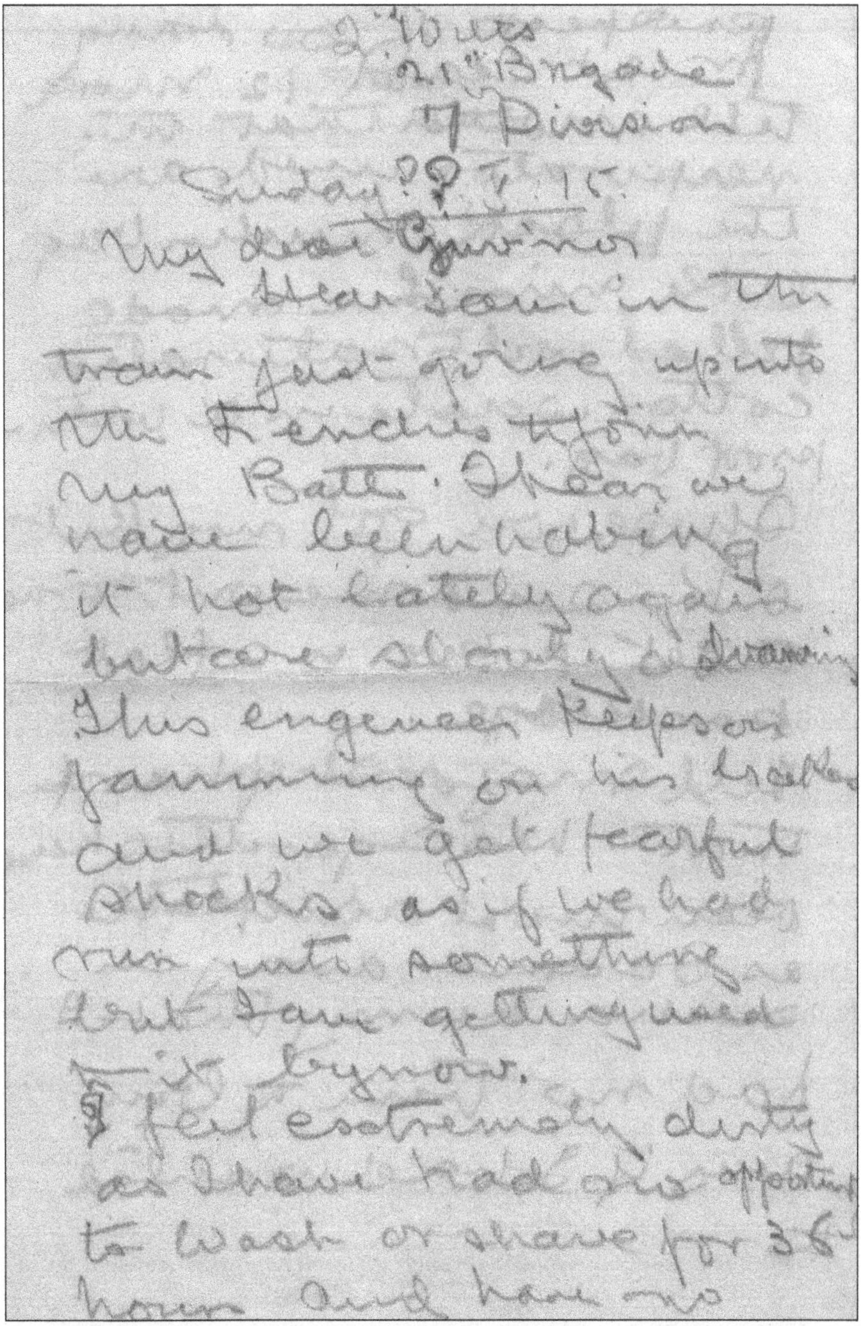

G. Watts
21st Brigade
7 Division
Sunday 9.V.15.

My dear Guv'nor
Here I am in the train just going up into the trenches to join my Batt. I hear we have been having it hot lately again but are shortly [illegible]. This engineer keeps on jamming on his brakes and we get fearful shocks as if we had run into something but I am getting used to it by now.
I feel extremely dirty as I have had no opportunity to wash or shave for 36 hours and have no

The opening page of Charlie's first letter from France. The paper is flimsy, allowing some of the writing on the other side to show through.

thing to wear in the trenches. Let me know what they cost, and I will send you a cheque.

I saw Wheeler about the photographs, and he had not received your order, so I told him to send you some more proofs. When you get them send one of myself standing to Mollie as I promised her one.

What has become of Dick? Was he at Havre? This writing I know is awful, but the line is extremely bumpy and the train sways about, although it is only going about 10 m.p.h. My best love to mother. I hope she got my last letter. By the look of the country round, one would not think that war was going on less than 15 miles off. Everything is so peaceful.

Well cheeroh, ever your loving son, Charles.

It was the first time in his letters that Charlie had addressed his father as 'Guv'nor'. It shows, perhaps, a cocky confidence about him now that he was in France. The letter also contains interesting information about the type of respirator being used on the Western Front at that point.

The German use of chlorine gas at Ypres on 22 April 1915 had sent shock-waves through the Allied ranks and caused great concern amongst the British public at home. Chlorine is a powerful irritant that can inflict damage to the eyes, nose, throat and lungs, and can cause death by asphyxiation if a victim experiences high concentrations and prolonged exposure. At Ypres, the gas had been released from storage cylinders along a four-mile front after the Germans had waited several days for the weather conditions to be right. The easterly breeze had then carried the large, dense, yellowish-green gas cloud across no-man's land and into the Allied trenches. Men were seen staggering out of the trenches and away from the cloud, coughing, spluttering and vomiting as they went. Lips and faces turned blue as blood became starved of oxygen. Some died before they could be given any medical assistance. Victims literally drowned in their own fluids.

The Germans had come close to a breakthrough that day. Although Sir John French immediately demanded chemical weapons, his request had first to pass the politicians because the use of poison gas in war was against international agreement. French ultimately got his way and so his forces would also get chlorine gas. It was now only a matter of time before supplies were built up and it would be ready to use.

The use of gas on the Western Front would always have its limitations (wind conditions being a major one) and it would not always prove fatal,

The German use of chlorine gas at Ypres in April 1915 had sent shockwaves through the Allied ranks on the Western Front. It led to the introduction of the British Smoke Hood, or Hypo Helmet shown here.
(*Courtesy of the Passchendaele Museum*)

but it did have a huge psychological effect on those targeted. Even the sight of a gas cloud, or anything looking like a gas cloud, was enough to put fear into those occupying the opposing trenches. Just as soon as gas had been used by the Germans at Ypres, the British started issuing cotton wool pads wrapped in muslin to be dampened and held over the mouth to their front-line troops. It was only a short-term solution and soon a respirator appeared. Known as the Black Veil Respirator, it was a cotton pad soaked in an absorbent solution and secured over the mouth using cotton veiling; the veiling being used to cover and offer some protection to the eyes, with string used to hold the mask in place. Treated in a mixed solution of sodium hyposulphate, sodium carbonate, glycerine and water, the respirator was stored in a purpose-built waterproof satchel, keeping it moist for immediate use when required. This was the 'black muslin bag' that Charlie described in his letter, and he was amongst the first to have it issued as it had only been introduced to the front line a couple of weeks or so before he arrived in France. But troops would soon find the Black Veil had its limitations, not least that it was fragile, and it effectively immobilised the individual because of fear of the mask becoming loose; wearers would try to hold the mask in place. The Black Veil was therefore soon replaced by the Smoke Hood, a canvas hood donned over and fully covering the head, treated with chlorine-absorbing chemicals, and designed with a single rectangular eyepiece.

Charlie had finally arrived at the front and gas was already on his mind. But there was to be no immediate rush to the trenches. That would have to wait.

Chapter Six

'I shall soon be in something pretty thick myself'

Today, Robecq is a quiet commune in the Pas-de-Calais department in the Hauts-de-France. With a population of little more than a thousand people, it is situated nine miles to the north-west of Béthune, close to the Belgian border. Its focal point in 1915 was the Église Catholique Saint-Maurice à Robecq, a fourteenth-century church, which still stands on the Rue de l'Église where it meets the Rue de Saint-Venant, now the D937. And on the D937, the Commonwealth War Graves Commission's St. Venant–Robecq Road British Cemetery, containing 479 burials and commemorations from the First World War, serves as a reminder of the intense fighting that once took place near here more than a century ago.

When Charlie arrived at Robecq at the end of May 1915, he found the commune practically unscathed. The 2nd Wiltshires had by then been billeted in and around the area for ten days. It was an ideal place to rest and recuperate as Robecq was generally considered to be a quiet spot. Troops could be billeted almost anywhere, depending on the availability of public buildings and private property in the area in which they had been sent to rest. The standard of billeting varied enormously, ranging from châteaux with wine cellars for senior officers to roofless farm buildings, draughty huts, tents or hay barns for the men. And a bed could be anything, from an actual bed to packing cases or bundles of hay. In small communes, such as Robecq in 1915, most of the local population had long left the area and so whatever houses that survived could be used. But there was never going to be enough accommodation for a thousand men and so farm buildings and tents were also used to the west of Robecq, close to the Canal d'Aire à la Bassée (known to the British as La Bassée Canal), where the men could swim and relax.

With the arrival of Charlie, John Cortis, and Edgar Mack, and the accompanying draft of ninety-nine NCOs and men, the 2nd Wiltshires were all but back to full fighting establishment. The War Diary records the battalion's strength on 31 May 1915 as 27 officers and 900 other ranks.

Alongside the 2nd Wiltshires, three other regular infantry battalions made up the 21st Brigade: these were the 2nd Bedfordshires, 2nd Yorkshires (formally the Princess of Wales's Own West Yorkshire Regiment, and also known as the Green Howards), and 2nd Royal Scots Fusiliers; a Territorial unit, 4th Cameron Highlanders, was also attached to the brigade. With two other brigades – the 20th and 22nd – the 21st Brigade was part of the 7th Division, under the temporary command of Major-General Hubert Gough. The division was part of Lieutenant-General Henry Rawlinson's IV Corps, which came under the overall command of the First Army led by General Sir Douglas Haig.

Haig was a cavalryman and at the outbreak of war was General Officer Commanding Aldershot Command, which had formed a large part of the BEF. Haig had helped Sir John French with the organisation of the BEF, with Haig's command becoming I Corps and he had gone with it to France. Soon after Haig was promoted to the rank of general and in December 1914, when the BEF was divided into two armies, he was given command of First Army with Second Army going to General Sir Horace Smith-Dorrien. Haig's First Army would take the major role in the campaigns of 1915, supporting the synchronous French operations in Artois and Champagne.

When Charlie joined the 2nd Wiltshires at Robecq the battalion was then under the command of 37-year-old Captain Ernest Makin due to the temporary absence of the CO, Lieutenant-Colonel Walter Brown. Brown, a 44-year-old veteran of the South African War, had joined the battalion at the beginning of April at La Gorgue, but had been admitted to hospital with measles following an outbreak in the brigade. It was not the first time that Makin had taken command of the battalion since his arrival the previous December, as it was to him the brigade commander turned whenever the battalion CO was out of the line.

A fourth officer joined the 2nd Wiltshires on the same day as Charlie and the others had arrived. This was 2nd Lieutenant James Badgley, the 27-year-old son of an army colonel who had initially enlisted into the Canadian contingent at Quebec. The new arrivals were spread across the battalion's four companies with Charlie put into 'B' Company, the company which had suffered the heaviest losses at Festubert, while Mack went to 'C' Company, Cortis joined 'D' Company, and Badgley was put into 'A' Company.

Charlie's company commander was 48-year-old Captain Bernard Cave-Brown-Cave, a member of the ancient family of Cave-Browne-Cave,

Baronets of Stanford, Northamptonshire, and a friend of the Hodgins family through Charlie's father. Cave-Brown-Cave was a highly respected veteran of the Wiltshire Regiment. He had seen active service in Egypt and in India, and on operations in Sierra Leone during 1898–9, where he took part in the Mendiland Expedition and the Kwalu Relief Column, during which he was severely wounded. He had then served with the Mounted Infantry in the South African War and was recalled to service at the outbreak of the First World War, joining the 2nd Wiltshires in November 1914.

Cave-Brown-Cave was not at Robecq on the day Charlie arrived, but he was soon to return to the battalion following a period of sick leave. It might well have been through Cave-Brown-Cave's influence that Charlie had decided to add the Wiltshire Regiment to his list of choices while at Sandhurst, and this might also be the reason why Charlie was put into 'B' Company, so that Cave-Brown-Cave could keep a watchful eye over him. Second-in-command of 'B' Company was 21-year-old Lieutenant Geoffrey Wilson from Chippenham in Wiltshire, who had been with the battalion since February. And alongside Charlie the company's other subalterns at that time were 2nd Lieutenants Fred Bone and Leonard Schultz, both from London and both aged twenty-five.

There was very little experience amongst the battalion's junior officer ranks, such had already been the wastage of war. The other subalterns included George Bryer-Ash and Frank Verran, of course, both of whom Charlie knew from their training days at Sandhurst. They had now been in France for nearly two months and so might help the newcomers to some extent. Both had already spent time in the trenches; Bryer-Ash with 'D' Company and Verran with 'C' Company. There was also 22-year-old James Janasz from Bournemouth, an officer of the Dorset Regiment who was now attached to the 2nd Wiltshires. He was with Cortis in 'D' Company. And 21-year-old Gerald Stamford from Eastbourne was in 'C' Company with Verran and Mack, while in 'A' Company there was 21-year-old Frank Friend from London. These officers were not just 'young' in terms of experience; they were young in age, too – eight of them were twenty-one or younger. Charlie, still not quite twenty, was the youngest of all.

June began with the return of the CO, Lieutenant-Colonel Brown. That afternoon the battalion paraded and lined the road for a casual inspection by the British Prime Minister, Herbert Asquith, who was in the area for the day. Having had lunch with Haig, the Prime Minister had then been briefed on the situation in the First Army's sector, after which Asquith and Haig motored through the Indian Corps area and that of the Canadian

Division to meet the corps, divisional and brigade commanders at Robecq. It was their arrival in Robecq that Charlie witnessed. Asquith then looked at some of the support and communication trenches in the area before enjoying tea at Busnes Château with Haig and Gough, after which the Prime Minster left, seemingly most enthusiastic about all that he had seen.

Such visits to the front as Asquith's on 1 June 1915 seem to have been more popular for the senior politicians and generals than they were for the men. The following day the 2nd Wiltshires moved to new billets at Hinges, five miles to the south-east of Robecq. Charlie's next letter, written from Hinges on 3 June, includes his brief thoughts about the event:

> My Dear Father & Mother
>
> We did not go into the trenches after all as the day we arrived up here the Battalion had just come out and we are at present resting or supposed to be resting. We do parades here all day and all day long the guns are booming in the distance. The other day we watched the Germans shelling one of our aeroplanes and it was marvellous that the thing escaped for the air was thick with bursting shrapnel. We advanced quite a bit as you can probably see by the papers. We were relieved by the Canadians who, though not popular out here, are doing very well.
>
> Did you see in all the papers that Basil MacLear – the celebrated Irish international was killed? He used to sleep next door to me at the RMC. He was in charge of the PT and games and an awfully nice man. That is the second one of my company officers to be killed out of three.
>
> How is Dick, is he well again? I did not see Douglas at the base when I was there, which was about three days. Will you get me a quantity of insect powder in small packages to distribute round my platoon as all the poor things are one mass of livestock, and it is quite a sight to see them hunting for them, sitting in rows without their shorts on. I think Boots Persian powder is the best.
>
> We have moved up nearer the firing line again and are expecting to move onto the trenches next. The Germans seem to have no shortage of H.E. shells as was shown by the way they used them on us last time. We had to line the roads the day before yesterday for Sir Douglas Haig and above all persons Asquith the Prime Minister. They both took our courtesy very coolly, in fact took very little notice of us.

> I wrote and paid for an electric torch from S. Smith & Son about a week before I left. I got his receipt for the money but have not yet received the light. I would be very glad if you could make some enquiries for me. The address is 68 Piccadilly and the light a field service light and case, price 2/7. It was to be sent to Weymouth but did not arrive. I have written there (to Weymouth) but had no reply yet.
>
> I see the Germans have bombed a part of London. Was that anywhere near Woolwich? If so, was Davies one of those killed? The weather remains more or less fine and we bathe in the canal which runs through our billeting area. This canal is a great boon as it is the only place to get a wash. By the peaceful look of the country one could have no idea that a war was going on.
>
> I have just heard that the Germans have just dropped 9 shells into the town, but the people did not seem to mind. One girl was slightly wounded in the arm.
>
> Send me those canvass leather field boots size 10, and also a small bottle of Fellowes syrup. Well best love to you both. Remember me to Major Sheppard. Ever your loving son, Charlie.

In addition to mentioning the visit of Asquith and Haig, the letter includes the sad loss of Basil Maclear, the former Irish rugby international whom Charlie had met at Sandhurst. Maclear had been killed a week or so earlier during the Second Battle of Ypres while serving with the Royal Dublin Fusiliers. He was the first of six former Irish rugby internationals to be killed during the war.

Two days later the 2nd Wiltshires were on the move again, this time to Locon, a couple of miles to the east. That same day three more subalterns – 2nd Lieutenants H.H. Morris, H.A. Price, and J.M. Martin – and a draft of eighty-nine men arrived.

The following day, being a Sunday, was church parade. Church parades were compulsory for everyone when out of the line, with churches being set up almost anywhere suitable to conduct a service. There were men from all religions in the trenches – Church of England, Roman Catholic, Presbyterian and Methodist to name but a few – and while they were not all regular church-goers before the war, many were from religious backgrounds or had been brought up in a religious way. Religious beliefs might not have been able to provide answers for the slaughter taking place on the Western Front, but many officers and men took comfort from religion, feeling that it gave them an inner strength and courage to face the horrors of war.

The following days were spent route marching and drilling. Even in June 1915 there was time for parades and drill. Charlie was still several miles behind the front-line trenches, but the distant sound of the guns was a constant reminder that the war was not far away.

Being in billets meant Charlie had time to write home, and he soon wrote to his father again. His letter dated 9 June reads:

> My Dear Father
>
> Received kit bag etc o.k. and also a letter. Am so glad to hear Dick is better now. I think I told you I am in the same part of the line as he was and will soon be in the thick of it. As far as I can see my birthday will be the thickest part.
>
> The Germans, so we are told by own intelligence corps, have rigged up a nice little gas plant, which is ready today. We all have these respirators, which are a black muslin bag like Miss Lee made and in it some cotton waste soaked in a solution of hypo washing soda and glycerine and water, and the latest order is company – gags! This means that every man must take out his gag from the waterproof bag and put it on in less than 20 seconds.
>
> I have heard nothing about my electric light yet. I explained the situation last time, I think. I also explained I wanted a pair of green canvas field boots size 10, an occasional grub box as one gets rather tired of bully beef and bread. We sometimes are able to buy eggs off the people around. One thing I particularly want is about one flat tin of plain chocolate about once every ten days, an occasional periodical or magazine. No newspapers or tobacco until I send for it. A left-hand side revolver holster, which may have to be specially made. A quantity of small packets of Boots Persian insect powder for my platoon. A pair of socks as I can usually get my things washed while in billets. Also, above all things, let me know how much all of these requisites come to and I will send a cheque for them. Now do not forget this as my order is a long one and I wish to pay for the things.
>
> I remember you said at one time that if any of us got knocked out in this war you would come out and avenge us. I must ask you if anything should happen to me on no account to come out here because the life is very strenuous, and it is not men we want but H.E. shells and shells only, and until we get them we will not advance a yard except with extremely great loss of life. Now I have

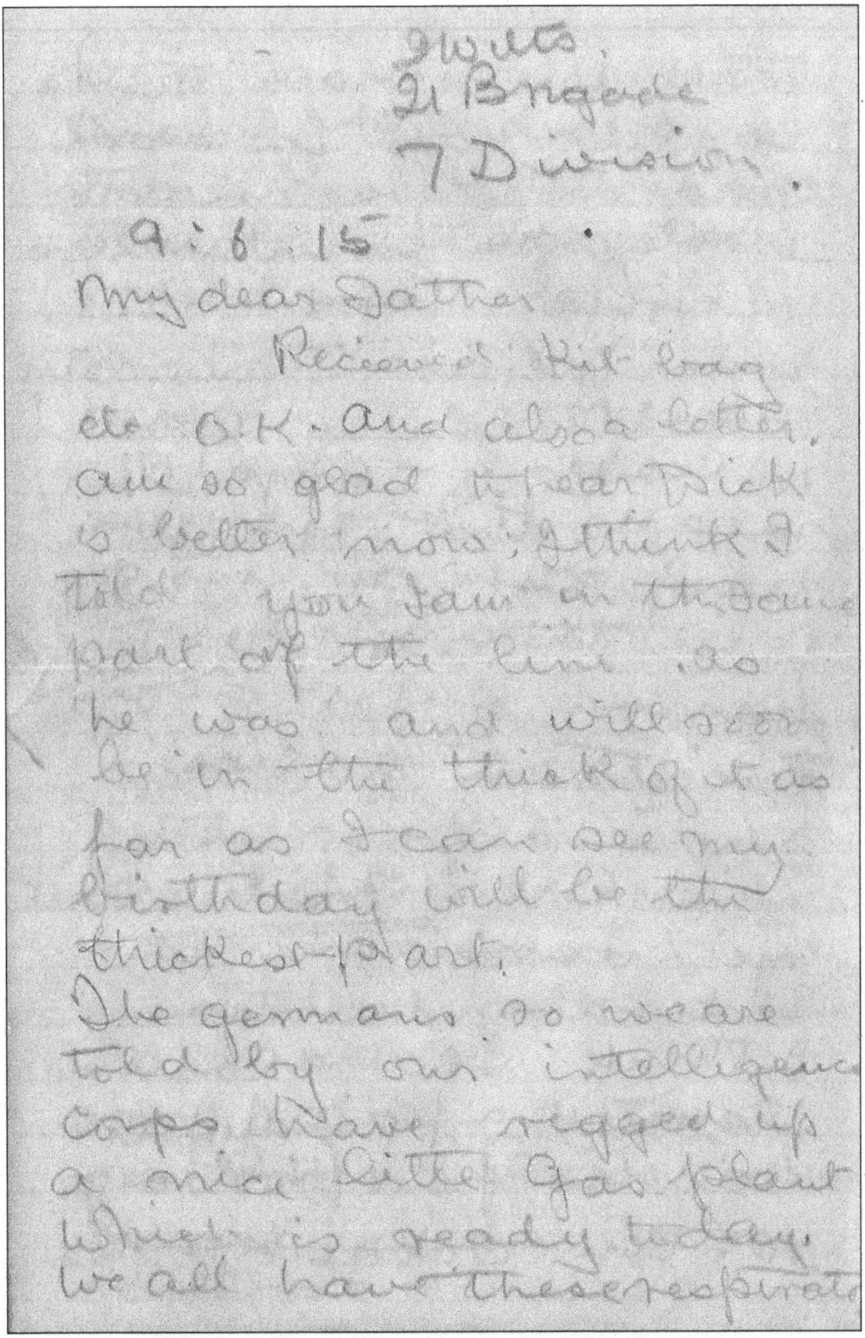

2 Wilts.
21 Brigade
7 Division.

9 : 6 : 15

My dear Father
Received kit bag etc O.K. And also a letter. am so glad to hear Dick is better now; I think I told you I am in the same part of the line as he was and will soon be in the thick of it as far as I can see my birthday will be the thickest part.
The germans so we are told by our intelligence corps have rigged up a nice little gas plant which is ready today. We all have these respirato

The start of Charlie's letter to his father of 9 June 1915.

asked you this so please do not forget it. You have mother and Pat to think of.

Old Cave-Brown has turned up here again and as luck will have it is again my company commander, but as there is a scarcity of drink around here, he will have to behave himself.

This will be the last letter I write before going into action and have no news so cheeroh and best love to mother and yourself. Also, hoping Dick is fit again. Give my regards to Major Sheppard and tell him there is a subaltern in the Middlesex attached to us named Belsham, but I have not yet asked him if he is any relation yet. Well cheeroh again. Your ever loving son, Charles.

The envelope from Charlie's 9 June letter showing the stamp of the field post office and the triangular stamp confirming that the letter had been passed by the censor.

This latest letter was written before Charlie went forward to the trenches in preparation for an attack at Givenchy, in fact on the very day that Cave-Brown-Cave returned to the battalion from sick leave. The subaltern called Belsham referred to was 2nd Lieutenant Sydney Belsham, originally of the Middlesex Regiment.

However, by the following day, 10 June, the battalion had still not moved up to the trenches. Instead, the day was spent parading for drill and then relaxing in the excellent weather, with many of the men taking the chance to bathe in the La Bassée Canal. Charlie took the opportunity to write another letter home, rather a very brief one on this occasion:

My Dear Father & Mother,

I just have time to write a hurried note before leaving for the trenches and something else. It is ammunition the whole time that is holding us up and will go on doing so until we get more of it.

We had a German aeroplane over here yesterday and shortly after a Bristol biplane appeared looking for it. After that the Hun cleared off. Can you send out about half a dozen mouth organs as soon as possible? Also, I think I asked for a felt slouch hat.

> Well must end now to catch the mail. So cheeroh and goodbye for the present. Take care of yourself mother. I shall soon be in something pretty thick myself. I wish those people would hurry up with that electric light. It is the one thing I miss. Well, I must end now as I have said before. Ever your loving son, Charles.

This letter was clearly rushed, and it was written to his mother and father, something Charlie rarely did. But he seemed to want them both to know that he expected to be in 'something pretty thick' quite soon. However, there was still no move forward to the front. Charlie spent 12 June, his twentieth birthday, doing drill at Locon. It must have felt a world away from the peace and tranquillity of the family farm in Canada where he had celebrated his nineteenth birthday only a year before. He had grown up so much in that time. He had to. But whether there was an opportunity for Charlie to grab a quick drink with his friends to mark him hitting his twenties is not known, although it is unlikely.

The following day was the battalion's last full day in billets at Locon. Another officer and a draft of thirty men arrived, bringing the 2nd Wiltshires war-fighting strength to 35 officers and 1,000 other ranks. The officer was 37-year-old Captain Robert Gillson, married with two young children and another veteran of the South African War. Gillson had been away at the time Charlie joined the battalion, but now, since he was senior to Makin, he became the 2nd Wiltshires' second-in-command.

The following afternoon the men paraded before setting off for the trenches at Givenchy. The 2nd Wiltshires were ready to fight. Charlie had been in France for just two weeks.

Chapter Seven

Givenchy

The Imperial German Army had been formed in the wake of the Franco-Prussian War of 1870–1 and was composed of the armies of the numerous states that made up the German Empire, the dominant state being Prussia with forty-two regular divisions in its army at the outbreak of the First World War. A German division comprised two brigades. Each brigade had two infantry regiments as well as cavalry and artillery, with each infantry regiment having three battalions. And so, despite the slight differences in structure, it meant that a German regiment was broadly similar in size to a British brigade. The Germans were fighting on two fronts and so large numbers of men had been sent to the Eastern Front to fight the Russians, but a formidable force had remained in the heavily fortified defences in the west.

The situation on the Western Front in mid-June 1915 was one of stalemate. The Allies believed the war could only be won by removing the Germans from French and Belgian soil, but whereas the opening weeks of 1915 had been a period of hope, the once grand schemes and intentions of the generals had now been replaced by deadlock and loss. With nearly half the year already gone, the battles at Neuve Chapelle, Aubers Ridge, Festubert and Ypres had seen all the great ideas and ambitious plans disappear. The most recent action alone, at Festubert on 15 May, had cost the British, Canadians and Indians, more than 16,000 casualties.

The BEF on the Western Front was still relatively small, consisting of just two armies made up of regular and Indian divisions. Partial British successes here and there had suggested that with more men, more ammunition, better communications, and with better planning and stronger leadership, victory could be won. But it was not that simple, as the British public well knew. News of a shortage of artillery ammunition had made the front pages back home following the attack on Aubers Ridge, when the newspapers reported that its failure had been due to a lack of shells.

As far as getting more men was concerned, there was hope on the horizon with the arrival in France of the Territorials and the first of the many thousands of volunteers who had answered Kitchener's call to arms. The volunteers, however, would not be considered ready to throw into the mix until later in the year; to send them into battle any earlier would risk severe losses in fruitless attacks, but with vastly increased numbers a first major British offensive of the war might be possible before the year was out.

The French, however, wanted an offensive as early as July. But although the French wanted to get things moving sooner rather than later, the British senior staff believed it would be early the following year before they had enough divisions available, maybe up to fifty, and at least a thousand heavy guns, to deliver a concentrated and coordinated offensive along a front. Not only that, but the front would need to stretch across at least twenty-five miles if such a battle was to have any chance of success.

The thought of waiting until 1916 for the BEF to be at sufficient strength to mount a major offensive did not go down well with General Joffre who was committed to further offensives in 1915 rather than delaying until the following year. Simultaneous attacks in Artois and Champagne would, he believed, be hammer blows for the German Army and a breakthrough in these areas could be achieved. Instead of holding back until 1916, Joffre urged Sir John French to prepare for a major offensive to the north of the French Tenth Army between the mining village of Loos and the La Bassée Canal before the winter could set in.

The British did not agree with Joffre's suggestion. Overlooked by German-held slag heaps and colliery towers, and with many fortified villages, the ground Joffre was suggesting was far from suitable for an advance. The British instead preferred an attack to the north of the canal, although that would mean attacking some ten miles or so to the north of the French Tenth Army.

There would be much political intervention to come, but even if there could be some agreement a major coordinated offensive was still some weeks, even months away. For now, attention turned to the part of the British line where the La Bassée Canal crossed the enemy trenches, to the south of where the Festubert battle had taken place. The final act of what had started at Neuve Chapelle and had continued at Aubers Ridge and Festubert, was to be at the much-battered village of Givenchy-lès-la Bassée.

Having already fought at Neuve Chapelle and Festubert, it was to be the 7th Division's third major assault in four months. The division was first ordered to take over the sector where the front line ran east of Givenchy and on a slight rise in the ground, which meant troops could be moved along the canal banks in daylight without being seen from German positions. From there it would attack enemy positions to the east of Givenchy, while on its right the Canadians were to attack an enemy strongpoint and the 51st Highland Division would be advancing on its left. However, the position also had its disadvantages for the British artillery spotters as it made direct observation of the German line difficult. Nonetheless, the attack was planned to take place on the German positions opposite this sector during the afternoon of 15 June.

Everything was soon in place. For the 2nd Wiltshires Lieutenant-Colonel Brown would lead the battalion with his staff of seven officers and a further eighteen officers were spread across the four companies to take part in the attack. But Charlie was disappointed to be told that he would not be going over the top that day. The excessively high casualty rate amongst officers in recent months had led to an order coming out that not all officers were permitted to take part in attacks. Some were to be kept back to pick up command of the battalion should losses be high. In the event, five officers were to remain with the 2nd Line Transport, including Charlie and Bryer-Ash. Makin was also held back to take command of the battalion should Brown and Gillson become casualties.

The decision to hold Charlie back from what might turn out to be another disaster would probably have been made by his company commander.

Charlie's next letter home was written in two parts on either side of the attack and therefore separated by four days. In the first part, dated 13 June, he writes:

> My Dear Guvnor
>
> I have now a little time to spare while off duty to write. The bursting of these German shells is something terrific, extremely sharp with a drawn off ending. We have been shelling the German trenches since 11th inst. and are going to continue. Dick will know why, and so will Kaiser Bill before this time next week and serve him right. He has started gassing us here and this gas has a most awful choking smell and when once you start you choke yourself to exhaustion, then you gasp solidly until you die, which you usually do in the form of a fit. The colour of one's complexion is a beastly coppery grey colour. There is a new law out that only 20 officers are to be taken. This means that a lot of junior subs will be dropped before going into action. This means most likely yours truly will not go through with the battalion. When – you will

soon know when, though I can't tell you the date. So, I will be snug in the trench, which I dare say will please you but not me.

I heard from Aunt Win today, at the same time as from you. Thank her for her letter and tell her that there were quite a crowd of little things in the last parcel, which I did not want but the best part of it was the thought. To be continued in our next.

During the afternoon of 14 June, the Wiltshires paraded at Locon before moving off during the evening to take up positions in the firing line and support trenches at Givenchy. They were to relieve sections of the Scots Guards and Border Regiment in the forward trenches ready to 'jump-off' at the appropriate time. At 7 p.m. 'C' and 'D' Companies left a point called Windy Corner, the name given to a small group of houses situated on the low ground to the west of where the fighting was to take place, with 'A' and 'B' Companies following on two hours later. But owing to congestion, particularly in the narrow communication trenches where parties of men were moving in both directions, the relief was not complete until 2.00 the following morning – the day the attack was due to take place.

The 2nd Wiltshires were to form part of the 21st Brigade's leading wave, but it seems that any element of surprise had already gone as during the day of the attack, 15 June, the British trenches were heavily shelled. The men of the battalion could do nothing but wait for the time of their attack, which was to be 6 p.m., and so casualties were suffered even before they set off.

As Charlie waited in reserve he must have wondered what his friends and colleagues were going through, not only physically with the shelling but also mentally as they waited to go over the top. There was his closest friend, John Cortis, whom Charlie had known from the start. Together they had waited patiently in Dorset to be ordered to the front. And then, having arrived in France, they had waited again for this moment to arrive. Cortis would be going over the top with 'D' Company, having volunteered to take part in the attack after Bryer-Ash, who was ahead of him in the pecking order, had fallen ill. Also going over the top with 'D' Company was Janasz, the young Dorsets' officer attached to the Wiltshires for the attack, and Belsham from the Middlesex Regiment. Edgar Mack, whom Charlie and Cortis had travelled with to France was with 'C' Company and would be going over the top alongside Frank Verran and Gerald Stamford. All these were in the two leading companies. From Charlie's 'B' Company there was the company commander, Cave-Brown-Cave, and two subalterns, Fred Bone and Leonard Schultz, while Frank Friend would be going over the top with 'A' Company. As far as Charlie was concerned, they were the lucky ones. They had been given the opportunity to lead their men into battle. Charlie would get his chance, of course, but held in reserve he could only imagine what Cortis and the others must be going through as they waited in the trenches for 6 p.m. to arrive. Every minute must have felt like an hour. It must have been a desperately long day for them all.

Finally, at 6 p.m., it was time for the 7th Division to attack, with the 21st Brigade leading; the 2nd Wiltshires were on the left and 2nd Yorkshires on the right. At the same time the British guns opened up on the German front line. The War Diary for the 2nd Wiltshires best records what happened next:

> At 6 p.m. the battalion commenced to attack the line I.12, J.14 – J.13. On quitting their trenches, the leading companies (C & D) were subjected to a heavy frontal and enfilade fire, the latter from I.14 – I.19. As the advance progressed it was enfiladed by machine gun fire from both flanks, on the right from the foot of the hill between I.12 and 13, on the left from machine guns concealed in the grass somewhere west of J.13. 'B' Company followed in support of 'C' and 'D' and occupied J.7 – I.5. 'A' Coy in reserve in Scottish Trench.

'A' Company had been kept back as it was to carry out a reconnaissance of an enemy trench called Violaines after the enemy position had been captured, but the attackers were mostly shot down within a few yards of their own front line. Only handfuls made it to within fifty yards of the German trenches, having crawled through the long summer grass. The War Diary commented: 'The firing line reached a point about 50 yards west of German trench at J.14. There was then only one officer not hit in the two leading companies.'

An hour after the leading companies had gone over the top, half of 'A' Company went forward to push on the attack, which had been held up. These men, together with the survivors of 'D' Company, then advanced, but they were subjected to enfilade fire from a crater and could not advance beyond an old disused German trench. The War Diary summed up the situation three hours after the battalion had first advanced:

> The Regiment was occupying the old German trench, with 'C' and 'D' Companies in front of them, and the trench J.7 – I.5, and were in touch with the Grenadier Guards on left of J.7. Groups from 'C' and 'D' Companies were returning to old German trench from the front.

The battalion was then ordered to attack the next part of the German line. This was to take place at 9.15 p.m. in conjunction with the Bedfordshires and Yorkshires, although the time was subsequently delayed to 10 p.m. The 2nd Wiltshires' War Diary continued:

> In order to form up for the attack the companies which were holding the old German trench and were being enfiladed from the right were ordered back to Scottish Trench with orders to form up in rear of it to clear the field of fire of the company holding J.7 – I.5.

However, this attack order was subsequently cancelled. The 2nd Wiltshires were instead told to hand over the trenches to the Bedfordshire Regiment and return to Windy Corner, the point the battalion had set off from some twenty-four hours before.

By the time the stragglers returned to Windy Corner it was 3.00 the following morning, 16 June. From there the survivors moved into reserve dugouts for breakfast. The battalion was then ordered to proceed to Château Gorre where the troops would remain in the wood to await further orders.

The battle of Givenchy had been costly for the 2nd Wiltshires, as listed in the battalion War Diary:

> Officers – 4 killed + 5 wounded – total 9.
> Other Ranks – 25 killed + 127 wounded + 48 missing – total 200.

Most of the forty-eight missing were killed in front of the German trench, mainly from 'C' and 'D' Companies that had led the attack. Out of 180 men who had gone into action with 'C' Company, a hundred were listed as casualties along with all of its five officers. The company commander, Captain Edric Richardson, was killed, as was 2nd Lieutenant Gerald Stamford, while the three other subalterns – Frank Verran, Edgar Mack, and James Bales – were all wounded. It was a similar story for 'D' Company. Of the four officers who went into the attack, just one was left – the company commander, Captain E.P. Lewis. One subaltern was wounded – Sydney Belsham – but the other two were killed: James Janasz and John Cortis.

For Charlie it was the most devastating news. The second part of the letter he had started before the attack is dated 17 June and is written from Gorre Wood, just before the battalion set off for billets at Hinges.

17th June, a wood behind la trenche,

Here we are again all quite safe but extremely sad. I have lost my best friend and what is more I do not know what has happened to him. He fell beyond the German second line of trenches believed to be killed. But a captain swears he saw him afterwards with both his legs broken trying to crawl back to our lines.

We failed in our attack. More than half our officers were casualties, 5 killed and 6 wounded. We could have captured the wily Bosche's trenches if the Yorks had succeeded, but for some reason they retired leaving our flank exposed and the Huns turned machine guns onto our flank. All of us who had been left behind were then rushed up to take the place of the fallen officers. But it was no good. We had to retire. I lost in my platoon one man killed and seven wounded.

It is a most extraordinary thing that I have seen. Men absolutely blubbing like kids of four or five with their hands over their eyes. I missed the worst part of the show and do not feel I have done my share, but the next time we go in I will avenge some of our fellows and especially my friend J. H. Cortis. He was at Sandhurst with me and everywhere that I have been sent he was always sent there too. He was in the same company and was gazetted the same day, but higher up in the list than I was. I wish they had let me go through the whole thing instead of keeping us behind. Cortis was behind with me in the morning and in the evening was dead or believed so. He may be captured and having an awful time from the Bosches. It almost makes you hope he is dead.

Well I got the haversack quite safe last night. Thank you both very much for it, but I am afraid it is no use to me out here as we all have to wear the Webb equipment and are not allowed to wear Sam Browns because they give us away so, but still the thought is the most treasured gift. It is a fearfully depressing feeling to look around at your men and see them all mud stained and dirty, either asleep or cleaning their rifles. They had no sleep the night before last but are making up for it now. I must end now as it is time to get up and dress. I am writing this early in the morning. It is half past four now. Hoping you are all well. I am ever your loving but depressed son. Charles.

P.T.O.

> I received the electric light ok by this morning's mail. Also, I have just heard that the Bedfords and Scots Fusiliers have just captured the thing we failed to capture, although we paved the way for them. CFBH.

From Charlie's letter it appears that the officers left in the rear had been called forward at one stage, but to no avail. The following day a draft of seventy-one men joined from Harfleur, fifty of whom were re-joining the battalion having been wounded at Festubert. Then, during the afternoon of 19 June, what was left of the 2nd Wiltshires paraded at Hinges before setting off for their old billets to the west of Robecq, arriving there in the early evening.

So poor John Cortis was dead. Walter Brown, the CO, would later write of him – 'He was extremely keen to go into action and was a first-rate soldier. The regiment feel the loss of such men as this; when we are able to do so we will erect a cross over his grave.'

Cortis was just twenty years old and the first of the Hodgins–Cortis–Mack trio to fall. He had been in France just three weeks, and with the battalion for only nineteen days. Back in Beaconsfield, the telegram informing his parents that their son had been killed would have come as devastating news. Cortis was reportedly buried on the field of battle where he fell, but after hostilities were over his body was never found.

Charlie's friend, John Cortis is one of those named on the Le Touret Memorial. Also listed is 21-year-old Gerald Morton Stamford, who had been at Sandhurst with Charlie and Cortis and graduated on the same day. Cortis and Stamford were both killed at Givenchy on 15 June 1915.

John Halsted Cortis is commemorated on the Le Touret Memorial (Panel 33 & 34), which remembers 13,479 British soldiers who were killed in this sector of the Western Front from October 1914 up to the Battle of Loos in September 1915 and who have no known grave. The memorial is located at the east end of Le Touret Military Cemetery on the south side of the Béthune–Armentières main road. Cortis is also featured on the Bridge Street War Memorial in Hungerford where he had worked.

The Le Touret Memorial is located at the east end of Le Touret Military Cemetery on the Béthune–Armentières road and commemorates 13,479 British soldiers who were killed in the nearby battles. Their names are listed on panels set into the walls of the court and gallery.

As for the battle itself – later to become known as the Second Battle of Givenchy (the first having been fought in December 1914) – it was not a success. British and Canadian sappers had detonated a 3,000-pound mine under the German defences as planned, but it had also caught some Canadians in the blast and did not seem to cause any great damage to the German defences. Also, there had not been enough artillery and so the men taking part in the ensuing assault met intact barbed-wire defences, which resulted in heavy casualties from the start. As soon as the leading companies went over the top the German machine guns started cutting them down. Nonetheless, the attackers pushed doggedly on over most difficult ground – a mix of shell holes and long grass – and while some

British and Canadian units managed to reach, and even capture, some of the German front line, they were soon forced back again by the shortage of ammunition and the strong German defences.

The 2nd Wiltshires remained at Robecq for the next week. Once again the battalion had to build back up to fighting strength. Charlie was back at the same billet where he had first been sent less than three weeks before. The big difference now, though, was that several of his friends were dead.

Chapter Eight

'I may not be here very long'

Since he was back in billets once again Charlie had time on his hands. Later that evening, 19 June, he wrote to his mother. The letter reads:

> My Dear Mother,
>
> I wrote father the day before yesterday telling him about our little action. The absolute undreamt of horrors are beyond words. I told him that I had heard that the Bedfords had taken it, which has turned out to be untrue. They tried and did not get as far as we did. Last night the Welsh Fusiliers and Warwicks tried again, also failing. In three days time we will most likely try another shot at it. It is as you can see an almost impregnable place and as soon as we stop shelling the Huns all come tearing out of undreamt of places and they say that they have concrete 'dugouts' in which they hide.
>
> Tell father that Cave Brown Cave was badly wounded in the leg having his leg nearly taken off just above the knee by a piece of shell, but he took it very well, cheering on the men and making light of it. Even if he is an old drunkard out of the battle, he is an absolute gentleman in one. He lay out for four hours before the stretcher bearers could reach him and when they did he was saying at the time 'take a rest boys, don't tire yourself' etc, and as you can imagine he was being unmercifully jerked about with a terrific shell fire going on all around.
>
> I have heard that Cortis had his back broken and died two hours afterwards, poor fellow. God rest his soul. The colonel says he was the most cheerful of the lot when told to advance to certain death. The latest German atrocity is the use of incendiary bullets, which they fire at wounded men to set them alight.

The French are making an attack further down the line. One can tell this by the artillery fire going on. Just as we left the wood in which I wrote my last letter, the Germans put two shells into us. One luckily did not go off, the other one, a shrapnel, did very little damage other than grazing two men's heads and knocking a hole through the coat of my platoon sergeant.

When is my box of cakes and things arriving? We look forward to such luxuries from home. If you can manage it, once a week would be acceptable. Do not send any books as I have more than I want now. My boot size is 10 not 8. Tell father the hat is not what I wanted. I want something to wear with my uniform, a Stetson or that sort of thing. By the way, young Belsham was wounded. If he is a relation of Major Sheppard let him know.

Why do you not write sometimes? About the only one who writes to me now is father. I may not be here very long so a little ink slung this way will not be wasted. Must end now, with best love to you all. Ever your loving son, Charles.

It is a rare letter from Charlie to his mother alone. He describes the realities of being on the Western Front, maybe because he felt his father might have been economical with the truth when explaining to her what Charlie was going through. There is also reference to Cave-Brown-Cave and his courage. Cave-Brown-Cave would end up losing his left leg, and his right leg had been shattered. For him the war was over, although his personal struggles were only just beginning. Then the bombshell in Charlie's letter – 'I might not be here very long' – perhaps as a way of preparing his mother that there was a strong possibility he would not get through it all and that he might soon be wounded or dead.

The following day, 20 June, the battalion was resting in billets and so Charlie again wrote to his parents:

My Dear Mother and Father,

Again, I have some time to write, although I have not heard from either of you for about three days. If you knew how one looked for letters while stuck away out here, you would sit down and start writing and continue to do so 'right straight along' (as Joe would sometimes say).

We have had a fearful mix up here and I am afraid the good old 2nd Wilts has got into trouble. There were 36 men who broke down through this fearful shell fire and were consequently sent to the rear as being no good and having a bad effect on the rest. Now

I do not know whether General Gough is mad or got a bad liver but he blames the colonel for letting the men go back, although he has had nothing to do with it and has had him sent back to England. He came round this afternoon to us and quite broke down when he told us. He has been with the regiment twenty-seven years and is nearly heartbroken about it. But this is more of this wretched red tape of the army. This is a most fearful knock to the regiment as you can see, so do not go spreading it round mother.

I have now been moved back into billets and are about 5000 yards from the slaughter line. How is Dick? You do not say when you do occasionally write. I went up the other day to watch a fifteen-inch at work and found there that one of the chaps in charge was at school with me. He was very good and showed us exactly how it works. They are much better than the 42cm and only take 8 hours to effect. You can see the shell going through the air. It weighs ¾ of a ton and cost £150. I suppose really I should not tell you this much but I do not think that there is any harm; as the Germans are bound to know this much themselves but you had better put this in the fire when you have read it.

Well, I have no more news so cheeroh. Hoping to hear from you soon and to receive the parcel of cakes etc. promised so long ago. I remain ever your loving son, C. F. B. Hodgins.

P.S. The last part of this letter is written under difficulties hence the scrawl becomes worse. CFBH.

As well as discussing the effects of enemy shell fire on the men Charlie alludes to problems regarding how the battalion had performed at Givenchy. With the unit back in billets its part in the attack had come under scrutiny. A letter written by Gough had reportedly stated that 'the attack by the Wiltshires left something to be desired'. The outcome was that Lieutenant-Colonel Brown was recalled to England less than a week after the battle. He was to be replaced by 34-year-old Major Bertram Leatham, formerly of the 2nd Battalion, Yorkshire Regiment.

A Yorkshireman by birth and the son of a banker, Leatham lived in Richmond with his wife Everil and their young daughter. He had been commissioned into the Yorkshire Regiment at the age of nineteen and served with the Mounted Infantry in the Transvaal during the South African War. Now he was temporarily promoted to the rank of lieutenant-colonel to take command of the 2nd Wiltshires. Leatham had a good combat record and would soon receive the Distinguished Service Order for his service in the field with the Yorkshires.

Arriving with Leatham was 28-year-old Major Cusack Forsyth, also of the 2nd Yorkshires, who was to be Leatham's second-in-command. Forsyth was to replace Ernest Makin, who also returned to England with Brown, and the previous adjutant, Captain James Ponsford, who returned to the Divisional Cyclists Company. The entry in the 2nd Wiltshires' War Diary for 21 June records these movements and changes:

> Lt.-Col. W.S. Brown and Capt. E.L. Makin proceeded to England. Major B. H. Leatham, 2nd Bn Yorkshire Regt assumed command and Major C.G. Forsyth, 2nd Bn Yorkshire Regt appointed second in command. Capt J.M. Ponsford returned to 7th Divisional Cycle Company. Major Forsyth taking over duties of Acting Adjutant pro-tem.

However, there is no mention in the War Diary, or suggestion even, that Brown had been removed from his post for disciplinary reasons or that he had been sacked because of Givenchy. But whatever the reason, Brown was dismissed, although he would later return to France only to be killed in July 1916 while commanding the 1st Battalion, Wiltshire Regiment, during the opening days of the battle of the Somme.

On 22 June Leatham inspected the companies at Robecq. That same day, Charlie again wrote to his mother:

> My Dear Mother,
>
> I have just received your letter and a parcel of cake from Kunzle for which I thank you. It was very acceptable to us all out here in B Coy and we all had some for tea. Needless to say, there is not much left, but we all subscribe something and things get equalized up when you send something to me in the way of cake. All the others get a regular weekly parcel.
>
> The things I want here mostly (by the week) a small quantity of a good cut plug tobacco not my Mustin as it gets very dry and crumbles up very easily. Also, some matches and cake and a good bit of substantial chocolate. Do not forget to put in any magazines or periodicals you happen to have, but do not want, do not go out and get them especially to send out as some of the other chaps sometimes get them. Also, occasionally a good book, one of those seven penny novels are as good as anything, but mind it is a good one, none of this sentimental stuff.

I am very glad to hear Dick is alright again and think the longer he stays away the better, perhaps he does too poor chap. How did he get unconscious from it, a bursting shell? I saw about ten men knocked out and one killed by the concussion only of a shell. They were not touched by anything but compressed air or whatever it is.

Tell father I will not want the boots now as I have got all I want in that line but a pair of hose tops, which are just like stockings with the feet cut off would be very useful. I prefer greyish ones (if possible) to khaki. Also, not to forget the left-hand side revolver holster for a short Webley. This will probably have to be made and, if possible, of webbing like the Tommie's equivalent.

Do not forget to write as much as possible and if Dick is alright ask him drop a poor fellow a line as he must know how one hungers for something from home. Also, tell that lazy Jack to write as I wrote to him some time ago, but got no reply. Also, I did him a good service by forwarding on a letter for him addressed to me from our estimable cousin Mollie who wrote about 7 pages to him but only wrote about one to me, which is very rotten of her considering the pages of hair raising adventures I wrote to her. Also, I want a refill for my electric light. Get it from Smith & Co and send it out as soon as possible. It is no. 295.

The new CO we have is quite a smart officer but makes us do an awful lot of extra work as if we did not do enough in the trenches.

Well my dear mother I must end now so goodbye and best love to you all, especially father. I hate to worry you both for all my little necessities, but I know you do not mind. Well cheeroh everybody! Ever your loving son, Charles.

For the next three days the battalion carried out company parades, sporting activities, and route marches. On 24 June, Charlie again took time out to write to his parents:

My Dear Mother and Father,

Received today for once two letters which I was very grateful for and am sitting down right now to write one back, although there is absolutely no news.

My platoon won the Battalion inter-platoon football match, also the water polo. I have, therefore, the best platoon in the battalion. We have got a couple of majors from the Yorks for CO and Adjutant. They make us work twice as hard as if we did not do enough in the trenches. I do not suppose we will go in again for quite a longish time, say about three weeks.

I am sorry to say that my chum was killed, without doubt having had his back broken. I got hold of two men who had put their packs under his head and feet to ease him. He was dead before we were compelled to retire so I am told, and he asked for me before he died. But all the same a good many Huns will see the other side of hell before I have finished. As for going steadily, one cannot possibly do such a thing. One either goes mad or funks. There is no in-between as far as I have seen and from what others out here have found out also. It sounds rather unreal, but I think you are driven mad by a species of fright and terrible anxiety.

I can quite understand mother being rapt up in Dick just now and personally I would expect it of her. I do not mind being as you call it 'neglected'. My dear father also, as you are so busy.

I received a very nice cake, which I thanked you for last time I wrote. Re the syphon, I should be very glad of one as soon as possible and would also like the bulbs and a few of those soda & Lithia tablets to put inside the syphon. The water is not exactly good, but we all have bisulphate of soda to purify it if unpure. A filter would be no good thank you all the same. The felt hat you sent is very nice, but I am afraid is not quite the thing. I want a more military looking thing, something I could wear on parade for instance a 'Stetson' or 'Wideawake'.

My dear mother, you must understand that things take rather a long time to get here, therefore my letters to you and your letters and parcels to me crossed on the journey. We get soup squares issued to us occasionally so do not trouble to send them too often, but goodies are always acceptable.

It is quite correct about the concrete dugouts as I think I said in one of my letters and they are all nine feet underground. Very few shells can reach them they are so deep. We heard today from Sir J. P. D. F. [Field Marshal French] He said although we failed in our attack, we did all that was requested of us, namely the preventing of reinforcements from being sent up against the French. Hence this glorious advance lately. The Germans are just as badly off as we are for shells and worse off for aeroplanes so if we have a better supply of shells than they it will greatly shorten the war.

I am hoping not to get either killed or wounded just yet so do not think about it mother dear, but if we have many more work like this last I very probably will be. But sufficient with the day is the evil thereof.

Do not forget the mouth organs and bug powder for my platoon and quantities of the latter. I might say that this article is about the most needed thing now. No more of these 'woodies' but lice killer is the cry now. The poor chaps are literally infected with them. So, tell all your good friends to send a reliable vermicide out. With us officers who can get a change of clothes it is alright but for the men who only have what they wear, which they live in night and day, it is different. Send me out two pairs of cotton drawers and two cotton shirts and collars (attached if possible to the shirt). Well must end now as it is 10.30 p.m. and to bed. Cheeroh. Charlie.

From what he had written, Charlie clearly expected to be out of the line for a while, three weeks he believed, and he is clearly seeking revenge for the death of John Cortis. It is interesting that he also writes about his state of mind – 'One either goes mad or funks' and has learned about the strength deep concrete dugouts bring to the German defences and how little effect Allied artillery shells have on them. This realism is offset by hopeful rumours of the enemy suffering a shortage of shells and aircraft. Charlie's hopes for a shorter war if more ammunition became available made sense, but he could never have imagined that the war still had nearly three and a half more years to go.

Charlie obviously had time on his hands, for two days later, on 26 June, he wrote to his father: his parents now living at Frederick Road in Birmingham:

My Dear Father,

Just a short line to thank you for the syphon and sling etc. which arrived safely last night. In fact, I had more letters than I have had the whole time I have been out here. One from you, one from Aunt Winnie and one from cousin Mollie to say nothing of the parcel.

We are moving farther back from the firing line and will probably get a good long rest. You can see by yesterday's (24th) paper how many casualties we have had, and they only put about half of them in. I suppose this is to conceal our real losses.

There is absolutely nothing doing here except the Bosches are blocking up the canal above us and the water level is steadily falling. As all our food comes up by barges this is inclined to be

> serious. We are further south than we were. There is always some sort of an attack or counter attack going on, but the guns are the only thing we hear about it. Well you might send out a few mags like the Windsor etc.
>
> Well I have absolutely no news so must close down. Send me out some more thin envelopes. No writing paper as I can always use Army Book 153 and think I prefer it. Also, those mouth organs I asked for, a map case would be very useful out here, opening at the top and waterproof.
>
> Well must end in great haste as I always am now. I get orderly officer every three days as officers are so scarce and all our work is done by companies not battalion, except Battalion route marches twice per week. Well cheeroh everybody. Ever your loving son, Charles.

During their week at Robecq the companies were reorganised and then the Wiltshires were given orders to move once again. The battalion's War Diary records on 27 June:

> Orders were received for the Battalion to proceed to LUMBRES about 26 miles west of ROBECQ and 7 miles south-west of ST OMER, where they came into G.H.Q. reserve and detached from 21st Brigade.

That evening, the battalion paraded at 8.45 p.m. before setting off for Lumbres. It was going to be a long march.

Chapter Nine

In Reserve

By the end of the first day of marching the 2nd Wiltshires had reached the village of Aire, where the night was to be spent in barracks. It was always hard going when marching long distances to and from billets. At first the battalion would set off marching smartly but once out of sight the men could carry their rifles and march in a more relaxed manner. They were allowed to smoke their pipes or cigarettes. Then, when approaching a headquarters or any other key location, the battalion would smarten up once more.

The following morning the 2nd Wiltshires paraded and then marched off to complete their journey to Lumbres, passing General Haig's First Army Headquarters along the way.

The next couple of days were spent at Lumbres, the time being used for more inspections and allowing new arrivals to settle in. Then, on 1 July, the 2nd Wiltshires moved into barracks at Tournehem, marching the ten-mile distance via Quercamps and Boningues along what is now the D225. Since leaving the trenches at Givenchy a little over two weeks before, the Wiltshires had marched some fifty miles rearwards towards the Channel coast and were now just a few miles from the port of Calais. That evening, Charlie wrote to his father:

> My Dear Father,
>
> Again, I have some little time to sit down and write you a letter though under extremely great difficulties, i.e. on the floor of a barracks with nothing to rest my writing on except my knee. We have been on the move for some time since last Sunday night and are now about 12 miles from Calais. Hence my reason for not writing more often, although there is absolutely no news at all.
>
> I received another most delicious cake for which B Coy mess send their thanks. I do not think that bug powder was a distinct

success but would like half a dozen of the foot comfort soap which my men greatly appreciated. When are the mouth organs coming? I hope to see them soon. If you have not sent them yet you might put in two of those brass flutes. Certainly music on the march works wonders and the work is halved if the men have something to keep them amused. Send me out a razor strop also. I am afraid my letter is full of my wants, but I have nowhere else to send to and still less news to send with them to tone them down.

Did you get my request for some more bulbs for the syphon and also for another battery no. 295 from Smith & Son Ltd. Well must close so goodbye Trafalgar Square and hoping you are all well. Tell Dick to write. Charlie.

2/7/15
Since writing this letter I have received a parcel of bulbs and mouth organs etc for which I am very grateful. I have no more time to write as I am orderly officer today so must go and take the early morning parade. So cheeroh. Ever your loving son, Charles.

Charlie's battalion spent four days at Tournehem, during which more reinforcements arrived from Le Havre. It was a quiet time. Then, on 5 July, they were ordered to march to Wizernes some fifteen miles to the south-east, via Nordausques, Moringhem and Quelmes. The battalion arrived at their new billets in Wizernes at 5.30 p.m. That evening Charlie wrote to his father:

My Dear Father,

Again I have more spare time to write and do so, although there is still no news. We have moved back towards the east again and are quite close to Sir J. F.'s Headquarters, within two miles in fact. Have you been in for any of this row about the ordnance? Lately we have heard quite a lot about it here. We are properly in disgrace I am afraid and may be chucked out of the 7th Division. They say our discipline is bad, hence our being back here. We have been doing a lot of marching and have been complimented on it by more than one general OC, one of whom was D. Haigh.

The mouth organs were a great success and one man kept on blowing his the whole of our last march about 15 miles. I enclose a cheque to get some more – all Key D. I received a parcel last night on which was written 'Eatables from Mrs Col Hodgins', inside of which were one slouch hat for which I send my sincerest thanks as it is just the thing. Let me know what it cost. A revolver holster, a vest, two socks, butterscotch, chocolate, peppermints, peaches, sardines etc., for which thanks very much.

The Bosches are preparing a big attack for us and are going to try to get through, but I know will not succeed. We have another attack on tomorrow, but it is only a practice one this time. You need not send any more periodicals out as all the other chaps in my Coy get them before I do and it is not worth sending them when I can see them out here without you paying anything.

Tell Dick to write sometime. I think I asked you for some khaki hanks and cotton shirts and collars. Let me know what they cost also. Well I must end now so cheeroh, best love to all, especially mother. I am ever your loving son, Charles.

The 2nd Wiltshires remained at Wizernes for the next two weeks. The weather was good, and all seemed very pleasant. The war seemed a long way away.

Two days after arriving the battalion made its first visit to the training area at Helfaut, a mile or so to the south of their billets, to carry out battlefield exercises. Then, two days after that, there was a battalion parade, followed by a route march of twelve miles. Charlie's next letter is dated 10 July:

My Dear Father,

Why haven't you written for so long now? I have been looking forward to one from you to let me know how things are going at home with you and mother etc. We were inspected by some big brass hat this afternoon. I believe he was the Assistant C-in-C. He had never seen an attack done under the present circumstances, so my company had to show him. As a matter of fact, we did it very well and the general officer inspecting seemed highly edified. The CO told us afterwards it was very good. It is quite a business coming through imaginary wire entanglements as the tendency is to cut off corners, but we did that part the best. Fourteen of my men have even taken to go through a bombing course, but I will get them back in a fortnight. This leaves me at present with about 24 men all ranks.

This war is not over yet by a long chalk and the Germans have quite a lot of reinforcements handy, more than have been made out by the papers and plenty of ammunition, more than we have.

Well tell mother I am looking forward to the next parcel and as many letters as possible. I hope you are getting me those things I want, more handkerchiefs, two good HH pencils etc. I hope you got that cheque to get mouth organs with, key of D, they must all be the same key or they are no good. I will send you a cheque for the other things, hat etc, as soon as you let me know what they cost.

Well my dear father there is absolutely no news. I really must end now I am afraid. This letter is very badly written, but it is the same old excuse of having nothing to rest the book on. Best love to you all. Ever your loving son, Charles.

The 'big brass' Charlie refers to in his letter, who had carried out the inspection and then observed a company attack, was Major-General Percival, a staff officer of the 17th (Northern) Division, which was commanded by Major-General Walter Kenyon-Stanley and part of Kitchener's Second New Army (K2). The division was then still under training in England, but an advance party had been sent to France that month to observe tactical training exercises in preparation for the division's move to the Saint-Omer area the following week.

The following evening Charlie again wrote to his father. It was the fourteenth letter he had sent home since arriving in France just six weeks before. The letter reads:

My Dear Father,

Received your letter of 8th just this afternoon and was extremely sorry to hear you were ill. I hope you are better now. I said in my last letter that the Burberry Wideawake would do very well and asked you to let me know what it cost. I hope you succeed in getting into the munitions department as I think the job would suit you a lot better than this beastly worrying ordnance work. There should be plenty of jobs going in that line now for anyone who knows anything about shells.

Re the 12 tins you sent out, they were alright but did not succeed as well as they might have done and the new stuff I have not had a chance to use yet as not being troubled by bugs myself. I have given it away to one of my men to try if it works all right. I will write home for more, also some more foot soap. For the men say 10 tins would be useful. If the platoon commander does not look after his men who is going to? Hence all my requests for their necessities. I would like also a good map case opening at the top and doubling into three. Another thing I asked for some time ago was a pair of hose tops. They are just like stockings with the foot part cut off, a greyish khaki would be a very nice colour.

Do you not think this taking of S. W. Africa a great bit of work? I would like to hear the same thing said about this part of the world. I see in the paper that K [Kitchener] came out here for a few days and made a thorough inspection of all the troops and arrangement. We are attached to GHQ and never knew he was out here. Are you not sick of seeing Sgt O'Leary's name in the paper? We all are out here and that he is also.

I do not think the Bosche will try the Belgian part of the line so much as ours and the French's but that remains to be seen. It strikes me the Kaiser is a bit out in his calculations about the fourth of August. Do you not think so? I do not think that John Bull was quite right about us taking the offensive just yet, but one thing I did notice was about the Canadian contingent. Did you see that? It struck me as very true.

What is the name of that artist's man in your office engaged to Sir S.D.'s niece? We have a lot of artists round here. In fact, they are stationed at the next big town to us, and their school of instruction is quite close. We have three of them in this regiment.

Well I must end now as I am orderly officer and have to mount the guard now. Well I hope you are better again and going strong. You have no idea how letters cheer one. Cheeroh and good luck. My best love to mother and Dick. Ever your loving son, Charles.

Noteworthy here is that Charlie is up to date enough with world affairs despite his army work to comment on the conquest and occupation of German colony of South-West Africa by South African forces; his reference to the Kaiser and 4 August presumably relates to the first anniversary of the outbreak of the war.

Charlie's two weeks at Wizernes were coming to an end. There had been more inspections and parades, and more training exercises and demonstrations of company attacks at the training area at Helfaut for the benefit of the staff of the 17th Division. Charlie's last few days at Wizernes, however, were spent suffering with a fever.

Unbeknown to Charlie at the time, it was also at Helfaut during July 1915 that the Royal Engineers formed two units of a new kind, 186th & 187th Special Companies, in preparation for the first British use of chemical warfare. Two more special companies were formed the next month. The

Engineers also put on a demonstration of the use of chlorine gas in an attack, the same gas as the Germans had used at Ypres earlier in the year. Haig and other senior officers were at Helfaut that day and left with a positive and lasting impression.

For the 2nd Wiltshires, meanwhile, there had been more new arrivals, including the return to the battalion of 27-year-old Captain William Geddes. Geddes was from Liverpool and had been ill in Gibraltar when the battalion had sailed home at the start of the war. Now he was fit to re-join the battalion and would be Charlie's new company commander. Also re-joining the battalion was Edgar Mack who had recovered from the wounds he suffered at Givenchy.

After the losses at Givenchy, 34-year-old Major Bertram Leatham of the Yorkshire Regiment was promoted and given command of the 2nd Wiltshires. He was killed during the Battle of Loos. (*IWM*)

Because he had been unwell, it had been a week since Charlie last wrote a letter home, so his next letter is dated 18 July:

> My Dear Father
>
> I was very glad to get your letter. In fact, it quite cheered me up to see I was not totally forgotten. I have been, during the whole of this last week, been fighting a go of fever, but do not know yet who has got the best of it. I am feeling pretty cheap now and have a rotten pain behind my eyes.
>
> There are lots of K's army coming out now at last and we are only too glad to see them. They have nearly all brought their bands with them.
>
> Mother promised me a parcel and told me quite a lot of things she was sending in it, but it has not arrived yet. I suppose she has forgotten it with looking after Dick. Tell her my address is simply 2nd Battalion Wiltshire Regiment, British Expeditionary Force, France. No Brigade or Division.

I cannot get at the ordnance stores at Havre just now, so do not see how I am going to get the map case from them. Do not forget to send me out a razor strop as soon as possible as my old one is worn out. It only cost 1/6 new and has lasted me about 10 months.

Well I must close now as I have nothing more to write about, so with best love to you all. I am ever your loving son, Charles.

The following day, 19 July, the 2nd Wiltshires were driven in motor buses back to their billets at Robecq. It must have made a pleasant change from marching. There they re-joined the 21st Brigade and, in turn, the 7th Division in readiness to go back into action.

Contemporary drawing of Charlie by his brother Arthur.

At the time Charlie was born, his father, Charles (*middle row, far right*), was adjutant of the Cinque Ports Artillery Volunteers based in Dover.

Charlie in 1910 at the age of fifteen, by which time he was a boarder at the United Services College in Windsor.

Then: Berkhamsted School pictured in the early twentieth century. (*Berkhamsted School*)

Now: Berkhamsted School today. The building on the right contains the library and museum, built in remembrance of Old Berkhamstedians who died during the First World War. (*Courtesy of Berkhamsted School*)

When Britain went to war, Richard, the oldest Hodgins boy, followed his father into the Royal Artillery and went straight to Woolwich, but soon after was severely wounded at Festubert.

By January 1915, Charlie was at the Royal Military College Sandhurst. He is shown here relaxing with his pipe, probably in his own room.

Charlie pictured as a 2nd lieutenant shortly before leaving for France. He was still only nineteen years old, as were many of those who graduated with him from Sandhurst.

In his letter of 3 April 1915, Charlie says he was in command of the local guard with his base at the Spring Head Hotel in Preston in Dorset. It is still there, as is the pumping station he mentions (now a water treatment works), which can be seen in the background beyond the houses.

When Charlie joined the 2nd Wiltshires at the end of May 1915 the battalion was billeted at Robecq. A quiet commune in the Pas-de-Calais department, at its centre was the church of Saint-Maurice à Robecq, now with the local war memorial beside it.

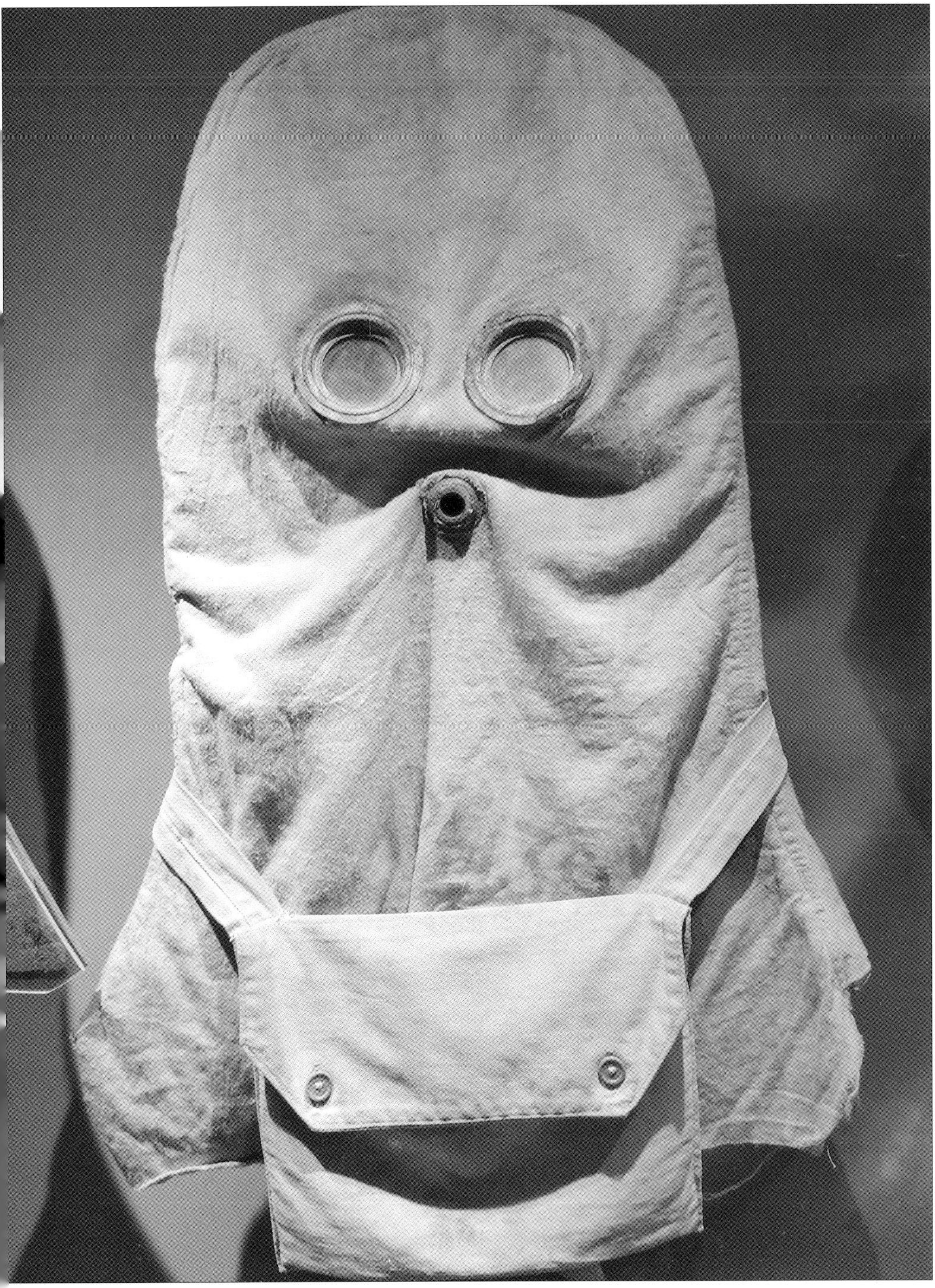

The P Helmet ('P' for Phenate) and then the PH (Phenate Hexamine) Helmet – shown here - replaced the earlier and simpler Hypo Helmet and featured two mica eyepieces instead of the single visor used previously and added an exhale valve from a metal tube which the wearer held in his mouth. (*Courtesy of the Passchendaele Museum*)

Left: The most poignant photograph in the archive is this one of Charlie with his mother, taken in mid-September 1915, shortly before Charlie returned to the Western Front. It was the last time she would see her son.

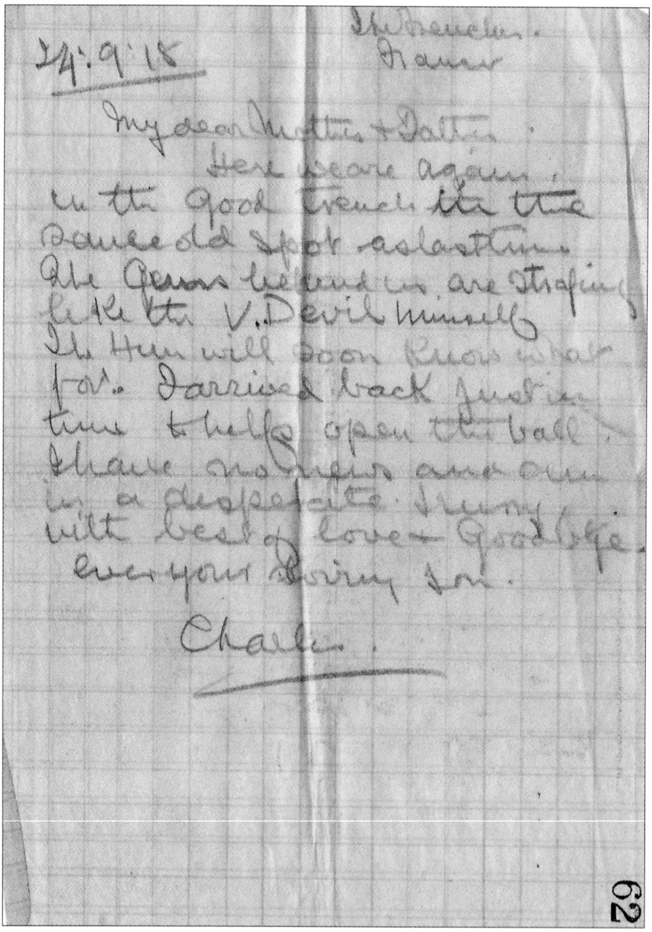

24.9.15

The trenches.
France

My dear Mother & Father.
Here we are again in the good trench the the same old spot as last time. The Germans behind us are strafing like the V. Devil himself. The Hun will soon know what for. I arrived back just in time to help open the ball. I have no news and am in a desperate hurry. With best of love & Goodbye. Ever your loving son.

Charlie.

62

Below left: And by far the most poignant letter in the archive is Charlie's last letter home. It is dated 24 September 1915, the eve of the Battle of Loos. Within hours of writing this letter Charlie would be dead.

Above right: The Vermelles British Cemetery contains 1,948 burials, including many who died at the château dressing station, which was situated here during the Battle of Loos. The château can be seen at the far right.

Right: Buried side-by-side in the Vermelles British Cemetery are Lieutenant Colonel Bertram Leatham, who commanded the 2nd Wiltshires at Loos and was killed on the second day of the battle, and Captain Murray Geddes, Charlie's company commander, who was killed on the third day. It was Geddes who had buried Charlie's body.

THE WILTSHIRE REGIMENT
CAPTAIN
W. MURRAY GEDDES
WILTSHIRE REGIMENT
27TH SEPTEMBER 1915
IN LOVING
HONOURED MEMORY OF
OUR ELDEST SON
LIEUTENANT COLONEL
B.H. LEATHAM, D.S.O.
YORKSHIRE REGIMENT
26TH SEPTEMBER 1915

Dominating the landscape near Loos-en-Gohelle and overlooking the former battlefield are two slag heaps together still known as the Double Crassier, which was in German hands in September 1915. The height was lower then and the orientation slightly different, but from this key position enemy observers held a commanding view across the British lines.

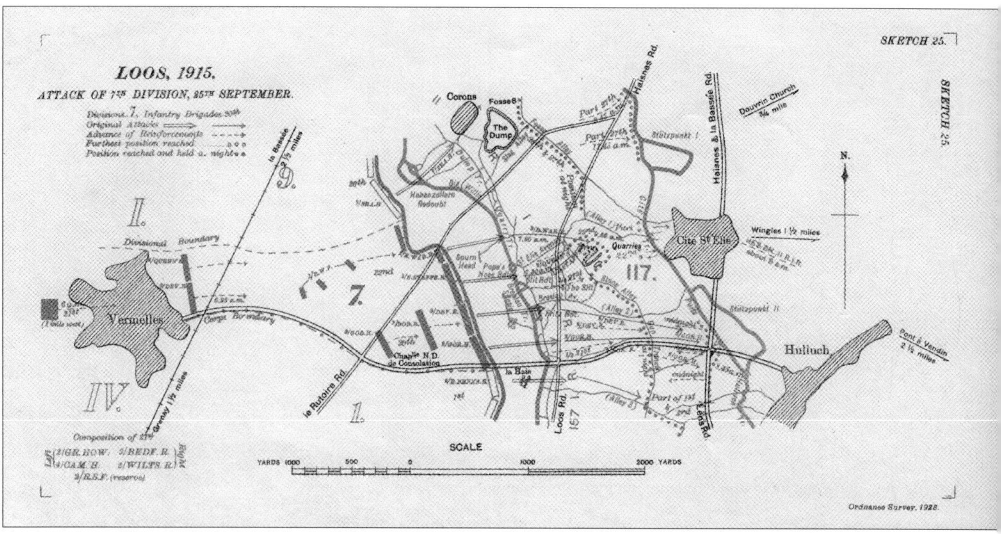

By late morning of the opening day the 2nd Wiltshires had crossed no-man's land to occupy what had been part of the German front line and support trenches. At 11.30 a.m. they left the German trenches and formed up here, on the northern side of the Vermelles–Hulluch road (its position is shown by the truck on the right), to assault the next line of German defences. Coincidentally, the farmer's tractor marks in the field indicate the line of advance across what was near-flat and very open ground. The German second line on the south-western side of Cité St Elie (just beyond the trees) was still strongly held and so the advancing Wiltshires were in full view of the enemy gunners and many were instantly cut down. The Quarries can be seen far left.

Left: Map showing the attack of the 7th Division on 25 September 1915, the opening day of the Battle of Loos. (*Compiled by Major Archibald Frank Becke and published by Ordnance Survey, 1928*)

During his time at Sandhurst Charlie formed a close friendship with 20-year-old John Cortis from Worthing. The two talked about going off to war together. Cortis was killed at Givenchy on 15 June 1915 when he and Charlie had been in France for just three weeks. (*IWM*)

M.S.3.Cas:) 45/E.F./1940.

December, 1915.

The Military Secretary presents his compliments to Mr. Mack, and begs to inform him that a report has just been received from Army Head Quarters in the Field which states that the late Second Lieutenant E.G. Mack, Wiltshire Regiment, was buried in Vermelles British Cemetery.

The Military Secretary ventures to send this information now, as Mr. Mack may not have previously received it.

Mack Esq.,
Swanmore,
Bishop's Waltham,
Hants.

Medals of Edgar Mack, the last of the Cortis–Hodgins-Mack trio to fall, and the letter informing his father that his son had been buried in the Vermelles British Cemetery.

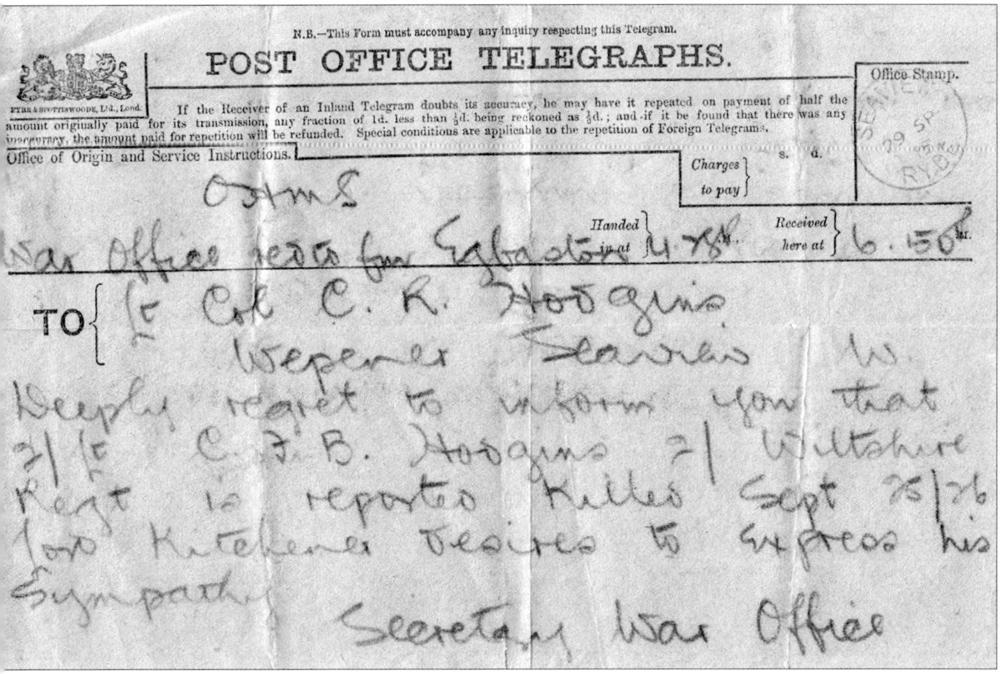

N.B.—This Form must accompany any inquiry respecting this Telegram.

POST OFFICE TELEGRAPHS.

Office Stamp.

If the Receiver of an Inland Telegram doubts its accuracy, he may have it repeated on payment of half the amount originally paid for its transmission, any fraction of 1d. less than ½d. being reckoned as ½d.; and if it be found that there was any inaccuracy, the amount paid for repetition will be refunded. Special conditions are applicable to the repetition of Foreign Telegrams.

Office of Origin and Service Instructions.

Charges to pay s. d.

OHMS

War Office Handed in at 4.28 M. Received here at 6.15 M.

TO { Lt Col C. R. Hodgins
Wepener Seaview IW

Deeply regret to inform you that 2/Lt C. F. B. Hodgins 2/Wiltshire Regt is reported Killed Sept 25/26 Lord Kitchener desires to express his sympathy

Secretary War Office

The telegram all families feared the most. Addressed to Lt Col C. R. Hodgins, it reads – 'Deeply regret to inform you that 2/Lt C. F. B. Hodgins 2/Wiltshire Regt is reported killed Sept 25/26'.

After the death of his son, Charles Hodgins raised the 120th Siege Battery, Royal Artillery, and went with it to France in June 1916 at the age of fifty-three. He subsequently suffered shell shock and was invalided back to Britain.

Charlie's medals and the collar badge of the Wiltshire Regiment. The medals are (*L–R*): 1914–15 Star, British War Medal 1914–20, and Victory Medal 1914–19 with bronze oak leaf denoting his Mention in Despatches.

In May 1926, more than ten years after the Battle of Loos, Charlie's body was exhumed from where it had been found on the former battlefield and reburied here in the Cabaret Rouge British Cemetery.

The Loos Memorial forms the side and back of Dud Corner Cemetery, which stands on a former German strongpoint captured by the 15th (Scottish) Division on the opening day of the battle. The cemetery contains nearly 2,000 burials, more than half of them unidentified, and the memorial commemorates over 20,000 officers and men who have no known grave and fell in the area between September 1915 and the end of the war. (*Rebecca Jacobs*)

The place where Charlie's remains were found – at, or extremely close to, the spot where he had been killed. The area has long overgrown, and the author is looking towards the enemy trench Charlie was attacking no more than a hundred yards or so away. (*Rebecca Jacobs*)

Charlie Hodgins's last resting place, in the Cabaret Rouge British Cemetery.

The Loos Memorial forms the side and back of Dud Corner Cemetery, which stands on a former German strongpoint captured by the 15th (Scottish) Division on the opening day of the battle. The cemetery contains nearly 2,000 burials, more than half of them unidentified, and the memorial commemorates over 20,000 officers and men who have no known grave and fell in the area between September 1915 and the end of the war. (*Rebecca Jacobs*)

The place where Charlie's remains were found – at, or extremely close to, the spot where he had been killed. The area has long overgrown, and the author is looking towards the enemy trench Charlie was attacking no more than a hundred yards or so away. (*Rebecca Jacobs*)

Charlie Hodgins's last resting place, in the Cabaret Rouge British Cemetery.

Chapter Ten

Trench Warfare

Charlie's stay at Robecq was brief. The day after the 2nd Wiltshires returned to their billets from Wizernes, Leatham and Forsyth went up to the trenches at Richebourg St Vaast. The 7th Division was taking over the sector and the 2nd Wiltshires were due to relieve a battalion of the Queen's Regiment in just a few days' time.

The following day it was the turn of the company commanders to visit the trenches to see for themselves where they were to be. They were able to talk to their fellow company commanders of the Queen's and learn about what the enemy was up to and what to expect when in the line.

During the afternoon of 22 July, the 2nd Wiltshires paraded at Robecq and then marched off to the trenches. Having stopped halfway for tea, the march was completed in darkness with the handover complete by midnight. Battalion handovers were usually conducted at night. The ongoing men were led through the labyrinth of trenches by a guide from the battalion about to be relieved. Men would often become separated in the dark, lost even, particularly on a pitch-black night or when the communication trenches were bogged down in mud, which slowed people down. Tape was often used for the men to follow so they would end up in the right place.

The Western Front stretched for some 450 miles, from the coastal dunes of Belgium to the Alps. The British held the northern part of the line from the coast, southwards across the fields of Flanders and the undulating hills of Picardy and Artois, and then along the Chemin des Dames, with the French holding the line thereafter. So entwined were the lines of trenches – the fire trenches, the support trenches, battalion reserve trenches, brigade reserve trenches, and communications trenches – that they were given nostalgic or otherwise popular names. Signposts were erected and maps issued to help the men find their way around, particularly when having to move about in the dark. Household names such as Piccadilly Circus, Hyde Park, and Leicester Square, or more unusual names such as Fork

Alley, Lovers Lane, or Idiot Row, had become part of the vocabulary on the Western Front.

By the summer of 1915, when Charlie first went into the trenches, the Germans were well dug-in opposite the British line and generally on higher ground. The ground was not only higher, but it was drier and gave a commanding view across large sections of the front.

A heavy artillery bombardment could change the landscape in a matter of hours, and so conditions in the British trenches varied considerably depending on the location and topography along the Western Front. Across the Flanders plain, for example, where the water table was high, the trenches soon filled with water every time it rained. Some trenches were constantly wet, whether it was raining or not. Trenches that were prone to getting very wet – the worst being around the Ypres Salient – had wooden planks running along their length to make it drier for the men to stand and making it easier to get around, and sump-holes every now and then to aid baling out. The parapet raised the height of the trench, usually by using sandbags, meaning that men could walk around without having to crouch down. It also meant they could keep out of sight of enemy snipers, and a fire step provided somewhere to stand to look out and when firing over the top.

For the men of the 2nd Wiltshires, daylight revealed the state of the trenches they had just taken over, which was not helped by the early morning rain. Trenches zig-zagged everywhere and although the sector had been relatively quiet at that time, the new arrivals found the trenches to be in a bad state of repair. The combination of having initially been dug very quickly and then the heavy shelling since, had left the trenches varying in size and in a far worse condition than Charlie expected from what he had earlier been taught to be a textbook trench. In some parts of the line, the arrangement was more like a series of connected shell holes rather than an established trench system. But to repair the trenches meant being out in the open, and that would mean the men being exposed to enemy snipers. Up to twenty men a day were being killed by enemy snipers along the Western Front, and so working parties had to carry out trench repairs at night.

Digging and repairing trenches had become a routine occurrence on the Western Front and could be particularly unpleasant in parts of the line where bodies, or parts of bodies, were unearthed having been buried during earlier bombardments. As the war dragged on, it could be months, years even, before a body was found, particularly where the dead lay covered by earth in what had become known as no-man's land, which could range from several hundred to just a few yards wide. And yet, despite the madness of war, birds would sometimes be seen strolling across no-man's land and birdsong could be heard along the quieter sectors of the front.

Officers lived in separate dugouts to their men. Subalterns would share, say in a group of four, and within their dugouts there was a youthful bond. They were, after all, still so young. Most were barely in their twenties, and most were experiencing the hardships of military life for the first time, certainly as far as trench warfare was concerned. But everyone usually had enough space for a bed and their own kit, as well as somewhere to carry out the administrative paperwork they were routinely required to deal with – such as casualty returns, operational and intelligence reports or personnel matters including writing letters to bereaved families or loved ones at home. An officer's dugout became an office as well as his home. Much depended on what the previous occupants had done to help improve conditions, but everyone would try and personalise their space in any way they could for the duration of their time in the trench. Candles and lamps were the normal form of light, but although some dugouts were made to feel quite homely and cosy – with floorboards, lamps, mirrors, gramophones, magazines, and newspapers from home – they were in the main rather uncomfortable and extremely dangerous places to be.

The time of year and the longer or shorter nights determined much of the routine. For Charlie on this occasion it was summer and so the days were very long – and of course the enemy also played a big part in determining how each day was spent. There was also the stress of being in the front line and having to cope with minimal sleep, and there was the weather. Rats seemed to plague the Western Front, the result of too many unburied or partially buried corpses. And there were lice, which fed off the human body, and their associated infectious diseases, as well as the germs – all because of the unsanitary conditions in the trenches. Dysentery, nephritis, enteric fever, and tuberculosis (the list goes on) could, and did, reduce a battalion's fighting strength within days – as much as, if not more, than losses due to enemy action. It was a war of attrition in more ways than one. But it was the same for both sides, such was the life of trench warfare on the Western Front.

It rained continuously throughout Charlie's first day of this tour in the trenches, which was good in some ways as it meant it was quiet and peaceful all day. That night Charlie led a working party to carry out trench repairs with his men and so there was little chance to sleep.

After this relatively untroubled opening day for Charlie the following afternoon, 24 July, brought a much different story when heavy German artillery fire left two killed and four wounded. That evening, Charlie wrote from his dugout to his father, who was now based at Ripon in Yorkshire and staying at the Spa Hotel:

> My Dear Father,
>
> Just a few lines to let you know all is well and I am still going strong, although I have only had three hours sleep in two nights and three days but hope to get some shortly. I was up all last night with my platoon building up a trench which the Bosch had blown about a bit. At first, I was quite jumpy of the bullets whistling round my ears but soon got used to it. I had one rather nervous escape and thought I had lost my servant, but all turned out alright. We were filling sandbags and building up the parapet when 'boom-boom-whoar-crack-crump-whirr-boom!' etc. I did not wait for the rest but shrieked to everybody to jump down. Into the trench leaped myself. My sergeant was next me on the top of the parapet but did not jump down until about ten seconds after. So, I stood up again to see if he was hit, but he just jumped in in time to loose a 'souvenir de Guerre' from a fresh outburst of 'straffering' from the German guns. It was composed of 'whizz-bangs' (which is a kind of H.E. and shrapnel shell in one, which goes off with two successive reports), shrapnel and case shot the latter, fired from field guns mounted right up in the German second line of trenches.
>
> Well this straffering went on for about five minutes while we all hugged the parapet. Keeping well down in the trench the balls and splinters whipped and pattered over our heads. When it was all over the working parties went out again to finish the job. A short time after this a bullet came whizzing past my ear and flattened into an old broken down house I was standing near. Well I was fairly jumpy after those shells came over and when I heard a bullet come cracking close to my head. Out of sheer kind of nervousness I would keep on finding myself ducking away, but soon recovered again. I do not mind bullets, but H.E. gets me. We had three black marias into our trenches yesterday about 60 yards off and the splinters came rattling down all round us. They were too hot to pick up.
>
> Well, as I said before, all is well. The snipers continue to snipe through the gap outside my dugout trying to get me as I go in and out and succeeding to remind me that the country is at war. The

shells go 'whewing' overhead just to remind us that the Kaiser's straffering process is in working order. An occasional one burst somewhere nearby making me wonder when the top of my house will be lifted off and carried away.

Must end now to get some sleep as we have got the same job on again tonight. With best love to you all. Thank you for the cake by the way. Ever your loving son, Charles.

Charlie appears keen to tell his father how he had been under fire and seemingly wanted him to know all the detail. It was quite a change from the letters that had gone before. Black marias were German heavy howitzer shells that exploded with a characteristic black cloud of smoke.

Organising and commanding working parties were key parts of a subaltern's life on the Western Front. Not only did the trenches and parapets need to be maintained, but so too the barbed wire out in front of the trench. Being sent on a wiring party meant tedious and hard work, not to mention the danger. The grass, where there was any, had to be kept quite short as if it was left to grow it could hide enemy patrols or attackers. It was better to remove any vegetation rather than keep having to go out into no-man's land to keep it short so that a good field of observation and fire could be maintained. Besides, the fewer times a working party had to venture out above the parapet the better, particularly on dark nights when it was easy to become disorientated. On such nights, when there was no moonlight or stars to provide any form of illumination, both sides might fire flares or star shells over no-man's land to see if any working parties were about. And if men were out there, they could become sitting ducks. Work in no-man's land was never-ending. Every time the enemy shelled the trenches and their surrounds it would destroy what had been done before, and the area would have to be put back into good order once again.

Patrols were also part of the night routine as a way of maintaining activity against the enemy. Small groups of men, often led by a junior officer, would go out into no-man's land under the cover of darkness to raid or reconnoitre the German defences, or to counter any enemy working parties. Both sides carried out patrols, trying to dominate the undominated ground. But patrols often led to men failing to return, having either become casualties of the enemy or the mud, or maybe having strayed into enemy trenches to become prisoners of war.

That second day in the line a draft of fifty-five men arrived from Le Havre to bolster the Wiltshires, but there was no let up from the shelling. The following day Charlie's 'B' Company suffered the worst of it, with the shelling lasting half an hour and killing one man. The War Diary for Sunday 25 July 1915 reads:

> France, Richebourg St Vaast Trenches – G.O.C. 7th Division and Brigadier General 21st Brigade went round trench lines held by the Battalion. Hd Qrs and 'B' Company shelled for about half an hour in the afternoon. One man of 'B' Coy killed.

The man killed was 31-year-old Private Edgar Stamp from Westbury in Wiltshire. He was the 2nd Battalion's only fatality that day. Stamp is buried in the St Vaast Post Military Cemetery, Richebourg-l'Avoué (plot I.H.2.).

Being shelled was for many the worst part of trench warfare. For the duration of the bombardment, they would have felt trapped in their dugout or trench, their nerves being ripped to shreds, wondering whether the next shell would fall on them, or maybe the next but one. There was nothing they could do, other than to hope and pray. Charlie, no matter how he must have felt inside, had to hold his nerve, and keep a stiff upper lip. He could not look weak to his men. On 27 July he wrote to his father:

> Les Trenches, BEF
>
> My Dear Father,
>
> Again, I write to you from this small rabbit warren of a place in which I live – or have been for the last 5 days and will be for the next two. The first letter I sent to 47 maybe mother opened it.
>
> Well I am still going strong but may not be in five minutes time as it is just about the time for the Hun to start his afternoon hate. I can hear he has started down the line with his 'crumpers', so called because they go off with two reports like this and which 'crump, crump'. We lost a man the day before yesterday, an officer's servant. He was hit in the side by the case of a shrapnel shell just outside the dugout we were feeding in. It was just about this time. He died from shock I think, not so much from his wound.
>
> My turn for leave should be along shortly in about a fortnight or so I hope. Then I may get seven days.
>
> The best (or the better) of large shells is that you can hear them coming and dive under cover, but shrapnel whizz-bang!! all over is about all one gets. With the bangs, unless one is in a suitable dugout is included at least half a dozen balls or a large chunk of sheet iron. The situation is better in regard to ammunition now, but the gunners are awfully rotten at hitting or even getting near

The pencil sketch Charlie sent with his letter of 27 July 1915.

aeroplanes. One flew over quite close last night, and the guns were painfully far away from it. The Bosch always gets jolly close to ours.

I spend all my night out with a working party building up a trench. I rather enjoy it so long as no shells land too near, but I do not mind the bullets so much. I am getting used to them. One came so close last night that it temporarily deafened me in one ear. You cannot keep your head down when on a working party as one spends more than half the night on the top of the parapet shovelling earth. I got a fearful shock the night before last as I went into a hole a shell had made a few hours before. I suddenly came across a blue coat. On close inspection I found it to contain the body or part of the body of a dead Frenchman, so I beat a hasty retreat. I also found a kukri near a place that a shell had been and have got it as a 'souvenir de la guerre', although it is rusty and has no handle on it.

I can hear a shell coming this way now, but needless to say it has now gone off somewhere behind me – 'whoooooeeesooow' = shell coming your way, either the last part you do or do not hear as the case may be – bang!!!!!

Well I must end as to get some sleep as I am going on with my trench tonight again. Re the cut tobacco it was not bad but not very good. I have got hold of some out here from another chap who has it sent out to him by the pound, which is not at all bad. The mosquitoes in these trenches are as worse than those in Canada. They are all enormous size and are very poisonous.

Well goodbye and best of luck, with best love to mother. I am ever your loving son, Charles.

If you would not mind writing to Cox and telling him that you were charged for camp kit at RMC, therefore credit me with £7-odd which you paid for it.

Charlie's letter includes a pencil sketch he had done showing the view from his trench towards the German lines. His view was across what is best described as uneven ground, probably due to shelling, in front of a building, presumably an empty dwelling of some kind and less than a hundred yards away, with a few trees in between.

Charlie had now settled into routine trench life, which was much the same from day to day. 'Stand-to' was an hour before first light with everyone fully armed in case the enemy tried to carry out a dawn raid. Breakfast was around 7 a.m. and would typically be porridge, eggs or maybe tinned bacon or sausage, bread and marmalade, and tea. After breakfast the men would be kept busy tidying the trenches and cleaning their rifles and kit ready for inspection. The standard weapon of the British soldier was the Short Magazine Lee-Enfield Mark III rifle. Its ammunition magazine held ten 0.303-inch calibre bullets and its development as a shorter weapon had meant that a longer bayonet, seventeen inches long, was required to ensure the British soldier would not be at a disadvantage should he ever come face-to-face with a lunging enemy soldier. The soldier's equipment webbing was a complex arrangement and included a belt, cross straps, ammunition carriers, water bottle, a bayonet sheath, and an attachment for specialist items such as an entrenching tool, although the webbing arrangement could easily be removed as one. The soldier was also issued with a large pack and a haversack, although these were not always taken into the trenches.

Subalterns inspected their men on a regular basis. This was in part to check the men's weapons were clean and in working order, but it was also to look at their overall health and cleanliness to make sure the men were maintaining their fitness for duty. Looking after their feet, for example, was critical when living in damp or wet conditions. Men were issued whale oil or lard to rub into their feet to help prevent the disabling condition known as trench foot. Platoon officers inspected their men's feet regularly to make sure they were changing their socks whenever possible and looking after their feet to prevent frost-bite from setting in.

Not only were there inspections for the junior officers to carry out, but food levels and ammunition reserves had to be checked to make sure the men were suitably fed and armed. Assuming things were relatively quiet, lunch was around midday and might typically be hard biscuits and jam. The afternoon would be spent carrying out any duties that needed doing without exposing the men to unnecessary risk, such as constructing better defences or completing repairs to dugouts or collecting rations and water. Everything had to be carried into the trenches, which could mean the ration party having to ferry supplies a mile or more forward from the transport line. There rarely seemed to be enough water to drink, let alone for washing or shaving. Moustaches were mandatory for officers and men, although those too young or unable to grow enough facial hair were exempt. Nonetheless, the rest of the face had to be shaved, although it was a regulation that could not always be enforced when water supplies were short.

Dinner was any time from 6 p.m. and would typically be soup or stew or bully beef or maybe sardines or kippers, followed by some tinned fruit. The standard of food was generally good because it helped maintain morale. Some cooking was possible in the trenches using a 'Tommy Cooker' or Primus stove, but most hot food was prepared behind the line and carried up to the trenches in dixies. Officers in the main ate the same food as their men, but it was usual for wartime army rations to be supplemented by items sent in food parcels from home, the contents of which varied enormously depending on the wealth of the family or friend sending it; food items were often shared amongst colleagues. Alcohol, though, was forbidden for the men, except for a daily rum ration, although officers were allowed to have privately-purchased alcohol for their dugout. Cigarettes and pipes were also part of the daily diet. Almost everyone smoked to some extent. Finally, there was another hour of 'stand-to' at dusk before the night-time working parties resumed their endless tasks. They might be given supper – maybe stew and tea – to keep them going through the night.

As well as the daily routine, there were also drills to practise, such as what to do in the event of a gas attack or a fire in the trench or how to deal with unexploded enemy shells. Everything smelled of explosives especially when enemy shells had recently burst nearby. The trenches had a smell like no other, partly of chlorine or lime used as disinfectants, or even something worse, or simply the smell of fear. There were regular visits from the battalion's senior officers, such as the company commander or the battalion commander or, perhaps, a visiting senior officer or red-tabbed staff officer who needed showing around.

Subalterns were required to read and censor their men's letters home as part of their everyday duties to prevent the betrayal of military secrets. Some young officers, faced with numerous letters to censor every day, skimmed through them as quickly as possible but others spent time reading them in detail as it provided an opportunity to learn more about their men. It was easier to command a man if the officer had some understanding of what was going on in his life. The originator of the letter might have lost a close relative in battle, for example, or was feeling down because of an illness at home or perhaps he might have been jilted by his sweetheart. By reading their letters it would often open the eyes of a young subaltern who might otherwise have had no previous connection with those of a different class.

Much of Charlie's time was spent doing his rounds, which could take a couple of hours or more every time. He was expected to be everywhere, keeping an eye on the tactical situation and looking after the everyday needs of his men. He might have just turned twenty himself, but the men looked up to the officers in command, even young subalterns like Charlie. Subalterns learned the importance of listening to their men, providing an encouraging word here and there, helping with a letter, or perhaps simply providing a cigarette or two to help lift spirits. They got to know their non-commissioned officers and men in a way that had never been seen in the British Army before. They were all side-by-side in the trenches, facing the same dangers and suffering the same hardships. Many young officers would not ask their men to do something they were not prepared to do themselves. That did not mean the men became over-familiar with their officers or lacked respect, because there was still a rank structure in place and discipline had to be maintained, but it was quite different to army life in the Victorian days. The older officers would often become more like fathers to the men and the younger subalterns like brothers. There was a bond between officers and men like never before, in a world where caring and personable leadership went a long way to help maintain morale in the trenches. Friendships formed and strengthened in the trenches. There was a strong feeling of camaraderie amongst those suffering the same hardships and where the expectation of survival was low. For some, life in the trenches – where there was food, companionship, and laughter – was better than the loneliness and poverty they might have suffered previously.

Charlie tried to catch some sleep whenever he could, but an officer might only grab a couple of hours' sleep or less in every twenty-four. It was one of the biggest strains of trench warfare. While the officers were mostly kept on the go during the day and night, routine trench life for the men could be tedious. It was important to keep the men busy. Much of their time was spent on sentry duty or in a working party. The routine differed from unit to unit, but typically the men would work in shifts. Two hours might be spent on sentry duty, for example, followed by two hours on a working party and then two hours of rest to catch up on sleep. This routine was often disrupted by enemy activity, of course, but in quiet sectors and on quiet days it was important to make sure there was never too much spare time for the men to get bored. Boredom and fear were not a good mix.

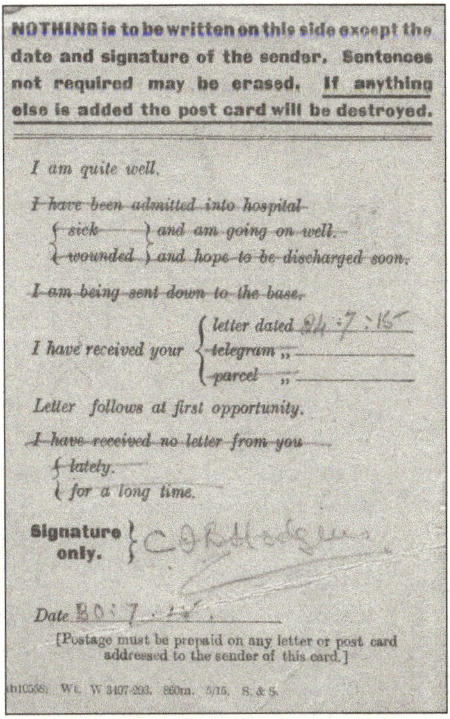
NOTHING is to be written on this side except the date and signature of the sender. Sentences not required may be erased. If anything else is added the post card will be destroyed.

I am quite well.

~~*I have been admitted into hospital*~~
~~*sick*~~ ~~*and am going on well.*~~
~~*wounded*~~ ~~*and hope to be discharged soon.*~~

~~*I am being sent down to the base.*~~

I have received your *letter dated* 24 : 7 : 15
~~*telegram*~~ ,,
~~*parcel*~~ ,,

Letter follows at first opportunity.

~~*I have received no letter from you*~~
~~*lately.*~~
~~*for a long time.*~~

Signature only. C F B Hodgins

Date 30 : 7 : 15

[Postage must be prepaid on any letter or post card addressed to the sender of this card.]

(h10558) Wt. W 3407-293. 860m. 5/15. S. & S.

Charlie's Field Post Card of 30 July 1915.

On 30 July, Charlie sent a Field Service Post Card with its set of standard comments to his father:

> *To: Lt Col C R Hodgins, AOD, The Spa Hotel, Ripon, England*
>
> I am quite well.
> I have received your letter dated 24:7:15
> Letter follows at first opportunity.
> *Signature:* C F B Hodgins
> *Date:* 30:7:15

This was the first of three such cards Charlie sent that have survived. These post cards were used by soldiers in the field as a quick way of getting a message home without the need for having it censored. As shown above, the card had pre-printed messages on it and the soldier simply crossed out those that did not apply.

The following day, Charlie sent another field post card to his father at Ripon:

> *To: Lt Col C R Hodgins, ADOS, 4th Army, Ripon*
> *[re-directed to Clotherholme Lane, Ripon]*
>
> I am quite well.
> Letter follows at first opportunity.
> I have received no letter from you lately.
> *Signature:* C F B Hodgins
> *Date:* 31:7:15

Charlie had been in the trenches for ten days and so it came as a relief when his tour came to an end. By the early hours of 2 August, the 2nd Wiltshires had been relieved by the 15th Sikhs of the Meerut Division, the relief again being completed under the cover of darkness.

The Wiltshires marched off to their new billets at Les Harisoirs, near Hinges, a few miles to the rear. There were some nervy moments after leaving the front-line trenches before reaching the safety of the billets at the rear, but once the bright flares and noise of the guns had been left far behind even the simplest of things in life were something to look forward to. Most of all, though, it was good to be alive.

Chapter Eleven

'We are at last out of those evil smelling trenches'

By the time the 2nd Wiltshires arrived at their new billets it was 7 a.m. The war was not far away yet there was peace and quiet at Les Harisoirs. It was now time to rest and look forward to a good long sleep.

Charlie was keen to share his recent experience with his father. On 4 August he wrote:

> My Dear Father,
>
> At last I have some time to write you a short letter. When you write me I think it would be best if you stuck the name of my company on the address as it better insures my getting the letter etc.
>
> We are at last out of those evil smelling trenches and I am jolly glad. The last morning we were in the Hun started to strafe an artillery observation post which he missed every time he put 70 large H.E. shells into the ground around but only succeeded in knocking down the trenches and spoiling my work of two nights.
>
> Two days ago he tried the same again but only knocked about the trenches in the same way. So in the night I took a working party of sixty men and one officer down to repair the damage. Now this officer is a very nice fellow but deaf and therefore cannot hear when bullets are coming his way. He is also very careless. You cannot call him brave and just as I was running round the damaged spots and apportioning off tasks to the men a star shell was fired by the Hun and the only thing to do is to crouch down wherever you are but he goes on walking along the trench with his head well above the broken down parapet. Of course the Bosche sees him and fires three volleys over. You can guess how

quick I came down off that parapet. But still all the evening I was expecting to get someone hit or a lot of whizz-bangs over, like they did on the first night I was out.

Well to go on we made quite a fair job but had rather trouble with the Indians that had been buried along the bottom of the trench by some D.F. and dug up again by the shelling. You can imagine the stink the next night. We went on with it and finished it about 1 a.m. so took the party home and then went out in front to see how the other working party was getting on. They were well below ground, so I took a crawl round in the field between the jolly old Hun and our lines. It had once been an oats field and the crop was still standing though rather thinned out by bullets. I found that between our line and the Huns was a stream and in this stream was piles of dead. Also between this stream and our line was any amount of dead and rotting corpses. They were mostly Huns, Indians or Highlanders. The only way you could recognise them was by their several equipments. The Hun by his jack boots, the Indian by his leather belt and pouches, the Jock by his pieces of kilt lying round, also by his cap or what remains of it. They must have been there since the 13th March. I was sickened by the smell and the sensation of putting my knee or hand on a body nearly every other step so returned hastily with bullets zipping round me and got back just in time to see Fritz start his morning hate on our artillery observation post. This time he used larger shells, Jack Jns and Black Marias and Coalboxes. He started about 7 a.m. and continued until 8.30 a.m., firing 72 shells. Eleven were 'duds' or shells which do not burst. I dived for my dugout just as the splinters commenced to fall and in my haste left my equipment just outside. I kept on popping my head over the top to see where they fell and then bobbing in again before the splinters reached me. But the observation post bore a charmed life and only my work of two nights was 'strafened' to pieces but I do not mind so much as we came out the following night and the relieving corps can see to them. They belong to Douglas' Division and will be among their own Kith and Kin in those trenches. By the way he is in just up the line, but I was too busy to pay him a visit. I heard from the CO of the relieving regiment that night that they had combined both battalions of his regiment owing to lack of recruits. I was OC guides that night and had to take the guides up to guide in the relieving troops.

By the way, also I have to report that a large piece of a Jack Johnson landed on my electric torch and jammed it into the ground, smashing it up to smithereens. It was with my kit outside. I have got that piece of shell as a 'souvenir de la guerre.'

My leave will not be for a fortnight or more now as quite a lot of chaps who have been sick and come back after I arrived I find have a precedence over chaps who come straight from England. Will you send me out a good cheap electric torch if possible to fit on my belt to replace casualty. Also a razor strop and a good pipe, one you can recommend, not too heavy or too light, also not with too large an inside to the bowl as I do not care for too large a pipe at a time.

Mother tells me that she has a parcel for me, tells me all the good things inside but having made my mouth water no parcel turns up. I wrote her yesterday. Can you tell me exactly what did happen to Dick to make him so bad a casualty? He was not in the List of the Empire Roll of Honour as far as I saw.

Well must end now so cheeroh and best of luck to you. Ever your loving son, Charles.

This long and detailed letter was by far the longest Charlie had written from France up to that time. The graphic description of the hastily buried Indian dead suggests that they were probably killed during the battle of Neuve Chapelle. The bodies would have been lying there for nearly five months. Charlie's opinion of the matter is clear – his abbreviation 'D.F.' may well stand for 'damn fool'.

Having rested and cleaned up after ten days in the trenches, the 2nd Wiltshires resumed the routine programme for a period spent in the rear. As well as giving the men a chance to relax, the army always believed it was important to occupy their time. There was more company training and, of course, inspections, one being on 6 August by Major-General Sir Thomas Capper. Capper has been described as an active and vigorous soldier and had served with distinction at Ypres while in command of the 7th Division, for which he was knighted. But having been wounded in April 1915 he had temporarily returned home to convalesce before resuming command of the 7th Division in July, replacing the now promoted Lieutenant-General Hubert Gough who had taken over command of I Corps.

That same day, 6 August, there was a football match between the 2nd Wiltshires and the regiment's 6th Battalion, which had recently arrived in France with the 19th Division. Although sport was not organised from the top, battalion commanders used it as a way of trying to cancel out the horrors of war. Sporting activities would range from inter-battalion or inter-company football, rugby, cricket, or tug-of-war, to more simple and often comical races between the officers and men. For the record, the 6th Wiltshires won the football match 2–1.

Being out of the line provided an opportunity to have rest and proper sleep without the worry or fear of being shelled. It was good to be dry and clean once again after spending so long in the dirt. Some took the opportunity to take a bath in a nearby town, while others took their turn in one of the divisional bath houses. Being out of the line also meant fresh

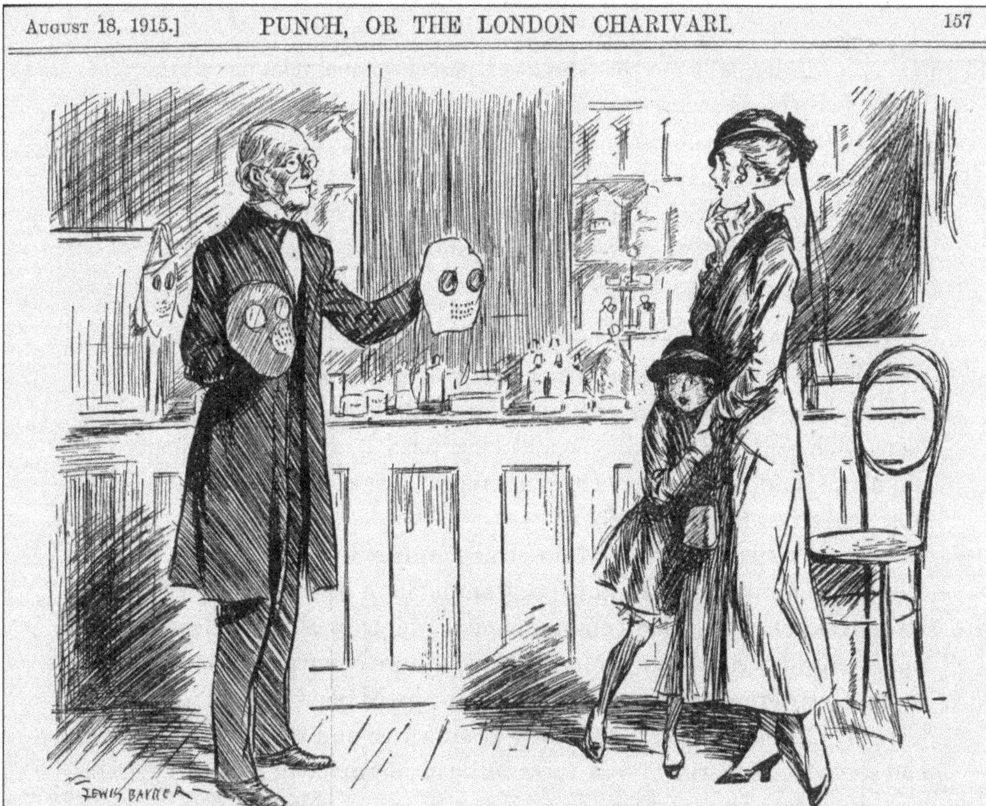

News of the German use of gas on the Western Front soon spread concern amongst the British public back home, although some chose to take a light-hearted view of the need for respirators, as shown in this cartoon of August 1915, published by *Punch, or The London Charivari*, a British weekly magazine of humour and satire. (*Punch*)

air and clean water and, above all, relative peace and quiet. There were also church parades, where a good sermon could help heal the psychological wounds of the men. Otherwise, some took comfort in painting, reading or writing poetry, or wandering around the countryside. Everyone had their own way of passing the time when out of the line.

For subalterns like Charlie there was also his turn as orderly officer, with duties including routine inspections of the men, mounting the guard and inspecting defaulters. And there were always letters to be written to families and loved ones of those who had been killed.

On 10 August, Charlie sent another field service post card home:

> I am quite well.
> I have received your parcel of 4th inst.
> Letter follows at first opportunity.
> *Signature:* C F B Hodgins
> *Date:* 10:8:15

Later that day, Charlie wrote the letter he had referred to in his post card:

> My Dear Father,
>
> Just a short line to let you know I received your parcel ok, also letter of 7th inst.
>
> The reason I sent the PCs [post cards] was that being in the trenches I thought you would rather have them than nothing at all. I was so dog tired after about four days that I found the only thing I could do was work and sleep, the greater part being work. I think I had about 20 hours sleep in ten days. The rest was doing some job or other. I am a great deal busier now as we have more work and I must leave this now to take a bathing parade.
>
> So goodbye and cheeroh. Ever your loving son, Charles.
>
> P.S. Do not forget the strop. Also the accordians which I wrote for yesterday. Sending cheque. They must both be the same key. If you could send them out quickly I would be very grateful. They are not concertiners but accordians that I want.

The 2nd Wiltshires spent two weeks at Les Harisoirs, during which more reinforcements arrived from Le Havre. There was even time to send handfuls of men and an officer home on leave. On this occasion it was Cusack Forsyth's turn to go. He had been on the Western Front since October 1914. Charlie had only been in France a little over a couple of months and so he would have to wait for now.

It was now time for the 2nd Wiltshires to go back into the line. On Monday 16 August, the battalion War Diary records:

> 7th Division relieved 9th Division in trenches in FESTUBERT section. Battalion was in Brigade reserve and occupied Old British Trench either side of RUE DE CAILLOUX. 'C' Company less 1 platoon occupying keeps on RUE DE CAILLOUX. Battalion relieved 5th Cameron Highlanders; relief completed about 1 a.m. Position about 1,400 yards in rear of firing line.

Fortunately, this was a quiet sector at the time, although during the second night a working party came under rifle-grenade fire and suffered a few casualties; five men were wounded, one of whom died on the following day.

On the 21st, the battalion relieved the 2nd Yorkshires and took up position in the firing line, while its headquarters remained in Old British Trench about 400 yards to the rear of its companies. The War Diary entry for the day includes a paragraph on just how dangerously close to the enemy's trenches Charlie's 'B' Company were:

> The centre of line held by Battalion and occupied by 'B' Company ran out to a point about 40 yards from enemy trench. This point came very frequently under rifle-grenade fire, which was returned. 1 Sgt and 2 men wounded.

Despite these losses it was a relatively quiet period in the trenches for the Wiltshires, with just three men killed and nineteen wounded during the eight days. On 26 August the battalion was relieved by the 2nd Gordon Highlanders of the 20th Brigade and proceeded to billets in Les Robes, from where it then moved to new billets at Les Preol.

With the battalion out of the line again Charlie could finally go home on leave. For junior officers home leave generally worked on a rota system. Charlie would have been at the bottom of the list when he arrived in France back in May, but with each departure home his name would have moved up a place. How often leave came round would depend on many things, of course, but for junior officers it would typically be every six months or so. For the other ranks, it might only be once a year, or even less. Again, it would depend on what was going on at the time and the number of casualties suffered. Leave was typically a week to ten days, maybe a little longer if circumstances allowed. Travel time had to be considered and so every day spent travelling was a day less at home with family and friends. Accordingly, not everyone would go home when given a period

Charlie with his father, Charles, then a lieutenant-colonel, outside the family home during Charlie's leave. Within days of this photograph being taken Charlie would be dead.

Charlie enjoying a moment of relaxation with his mother in the garden of the family home in Birmingham during his leave. It was September 1915.

of leave. Some chose to stay in London, particularly young officers who could afford to, and spend time enjoying all that life had to offer while they could. Others, though, would struggle to enjoy their time on leave. They would constantly be thinking about their friends at the front. It was not always simple to switch from one world to another. It was also difficult for families and friends who had not experienced the Western Front to understand those who had. Some officers chose not to take leave at all or to take their leave in France. But, in Charlie's case, he simply wanted to go home.

The exact date Charlie left France for home leave is not recorded in the War Diary, nor is it mentioned in his letters, but he left sometime around the end of August. Given he had only been in France for three months at that stage, his leave had almost certainly been brought forward for a reason, and that reason was because a major offensive was coming up. Rumours might well have already started amongst the men, but a major Allied offensive was now less than a month away.

Charlie's journey home would have taken him to one of the Channel ports and then by train to London. The landscape of southern England would have seemed a different world to what he had experienced on the Western Front. And from London he headed north to Birmingham to stay with his parents in Edgbaston.

Before Charlie returned to France, he had photographs taken with his parents in the garden. They would have been such precious moments. His parents could only wonder when, if ever, they would see their son again.

Chapter Twelve

Loos – Why Loos?

The debate about a possible British offensive between Loos and the La Bassée Canal had been going on for a while. The potential battleground was an undulating and rather featureless plain, except for the occasional ridge or small hill, but the whole area had once been one of the most important coal-mining regions in France.

The small mining communities that dotted the landscape, known collectively by the name Cité as if to give them some significance, were now in the main insubstantial, but although the mining had stopped because of the war the dominant features remained. These were the six towers supporting the winding gear for the shafts and coal slag heaps close by. The towers, known as '*fosses*', rose to a majestic height of a hundred feet or so, from where observers could enjoy an unrestricted view for miles around, while the slag heaps, called '*crassiers*', were also high enough to be used for observation purposes and to mount defences. One of these key positions, Fosse 8, was in German hands and dominated the northern part of the battlefield, while in the south another German-held *fosse*, known to the British as Tower Bridge, held another dominant position there.

From these towers and slag heaps close to their own front line, the German observers overall enjoyed a commanding view over the British positions. Furthermore, beneath the clay-like surface a layer of chalk made it relatively easy for the Germans to dig down to create deep defensive trenches and dugouts, which in some places were twenty or thirty feet deep.

Although the undulating and featureless plain meant there would be no major obstacles for the British attackers to overcome, it also meant there was little, if any, cover from enemy fire. It was not a good area to mount an attack, but the ground was considered even less favourable when the British discovered the Germans had constructed a strengthened second line of defence behind their front-line trenches, which essentially ran parallel to the Lens–La Bassée road. These second line defences were well placed on downward slopes, making them all but impossible for British observers to see, and were well protected by even stronger and deeper stretches of barbed wire. Furthermore, the Germans had established a chain of mutually supporting strongpoints along this sector of the front; the two most notable being the Hohenzollern Redoubt, situated between Haisnes and Hulluch in the northern part of the battlefield, supported by the key observation point of Fosse 8, and secondly a natural feature in the south, Hill 70, forming the backdrop to the village of Loos.

Haig, for one, was deeply concerned, not only because of the bare and open ground across which the British infantry divisions would have to advance, but also because the German defences were so strong. Haig believed that to mount a major offensive such as this would require perhaps twice as many divisions as were available at the time and a greatly increased establishment of heavy artillery. The BEF had fewer than a hundred heavy guns and 1,500 field guns available. Ten times that number of heavy guns would be required to support such a large offensive and probably twice as many field guns. Haig believed that sort of attack would only be possible the following year, after Kitchener's new armies had arrived in France.

The offensive was initially planned to begin at the end of August 1915. With a month to go, the senior French and British generals met at Frevént. Sir John French tried to convince Joffre that the British should attack to the north of the canal, where there was some chance of achieving success, but his argument gained little support. After all, the BEF had already carried out three abortive attempts earlier in the year. Other options were also proposed by French, such as a further British attack at Aubers Ridge, or maybe an attack in the Ypres sector, which would potentially remove the Germans from the advantageous heights of the Messines Ridge overlooking the Ypres salient. But none of these ideas gained any momentum. Joffre, in fact, went one step further and claimed there was no more favourable ground for the attack than what he had already proposed.

It was clear from the outset that Joffre and his senior generals, notably General Ferdinand Foch, commander of the northern group and deputy to Joffre, believed that an attack by the British First Army to the south of the La Bassée Canal in support of the French Tenth Army was the only way ahead. It was as if it had already been decided. French even suggested the British should commit to artillery support only, but this idea was always going to fall on deaf ears.

The discussions continued into August before the British senior commanders in the field – namely French and Haig – were overruled by Kitchener, the British Secretary of State for War, who reluctantly, or otherwise, decided to go with the French plan. In part this was because there was little good news coming from elsewhere. The Russians were struggling to hold the Germans in the east, the Italians had failed to advance against the Austro-Hungarians along the Isonzo River, and reports from Gallipoli suggested that the Allied landings there against strong and determined Turkish opposition had failed. And so, a coordinated major offensive on the Western Front would take some pressure off the Allies elsewhere.

Sir John had been left with no choice than to agree to Joffre's plan. The BEF would support the French, but on the understanding that the French attack to the south of Loos would be of sufficient strength to tie up the strong German artillery positions around the town of Lens, which marked the southern extremity of the British attack.

The decision had put Sir John in a position that no general would ever want to find himself in. Unrealistic demands were being placed upon him, but the bottom line was the British were to support the French – whatever the cost. French would have to order an attack without having enough men to achieve the aim, while being seriously under-gunned, and over ground that he knew was not suitable for there to be any real chance of success. Not only that, but he would have to go against the advice of his own senior subordinates, most notably Haig who commanded the First Army who would be the man to carry out the orders.

Who would ever want to be placed in such a bind? But that was where Sir John French found himself and this was the backdrop for the Battle of Loos.

On the other hand, the Chief of the German General Staff, General Erich von Falkenhayn, had been expecting a major Allied offensive. With not much having happened since May, he had for a while expected something new before the winter set in. As the summer wore on, it became increasingly likely that an Allied attack would take place and so two German corps were transferred from the east to the west, meaning the area to the south of the La Bassée Canal and around Loos was one of their strongest, if not the strongest, defensive positions along the Western Front. Well dug-in divisions of General Sixt von Armin's IV Corps of the German Sixth Army faced the area over which the British would attack.

The overall Allied offensive was to consist of two major thrusts into German-held territory. The main assault was to be carried out by the French in the Champagne region, heading northwards, while the attacks in the Artois area, heading east, would be an Anglo-French effort by the French Tenth Army and the BEF's First Army. All this was under the overall leadership of Joffre. These two thrusts would meet somewhere in

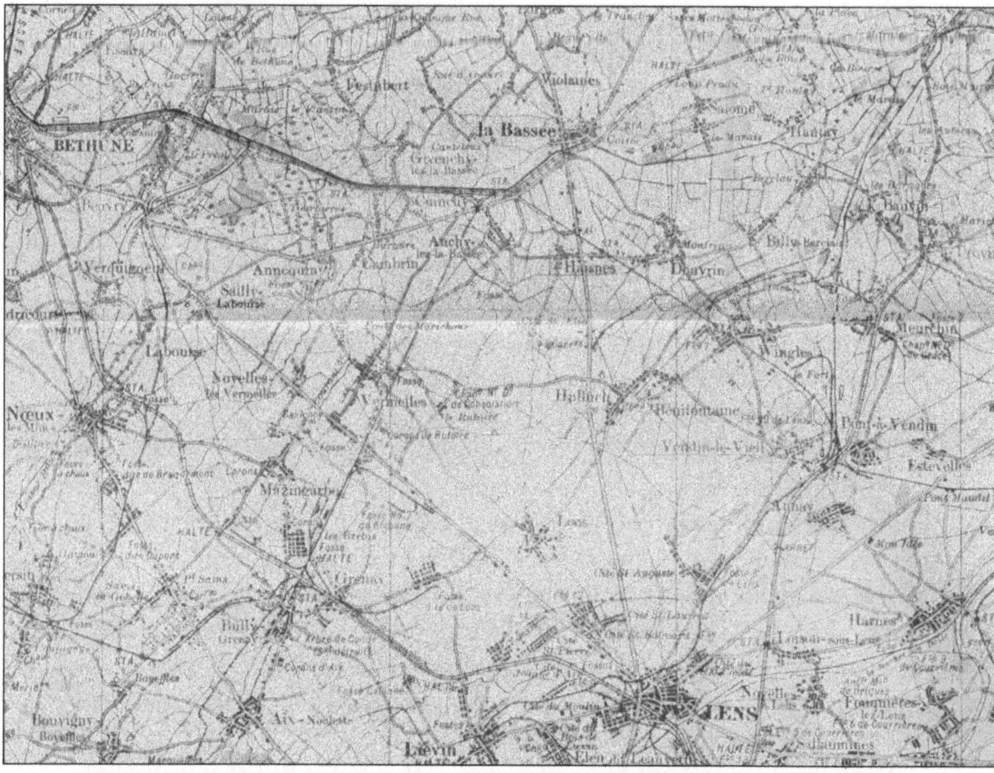

Map showing the area of the Loos battlefield. Loos itself is just north of Lens. The slaughter that took place within this relatively small geographic area is hard to comprehend today. (*Service Géographique de l'Armée*)

the region of Namur, it was hoped, cutting off and isolating three German armies as they went. This was to be a decisive breakthrough that could bring an end to the war, or at least put the Germans on the back foot and pave the way for an Allied victory.

The Anglo-French attack in Artois was to take place along a front of some twenty miles, stretching from the La Bassée Canal at its northern extremity to Arras in the south. Attacking over a wider front, rather than trying to punch a hole in the enemy's defences, as had been tried before, should decrease the effectiveness of the enemy's artillery and machine guns, because there would be no flanks from which they could oppose the attack. Equally, though, it meant there was a much wider front for the Allied artillery to support.

The French Tenth Army, which was to advance south of Lens, had seventeen infantry divisions available to it plus a thousand guns, with two cavalry divisions in support to exploit any breakthrough in the line. Haig's First Army, meanwhile, had seven infantry divisions and a cavalry division available for the attack. These came from I Corps, commanded by Hubert Gough, and Sir Henry Rawlinson's IV Corps, while a strong reserve force – consisting of the Cavalry Corps, the Indian Cavalry Corps, and XI Corps – was to be kept under the control of General Headquarters. The dividing line between the British and French armies was the Lens–Lallaing road. The plan also included the British carrying out subsidiary attacks to the north of the La Bassée Canal and at Ypres.

The aim of the British attack was to break the enemy's front and then prevent the Germans from re-establishing their line by decisively defeating their forces. Haig's plan was for six infantry divisions to attack across the British front, with I Corps allocated the northern sector and IV Corps the south; the dividing line between the two corps was to be the Vermelles–Hulluch road, which ran west to east through the battlefield.

The I Corps sector extended from the road northwards to the La Bassée Canal to join up with the Indian Corps. The 7th Division, which included the 2nd Wiltshires as part of the 21st Brigade, was to attack along the right of this sector, immediately to the north of the Vermelles–Hulluch road. To the left would be the 9th (Scottish) Division and attacking furthest north would be the 2nd Division. To the south of the Vermelles–Hulluch road were the three attacking divisions of IV Corps; its sector extending southwards to the Grenay–Lens railway to join up with French Tenth Army. The 1st Division was to advance along the southern side of the road, while 15th (Scottish) Division would be in the centre, and 47th Division furthest south.

Each division had its own artillery units. The 7th Division artillery, for example, consisted of the 14th Brigade Royal Horse Artillery (F & T Batteries), the 22nd Brigade Royal Field Artillery (104th, 105th and 106th Batteries), the 35th Brigade RFA (12th, 25th and 58th Batteries), and the 37th Brigade RFA (31st and 35th Howitzer Batteries). The field batteries of the RHA and RFA were equipped with quick-firing 18-pounder field guns. These had a maximum range of more than 6,000 yards and were capable of firing high-explosive, shrapnel and star shells at a rate of up to twenty rounds per minute. The field howitzer batteries, meanwhile, used 4.5-inch howitzers and fired a much larger high explosive shell at a rate of four rounds per minute, also at a range of around 6,000 yards.

The few heavier guns were to be spread along the front, a couple of miles or so behind the advancing troops due to the many German observation points in the area, with each gun typically covering a hundred yards or so

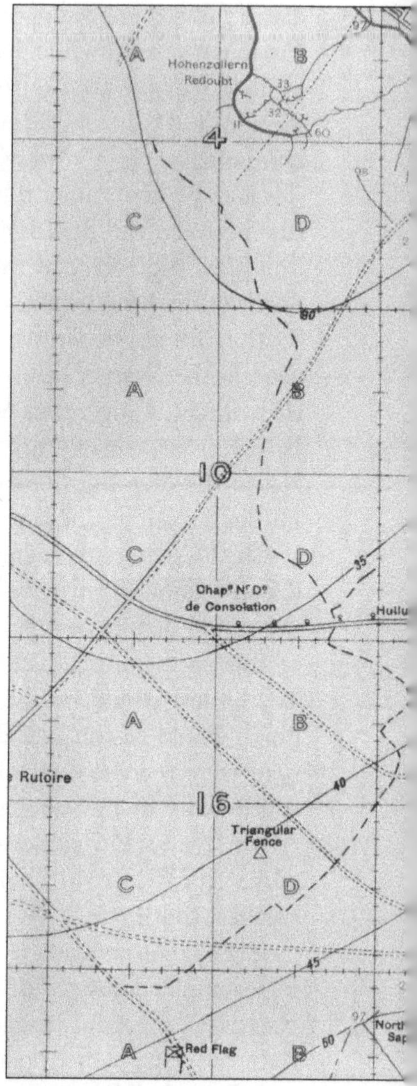

of front. The heavies were to target the enemy's strongpoints and second-line defences, which were out of range of the lighter guns of the field batteries positioned further forward; typically, half a mile or so in front of the heavies. They would target the barbed wire in front of the German front-line trenches and try to disrupt the enemy's lines of communication.

Artillery was considered the key to success, but in 1915 the British never seemed to have enough heavy guns, nor enough ammunition. As many guns as could be spared were to be made available to the First Army for Loos and nearly ten times the number of shells supplied at Festubert only a few months before, but most of these shells were 18-pounders for the field artillery, with less than 10 per cent of shells being for the heavier guns.

With just over a hundred heavy guns and fewer than a thousand lighter guns to cover a front more than six miles long and help to penetrate two lines of defences, the British would again be hampered by a shortage of firepower. And, because of the hoped-for use of chlorine gas for the offensive, there were two fire plans produced for each corps: one if gas was actually being deployed and one without.

The opening phase of the artillery plan covered the four days leading up to the attack. This was to be a preliminary bombardment of the enemy's defences. The rate of fire would increase as the time of the assault got closer, but it was never going to be possible to destroy all the potential targets. Also, the smoke and debris from the shells would make it difficult for the forward observation officers to determine how much success had been achieved against the targets that were engaged. In some places it would look like the barbed wire in front of the trenches had been cut whereas in others it would appear the enemy's defences had been untouched. It is hardly surprising, therefore, that in some key areas the preliminary bombardment would prove to be insufficient, and in many places along the front the German wire remained uncut.

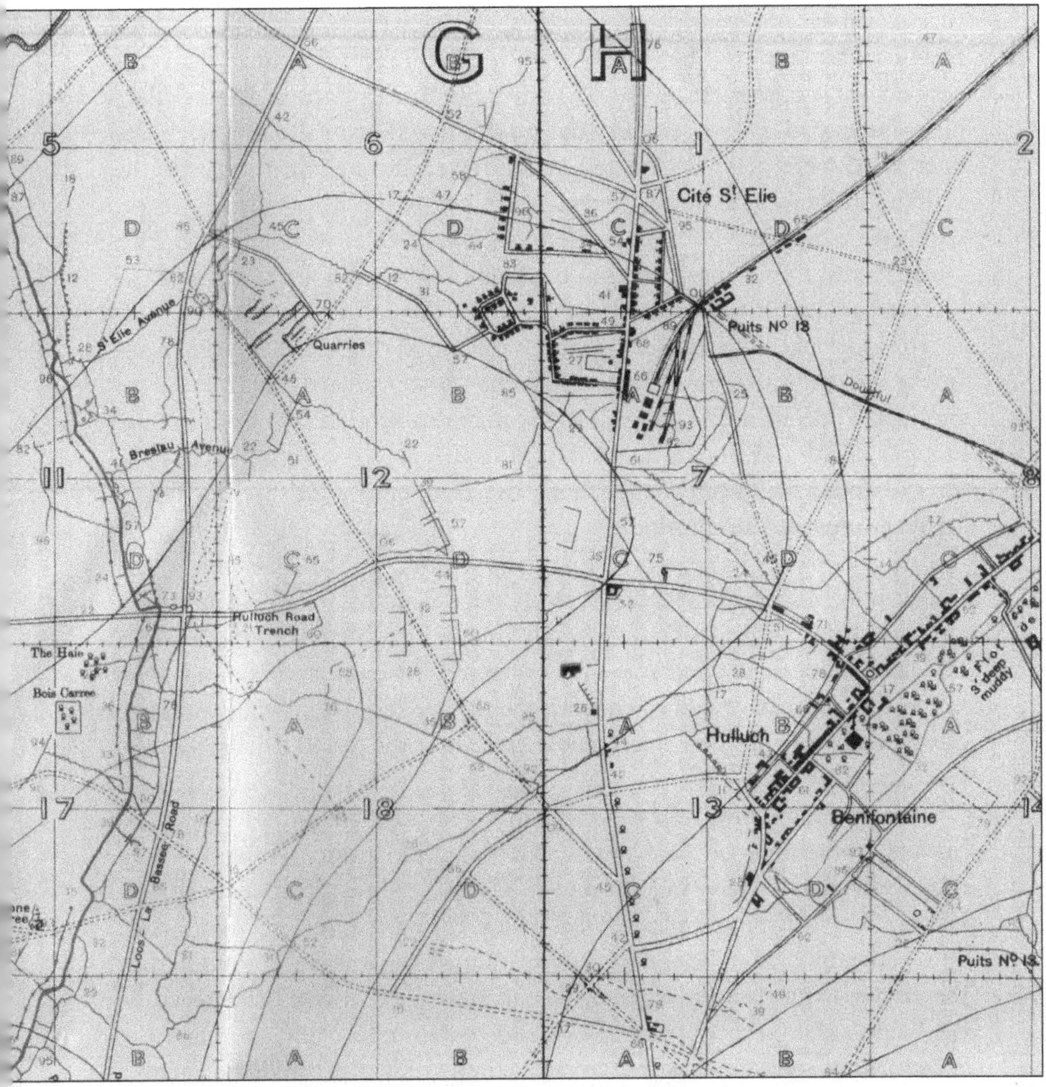

Map showing German trenches and key defensive positions in the part of the battlefield involving Charlie's 2nd Wiltshires. The map is corrected to 25 August 1915, just prior to the Battle of Loos. Of note is the Vermelles–Hulluch road (*running left–right across the centre*), the Hohenzollern Redoubt (*top left*), Cité St Elie (*upper right*), and the Quarries (*upper centre*).

The second phase of the artillery plan was to begin at H-Hour – the time when the first men were to go over the top – and last for forty-eight hours. During this phase the guns were to increase their ranges at various times. For example, at 'H+30' the guns were to fire more towards the German rear, and by 'H+60' they were to target the area 600 yards beyond the German front-line trenches. A third phase of the artillery plan, lasting four days, would take place after that to support whatever operations were being conducted at the time. Throughout the battle the artillery units were to be supported by aircraft of the Royal Flying Corps, with one wing carrying out artillery spotting duties to help the British gunners and two wings carrying out bombing operations to disrupt the German supply lines.

To help conceal the advancing troops the initial thinking had been to use smoke but given that gas cylinders had already started arriving in France it was instead decided that chlorine gas would also be used. The combination of a gas cloud and smoke, concentrated mostly in the central parts of the attack, would help protect the troops and compensate for the shortfall in artillery guns and ammunition.

This was to be the first time that gas was used by the BEF. But to use smoke and chlorine gas effectively it required favourable weather conditions, not least the wind direction and speed. For the opening phase of the Battle of Loos the desired wind speed was 8 m.p.h. or more and coming from as close as possible to due west, although anything from south-west to north-west was considered acceptable and cause the gas to drift across the German front line.

The gas was to be released forty minutes prior to the attack by the Special Companies of the Royal Engineers, from 5,000 cylinders – split roughly evenly between I Corps and IV Corps – while the intense artillery barrage was still taking place, after which the smoke screen would start. With favourable wind conditions it was hoped the gas cloud would cover the enemy's trenches for at least half an hour as this was believed to be the longest the German gas masks could remain effective. The longer the gas remained over the German trenches then the less effective the enemy's defences would be.

Throughout all this thc German front-line trenches would be under continuous shrapnel fire while the second-line defences would be hit by high explosive shells. Gas and smoke would be used concurrently until two minutes prior to the men going over the top when the gas would be turned off, while the smoke screen would be thickened up using triple candles. In areas where the enemy's defences were at their strongest a limited number of 4-inch Stokes smoke mortar bombs had been made available so that the screen could be fired into position rather than having to rely on the wind.

The six assaulting infantry divisions would then leave their trenches. The four divisions in the centre of the advance were to drive through the German front line and second-line trenches on either side of the Vermelles–Hulluch road and then push on eastwards as far as they could. The divisions on each flank of the attack were given limited objectives, the idea being to form a solid line of advance in the central sector covering both sides of the road.

To protect them from the effects of the gas, the men due to take part in the assault were issued with the new P Helmet ('P' for Phenate). Officially called the Tube Helmet it had replaced the earlier and simpler British Smoke Hood and featured two mica eyepieces instead of the single visor used previously, while adding an exhale valve attached to a metal tube which the wearer held in his mouth. The helmet had layers of flannel cloth dipped in sodium phenolate and glycerine and protected against chlorine. Helmets and respirators would evolve rapidly in the months ahead, with the 'PH (Phenate Hexamine) Helmet also soon appearing as gas became just another weapon that had to be endured in the trenches. But in 1915 gas warfare was still in its early days and was very much feared in the trenches, by both sides.

While the use of gas was the preferred option for the attack, should wind conditions be unfavourable on the day then a different plan was required. In this case, Haig wanted the width of the frontal attack to be significantly reduced and to use just two divisions rather than six. He even went one step further and suggested that unless the weather conditions were right for gas on the day then the attack should not go ahead at all. But his concerns again fell on deaf ears. The attack was to go ahead regardless – with or without gas.

Haig then tried another approach. If it was considered politically imperative for an attack to be carried out on the set date, but the weather conditions were not right for gas to be used, then a limited attack could be carried out and the main assault delayed until the following day when the weather conditions might be more favourable. And if they were not then the main assault could be delayed by a further twenty-four hours, or completely called off. This latest proposal was accepted by Sir John French, but it meant that two sets of orders would have to be issued – one set of orders for the use of gas and an all-out assault and the other set without the use of gas if weather conditions were not right on the day.

The large scale of preparation for the Loos offensive also applied to the medical services. Planning for Loos suggested that anything up to 40,000 casualties – killed, wounded and missing – might be expected and the battle might last several days. It would require an enormous effort to support such a large offensive. Additional horses, more wagons, more motor vehicles and more trains would be needed to move the wounded about.

Each infantry battalion had a medical officer and stretcher bearers. In everyday life on the Western Front artillery bombardments and enemy snipers caused casualties, but for a large-scale offensive like the one being planned for Loos the number of casualties would be on a scale not yet seen by the British Army in this war. Casualty care was based on a chain of evacuation in which the wounded and sick were moved from the battlefield rearwards. A wounded man would first either walk or be carried by stretcher bearers to his unit's Regimental Aid Post. This would typically be in a dugout in one of the reserve trenches and at this point the casualty would be assessed by the medical officer or another member of the Royal Army Medical Corps. Some basic treatment might be given, depending on the nature of the wound, the number of medical personnel available and the number of other casualties being treated at the time.

A casualty requiring further care would be taken to the relative safety of an Advanced Dressing Station where he would be cared for by men of a Field Ambulance (an 'ambulance' was a military unit rather than an emergency vehicle). Charlie's 21st Brigade, for example, was supported by 21st Field Ambulance. For the upcoming offensive at Loos the 7th Division's ADSs were set up in Hulluch Alley, with a simple line of wooden rails and trolleys being kept between the trenches and the château at Vermelles to ferry the wounded rearwards. If necessary, the casualty would then be moved to a Main Dressing Station for further treatment and care. The 21st Brigade MDS was at Gonneheim.

After that was the Casualty Clearing Station, with typically one CCS allocated to each infantry division. These were essentially basic hospitals, usually situated beyond the range of the enemy's guns, and were often set up in tents, with typically a hundred or more medical staff and personnel. These included nurses – CCSs were the closest to the front that women were allowed to serve. No. 7 CCS, for example, was at Merville and had the capacity for 500 casualties, although this figure could be more than doubled at a stretch. For the Battle of Loos, twelve CCSs were made available to the First Army alone, with a combined capacity for nearly 12,000 wounded. From the CCS the next move rearwards was to one of the large Base Hospitals along the coast of France, usually set up in existing permanent buildings and large enough for a thousand casualties. These were established with all the technical equipment required in a theatre of war. Finally, if the casualty's wounds required him to be sent home to

'Blighty' then a hospital ship would transport him back to Britain, and once there he would be sent to a hospital at home to receive specialist care or to convalesce.

By early September 1915 several divisions from Kitchener's New Army had arrived in France. Some battalions relieved more experienced battalions in the quieter parts of the line, while others took up positions in readiness to go into battle for the first time. Bertram Leatham now received orders to move the 2nd Wiltshires down towards Loos to take part in the preparations that had already begun. Along with the rest of the 7th Division, the battalion left the Béthune area on 9 September, arriving in Vermelles the following day, having stopped for the night at Le Bourse.

Vermelles is a former mining commune situated three miles to the north-west of Loos. Charlie had now come back from home leave, and he arrived to find Vermelles a rather battered village. Even though it was quite a large village for the area, most of its buildings had been levelled by enemy fire and the locals had long gone.

The 2nd Wiltshires occupied reserve trenches to the west of the village and for the next few days the companies joined in with the preparations that were under way. Every night the men went forward under the cover of darkness to dig assembly trenches and then returned to rest by day. Except for three days of rest, when the battalion was billeted at Verquin, this was the pattern for the 2nd Wiltshires leading up to the Battle of Loos.

Then, on 19 September, Haig issued his orders for the 'Big Push', instructing the First Army to 'assume the offensive on 25 September, and advance between Lens and the La Bassée Canal towards the line Henin–Liètard–Carvin'. It was now a matter of monitoring the weather closely and hoping the wind conditions would be right on the day. Rarely, if ever before, did an army commander have to pay so much attention to the wind direction and speed.

Chapter Thirteen

'The Hun will soon know what for'

The British front line was about a mile and a half to the east of the 2nd Wiltshires' positions near Vermelles, with both Loos and Hulluch then in German hands. The next few days were spent in and out of billets and a line of reserve trenches to the west of the village. The offensive was less than a week away, but things in the Vermelles area were still relatively quiet with nothing of note to report other than the arrival of a new draft of men from Le Havre. Each night the Wiltshires went forward to continue digging assembly trenches, before returning to the relative safety of the reserve line to rest by day. In the 7th Division's area alone, there were up to five parallel lines of trenches dug behind the British front line. These extra trenches were designed to make it easier and quicker for the attacking waves of infantry to form up prior to going over the top.

Charlie did not write any letters during these few days. Not only had he just returned to France from his home leave, but he would also have been busy and tired. British guns were arriving by the hour to take up positions in the ruins of Vermelles, ready to start the artillery onslaught in just a couple of days' time. This extra activity had come to the attention of the enemy artillery and their bombardments resumed, but for the Wiltshires the trench digging went on.

Haig's directive on 19 September triggered a set of orders that cascaded down the chain of command – through corps level to the divisional commanders who, in turn, passed their orders to brigades, and the brigadiers to the battalion commanders – until everyone knew what they were about to do.

The British artillery bombardment began at 7 a.m. on 21 September. Throughout what was a fine and warm late summer day, clouds of smoke and dust could be seen billowing above the German front-line trenches until it was difficult for observers to identify what was going on. The enemy retaliated with their own bombardment, although in the Vermelles area it was reportedly very weak. However, George Bryer-Ash was injured and had to be admitted to hospital. He would reluctantly have to sit it out on the sidelines and miss the 'Big Show'.

The fine weather, however, soon turned to rain, with the wind randomly changing direction and speed. At any other time, these variable weather conditions might not have mattered, but with the opening day of the offensive looming, and much depending on the effective use of gas, it was a worrying time.

On the 23rd it was again wet and the wind variable. The 2nd Wiltshires had finished their trench digging and later that evening marched back to their billets at Verquin under the cover of darkness. By then the weather had turned foul, with a raging thunderstorm and torrential rain, and by the time the men arrived at their billets everyone was soaked to the skin.

The following day, 24 September, was spent preparing for the attack, now just twenty-four hours away. The artillery bombardment continued all day. Fortunately, the weather conditions had improved, although the wind was again variable. At midday it was coming from the south and even round as far as the south-east. For the generals and planners, this was not good news.

At 3 p.m., Leatham gathered his officers. He told them what was expected of the 2nd Wiltshires and briefed them on the detailed plan of attack, which they were to pass on to their non-commissioned officers and men. The frontal width of Gough's I Corps was around two miles. Capper's 7th Division had been given an attacking front of around 1,400 yards between the Vermelles–Hulluch road on its right and the fortified Hohenzollern Redoubt on its left, although the redoubt itself was not one of the division's objectives; that hard nut was allocated to the 9th Division. Essentially, the men of the 7th were to seize and hold the enemy's second-line defensive trench positions at Haisnes, Cité St Elie and Hulluch, and from there they were to press on to the Haute Deule Canal, which ran north–south behind the German lines.

Within this sector the distance to the German front line varied from a thousand yards at its furthest, which was on the extreme left of the division's attack, where two battalions of the 22nd Brigade were to attack along a front of 600 yards, to just a few hundred yards on the right of the advance, where two battalions of the 20th Brigade were to spearhead the attack. The two remaining battalions in each brigade would then follow up the attack. It was to be a classic two-brigade attack. The 21st Brigade, meanwhile, commanded by Brigadier Herbert Watts and including the 2nd Wiltshires, would not be part of the initial assault. The brigade was to be held back as the division's reserve, but it would continue the advance after the two forward brigades had punched a hole in the enemy's defences, from where the 21st would then carry on to the Haute Deule Canal.

This was an ambitious plan, not only because of the lack of resources available to the British, but also because there were several key German defensive positions in the sector. The most notable of these defences was a fortified position known as the Pope's Nose Redoubt. It was in the centre of the division's attacking front and flanked by Spurn Head to its north and Breslau Sap to the south. From these strengthened positions the enemy machine guns could, and would, provide enfilade fire over a large area on both flanks. Beyond the German front-line trenches were two communications trenches – St Elie Avenue and Breslau Avenue – running rearwards to the second line of German defences, located about 600 yards further back, where there was Stone Alley and the Quarries, an old chalk mining pit a hundred yards or so wide. There was also the heavily defended area of Cité St Elie and there were two further heavily defended German positions – which they called Stützpunkt I and Stützpunkt II – situated respectively between Cité St Elie and the villages of Haisnes to the north and Hulluch to the south.

While being held in reserve was, on the face of it, a good thing for Charlie and the men of the 2nd Wiltshires, in that it kept them out of the initial assault, it did, however, make it more difficult for the officers to make plans for what they might encounter on the day. The assault battalions had been given clear objectives, which would have been briefed, planned, and even rehearsed, and so these objectives would have been firmly fixed in the men's minds, no matter how unpleasant a thought that might have been. But for the battalions following on there were so many uncertainties. They did not know exactly when they would be called upon nor did they know where they would be required to attack.

In addition to Leatham's overall brief, Charlie would have discussed the attack in more detail with his company commander, William Geddes, who would lead 'B' Company in the assault. There would have been much to talk about and many 'what-ifs' to consider, as their role could range from simply walking into the enemy's second line of trenches unopposed to having to fight their way out of the British front line should the initial assault be a disaster. And they might be required to fight on the left of the front or on the right, or in the centre. Anything could happen between the first men going over the top and the 2nd Wiltshires going in.

Thus the stage was set for what would become known as the Battle of Loos. It was to be the British Army's biggest offensive of the war to date. For the 2nd Wiltshires the rest of the day was spent making final preparations for the assault. It was important to keep everyone busy. The men were issued with everything they would need for the attack. Charlie's platoon was allocated sets of wire cutters, picks and shovels, and a pole with a coloured disc to indicate to spotters exactly where they were at any time during the advance. As well as their usual webbing and rifles, his men were laden with additional kit and each of them was issued with up to 200 rounds of ammunition, empty sandbags and extra food.

The young officers would have known that if anyone was going to be killed the following day then it was most likely to be them. The facts told them so. For some, the final day before going over the top would drag, while for others those final hours raced by. But whatever the individual's case, there was nothing anyone could do to stop the time uncontrollably slipping away. For many, it would be their last full day on earth. Some chose to write what might be a last letter home. Others thought it unlucky to write such letters. But at some point during that day, 24 September 1915, Charlie found a few minutes to write a short letter to his parents:

> The Trenches,
> France
>
> My dear Mother and Father,
>
> Here we are again in the good trench in the same old spot as last time. The guns behind us are strafing like the very devil himself. The Hun will soon know what for. I arrived back just in time to help open the ball. I have no news and am in a desperate hurry. With best of love and goodbye.
>
> Ever your loving son,
>
> Charles.

Charlie had decided to address this crucial letter to both his parents before going over the top. His habitual 'goodbye' at the end of his letter seems especially poignant here, when he knew what was about to come and that there was a strong possibility that he might be killed.

During the evening of 24 September, just hours before the assault was to begin, Haig met with his corps commanders. The wind was forecast to be favourable. It was moving round towards the west and expected to strengthen to anything up to 20 m.p.h. Conditions were forecast to be ideal for the use of gas and so Haig ordered the attacking brigades into the front-line trenches ready for the assault to begin, although the exact time the first men were to go over the top would not be decided until later that night.

Chapter Fourteen

The First Morning

Soon after midnight Charlie and the 2nd Wiltshires set off from Verquin in full battle array. It had started to rain, although it amounted to nothing more than drizzle for most of the night. They had a march of five miles to their allotted trenches, their route taking them via La Bourse and Sailly. The attacking brigades were now in place and ready while those in reserve were still marching towards their predetermined positions a few miles or so behind the front line.

By 3 a.m. the 2nd Wiltshires had taken up position in the trenches to the south-east of Noyelles, on the north-west corner of Vermelles. They were still a mile or two behind the British front line, but the men could hear and see that the artillery bombardment had intensified to a level they had never witnessed before. The first entry in the 2nd Wiltshires' War Diary for that day simply reads:

> Battalion moved at 12.30 a.m. marched via LA BOURSE and SAILLY, arriving at a reserve line of trenches S.E. of NOYELLES at point L.12 c 6.6 at about 3 a.m. Bombardment becomes intense.

The wind speed, however, had dropped and was reported to be less than 8 m.p.h. and there was a chance it could back to a more southerly direction once again. These were tense moments for Haig and his staff at Hinges Château as they agonised whether to release the gas. So much depended on the wind if the attack was to have any chance of success. Each hour that passed brought more uncertainty, although it was anticipated that the wind speed would pick up again soon after dawn. As for its direction, the longer they waited the more chance the wind would back round to the south and so the sooner the gas cloud could be released after dawn the more chance there was of success.

While the 2nd Wiltshires were taking up position on the edge of Vermelles, Haig issued the order that Zero Hour, the time the gas was to

This was the position taken up by the 2nd Wiltshires in the early hours of 25 September. The reserve trenches they occupied were on the extreme left of this image and ran along what is now the edge of the farmer's field, roughly parallel to the track (now the Chemin de Petit Marais) leading to the farmer's house.

be released, was to be 5.50 a.m., just around dawn. The infantry were to go over the top forty minutes later, at 6.30 a.m. But having announced Zero Hour, Haig would leave the final decision as to whether to use gas or not until nearer the time.

That crucial decision was finally made just after 5 a.m. In his War Diaries and Letters, Haig would later write about one of his staff lighting a cigarette and observing the smoke drifting in puffs towards the north-east. The wind was gentle, but it was coming from the south-west. And with that, Haig gave the order to carry on. Gas was to be used for the attack. It was a difficult decision, and a huge one at that, particularly as Haig knew how the wind had varied during the past few days. But difficult decisions in war are what senior commanders must make.

Within half an hour of Haig giving the order to carry on, the wind speed had increased slightly, but there remained the risk that should the wind direction change at all, or should it weaken, then there was a real possibility the gas would drift back towards the British lines and over the troops carrying out the attack.

Dawn arrived cold, damp, and with a heavy mist. To the north of the battlefield diversionary attacks were under way. The guns roared thunderously like never before and the ground shook all along the front. High explosive and shrapnel shells rained down on the enemy positions nearby.

The men of the 7th Division were ready to go. The four lead battalions had lined up from north to south: 2nd Royal Warwickshires and 1st South Staffordshires of the 22nd Brigade; and the 8th Devons and 2nd Gordon Highlanders of the 20th Brigade. Immediately behind these were the men of the 2nd Border Regiment (20th Brigade), while holding on the eastern side of Vermelles and ready to follow on as the second wave were (from north to south): 1st Royal Welch Fusiliers and 2nd Queen's, both from the 22nd Brigade; and the 9th Devons and 6th Gordon Highlanders of the 20th Brigade. The battalions of the 21st Brigade – 2nd Bedfords, 2nd Yorkshires, 2nd Royal Scots Fusiliers, 2nd Wiltshires, and 4th Cameron Highlanders – were all waiting in reserve.

Soon after 5.50 a.m. the heavy artillery bombardment intensified across the German lines and the gas was released, even though the wind remained variable and unpredictable at certain points along the front. This variation meant that the use of gas would be successful, or at least satisfactory, where the wind conditions were favourable, but far less so where it was not. In some cases, a change in wind direction soon after the gas had been released resulted in the gas being blown back across the British lines.

Across the I Corps front a wall of thick white smoke appeared from the shells, steadily increasing in density, and rising high into the air. In the 7th Division's sector, the two leading battalions of the most northerly brigade, the 22nd Brigade, began their attack.

At first things seemed to go as intended. The gas plan was working well, and the lead battalions were concealed by the smoke screen. But it then got to the stage where the men could barely see ten yards in front of them. Due to the inefficiency of their respirators many decided to remove them; they could not see through the fogged-up eyepieces and could barely breathe with them on. At such a crucial time in their lives, many decided to risk being gassed rather than be suffocated wearing the mask. It inevitably led to some of them being affected by their own gas. Furthermore, as the men got closer to the German front line it became apparent that the artillery bombardment had failed to cut the enemy barbed wire and this area was also clear of gas and smoke. The wind had not been as strong as had been hoped and so the gas had yet to drift as far as the German front line. And besides, the four days of preliminary artillery bombardment had meant there was no element of surprise.

As gallantly as they tried to cut the wire and break through the enemy defences, both battalions – the 2nd Royal Warwicks and 1st South Staffords – suffered heavily as they came under increasingly heavy fire from the Pope's Nose Redoubt, although some did manage to reach the trenches of the German front line. One of these was 33-year-old Private Arthur Vickers, a former brass carter from Birmingham, serving with the Warwicks, who would later be awarded the Victoria Cross, Britain's highest award for gallantry. His citation reads:

> On 25 September 1915 at Hulloch [*sic*], France, during an attack by his battalion on the first line German trenches, Private Vickers on his own initiative, went forward in front of his company under very heavy shell, rifle and machine gun fire and cut the wires which were holding up a great part of his battalion. Although it was broad daylight at the time, he carried out this work standing up and his gallant action contributed largely to the success of the assault.

Meanwhile, the two leading battalions of the 20th Brigade, on the right of the divisional front, had far more success. The artillery bombardment here had done its job and under the cover of the gas and smoke the leading companies swept through the German front line and were advancing towards Breslau Trench, the brigade's first objective. On the far right of the attack, the Gordon Highlanders were advancing along the north side of the Vermelles–Hulluch road. For the Gordons it had been a walk rather than a mad dash. On their left, however, the Devonshires had run into a major problem. Much of the barbed wire in front of them had been left uncut meaning the men soon became bunched together, making them easy targets for the defenders in Breslau Trench.

At around 6 a.m. the 2nd Wiltshires were ordered to advance through Vermelles and make their way up a long communications trench called Chapel Alley, which ran eastwards and followed the line of the Vermelles–Hulluch road, to occupy what had been the trenches of the British front line. It was drizzling with rain and there was a slight breeze.

The Wiltshires passed quickly through Vermelles, but progress slowed dramatically through Chapel Alley due to severe congestion as men tried desperately to move forward as quickly as they could. The enemy artillery bombardment was intense, and it was then that the battalion suffered its first casualties of the day.

The British use of gas during the opening phase of the Battle of Loos was reported in all its graphic detail back home. This artist's impression was by Samuel Begg and appeared on 30 October 1915 under the title 'Not Like Soldiers, But Like Devils'. (*Illustrated London News*)

Amongst the first to fall wounded was the 'A' Company commander, Captain A. St. J. C. D. M. King, known within the battalion as 'Boy King' due to his advancing years. He was nearly sixty years old and had relinquished a good position in Portuguese East Africa to return home and fight. King was carried off on a stretcher and would take no further part in the action, and so it would be left to 21-year-old 2nd Lieutenant Frank Friend, the London lad, to pick up the reins and assume command.

The battalion's War Diary summarises this early part of the day:

> At about 6 a.m. the attack was launched. Battalion ordered to advance through VERMELLES up communication trench (CHAPEL ALLEY) to occupy front line at point G.11 c 9.8. Capt King wounded 2/Lt F. H. Friend assumed command of 'A' Company.

At that stage Charlie was fine. The battalion had yet to go over the top, but had made it as far as the recently vacated British front-line trenches from where the attack had first started. The men had done well to get forward as quickly as they had, given the congestion in the communications trenches, but it had still taken them three hours to cover the two miles to the front. However, in this part of the line the preliminary artillery bombardment and gas appears to have had little effect. The variable wind conditions in this sector had meant that not all the gas cylinders had been turned on for fear of the gas drifting back over the British lines, and much of the barbed wire in front of the enemy trenches remained uncut.

Because of heavy losses suffered by the 22nd Brigade during the initial assault, the 1st Royal Welch Fusiliers were now sent forward to reinforce the two leading battalions. The first men to arrive were soon through the German front line and into the enemy's second line of defence. The 2nd Queen's had also been holding to the east of Vermelles and were also called into the attack. They, too, had reached the enemy's forward positions and were now pressing on towards the Quarries.

Back in the British front-line trenches, Charlie and the 2nd Wiltshires were ready to go. All the men could do now was wait, wondering when and where they would be most needed. It can only be imagined what Charlie must have been feeling at this point. The sound of the artillery guns had gone to another level. Shrapnel and high explosive shells were bursting all along the front so that the ground shook with every round detonated. The air was thick with smoke rising high above the battlefield. From the sound of the guns and the war raging nearby it would have been hell just waiting to go over the top.

By 9.30 a.m. the leading companies of the 2nd Queen's had taken the Quarries and the trench to the north known as Fosse Alley. But they did not stop there. Pressing on, they soon came up against the defenders of Cité Trench, which marked the western boundary of Cité St Elie. Meanwhile, the survivors of the 1st South Staffords had advanced on the right, following a line bordering Breslau Avenue, and were now also at Cité Trench.

It had been a monumental effort by the 22nd Brigade, but that was about as good as it would get. As the morning went on the number of casualties, already high, continued to rise. Although a small group of the 2nd Queen's would later enter Cité St Elie, they were soon forced back and there would be no further attempts to enter the village that day, although elements of the 22nd Brigade would remain at a forward position in and around the Quarries.

To the south, meanwhile, the lead battalions of the 20th Brigade were pushing on beyond the German front line and were advancing down the slope towards Hulluch. Despite heavy losses, the 8th Devons and 2nd Gordons had overrun Breslau Trench and had pressed along the northern side of the Vermelles–Hulluch road. Their leading companies were now at the junction with the La Bassee–Lens road and the brigade's second wave – the 6th Gordons and 2nd Borders – which had been waiting to the east of Vermelles, was now following on close behind the first wave.

With the battalions of the second wave now on the scene, areas of the German support trenches were soon in British hands. Although there had yet to be a breakthrough along the front, there had been significant gains. It was mid-morning and a crucial stage in the battle and had the battalions that had been held in reserve been on the battlefield at that moment, then a complete breakthrough of the German lines might have been possible. But they were not.

Nonetheless, it was important to maintain the momentum and so the 20th Brigade pressed on towards Hulluch. But the lead companies had barely made a couple of hundred yards when they came under extremely heavy crossfire from Hulluch and Stützpunkt II to its north. And the men of the brigade's fifth battalion, the 9th Devons, which had initially been held in reserve, also came under heavy fire as they made their way across the open ground. Less than half of the battalion made it as far as the German support trenches.

It was now 11 a.m. The 7th Division's two attacking brigades had reached the German second line and were within touching distance of Cité St Elie and Hulluch. It had been a huge effort, but the men were exhausted and there had been heavy casualties. The battalions had done as much as could have been expected of them by taking the German front line and the Quarries, but they were now facing yet another line of concentrated enemy defences, as strongly constructed as everything they had encountered before. With no chance of proceeding any further, there was little option but to take up defensive positions facing Cité St Elie and wait for reinforcements to arrive.

Chapter Fifteen

'Our poor fellows were scattered all over the slope'

No further advance could be made until Cité St Elie was in British hands. Inevitably, it was always going to be the case. With the attack in danger of stalling, Sir Thomas Capper, commanding the 7th Division, decided to order his reserve 21st Brigade to move forward.

Instead of attacking as a brigade, the 21st was to split into two as its battalions were required to support the full divisional front. Two battalions – 2nd Yorkshires and 4th Cameron Highlanders – were to go north, pass through the 22nd Brigade and go on to take Cité St Elie. At the same time a similarly sized force, consisting of 2nd Bedfordshires and 2nd Wiltshires, would head towards Cité St Elie and then pass through 20th Brigade to take Hulluch. The 2nd Royal Scots Fusiliers were held back in reserve.

Much now depended on just how quickly the men of the 21st Brigade could get forward and whether the artillery could support their advance. For Charlie, the moment had finally arrived. The trench he was standing in might have been damp and smelly, but at least it provided relative safety. Now he had to go out in the open, where there was no protection at all, and make his way towards the raging battle ahead.

To go out into no-man's land required extreme courage. It was about as perilous as it could be, particularly when Charlie knew that the German strongpoints were still active and that enfilade fire was sweeping across the front. The psychological strength he required to do this, as he led his men into battle for the first time, knowing full well that he might be killed, was immense. It was the same for everyone, of course, but everything Charlie had gone through before now had led to this point in his life. His men would be looking to him for leadership and inspiration, for guidance and direction, for courage and determination. There was no margin for error and to survive would also require a lot of luck.

Things at first went well for the Wiltshires with very few casualties. The leading companies were soon beyond the old enemy front line and reached the old German support trenches, as detailed in the Wiltshires' War Diary:

> Following the advance of the 20th Brigade the Battn occupied the front and support German lines. Lt Col B. H. Leatham D.S.O. then gave orders for the Battn to advance in open order in direction of CITE ST ELIE keeping to the north of HULLUCH ROAD, our right flank connecting with the 2nd Bedfordshires' left.

It was another crucial time in the battle, but Leatham clearly felt that one more push would break through the German defences and gathered his company commanders around him to brief them on what was to happen next. With Cité St Elie in the smoky and rather hazy distance, the 2nd Wiltshires were to press on towards the next line of German support trenches where elements of the Devons and Borders were only just holding out. Major Cusack Forsyth, the second-in-command, would lead the assault with two platoons of Charlie's 'B' Company, led by Captain William Geddes, on the left and two platoons of 'A' Company, led by 2nd Lieutenant Frank Friend, on the right. The width of the battalion's front was to be about 250 yards. Two platoons from each of the lead companies were to follow on as a second wave, about fifty yards behind the leading platoons. A short distance behind the two leading companies, 'C' Company, led by Major Robert Gillson, again with two waves of two platoons, would be in support. This would make the depth of the battalion's attack around 300 yards. 'D' Company, led by 44-year-old Captain Ernest Mudge, a veteran of the South African War who had been awarded the Distinguished Conduct Medal while serving with the Loyal North Lancashire Regiment, was to act as battalion reserve.

Leatham also briefed his officers that the 2nd Bedfords would be advancing on their right flank. They would be in the same formation as the Wiltshires, but on the other side of the Vermelles–Hulluch Road at a point where the road briefly takes a more north-easterly direction. The road would be the dividing line between the two battalions and would act as a guide to them both as they pressed on towards Cité St Elie. This made the total width of the two battalions' advance about 500 yards with 300-plus yards in depth. Artillery support – six 18-pounders of the Royal Horse Artillery – had already arrived along the same Hulluch road and were ready to support the advance.

Charlie and the 2nd Wiltshires left the old German trenches to form up ready for the assault around 11.30 a.m.. The battalion's War Diary continues:

> The Battn advanced in the following order. B Coy on the left, Capt W.M. Geddes in command. A Coy on right, 2/Lt F.H. Friend in command, two platoons of each Coy leading, two platoons immediately behind. C Coy in support. D Coy in reserve. Major R.M.T. Gillson in command of C Coy, Capt E.C. Mudge in command of D Coy.

The 2nd Wiltshires formed up and then set off, with Charlie's 'B' Company on the left, as described. The shelling from the enemy guns and stray bullets flying around would have made advancing across such open ground extremely frightening. One to be caught in the fire was Frank Friend who was getting his platoon into position when he received a bullet wound in the chest. But still the 2nd Wiltshires pressed on.

In the book *The 2nd Battalion Wiltshire Regiment: A Record of Their Fighting in the Great War, 1914–18*, Major Walter Scott Shepherd, who would be appointed adjutant after the battle, describes how the men moved steadily forward, but as soon as they reached 'the highest point in the ground' they came into full view of the German positions in and around the miners' cottages of Cité St Elie. Shepherd describes what happened next:

> At once the Germans poured forth a withering and deadly fire from their rifles and machine guns. Our lines advanced down the reverse slope facing this fusillade, and men fell in distressing numbers. The ground was free of any sort of cover, and the slope, though slight, presented the advancing battalions as most excellent targets for the Huns' shooting, which appeared to be steady and accurate. Those unhit pressed on, seeing their comrades continually falling to the right and the left, and each expected himself to be the next to fall. The bullets cracked so near their heads as to deafen them, and in some cases even pierced their caps and clothing. It seemed impossible that a single one of them could escape.

Major Shepherd's reference to the men reaching 'the highest point in the ground' suggests the terrain initially sloped upwards towards the German-held positions and then down 'the reverse slope'. But walking there today it is apparent there is barely any incline at all. However, as Shepherd described in the book, it is clear the ground would indeed have been 'free of any sort of cover'. It is near-flat and very open, as it would have been then, and a recipe for disaster, which it was.

The advancing 2nd Wiltshires were in full view of the enemy gunners, particularly those in the second-line defences on the south-western side of Cité St Elie, which was still strongly held. And, like the other battalions that had gone and suffered before, many of the Wiltshires were instantly cut down. Those lucky enough to survive the onslaught pressed on as colleagues fell on all sides. Enemy bullets were zipping all around, some whizzed over heads while others missed their target and thudded into the ground. Each one of the advancing Wiltshires must have wondered how long it would be until his luck ran out. Would they be the next to fall? How could anyone survive?

The survivors pressed on as best they could until they reached a line of German support trenches and gun emplacements where they were finally able to find some cover. The Germans had gone, but the Wiltshires came across abandoned field guns and ammunition, and they found small groups of men from other battalions already there. They had been advancing with the 20th Brigade but had been forced to take cover when the advance had stalled.

The 2nd Wiltshires' War Diary records the gallant advance as a simple entry, which reads:

> The whole were led by Major C.G. Forsyth, and experiencing extremely heavy rifle and machine gun fire from the front came to a line held very weakly by a mixture of 8th Devons and 2nd Borders. The trench contained 4 German Field Guns and ammunition.

Only minutes before the 2nd Wiltshires had started the advance in text-book tactical formation, but now the surviving ranks were depleted and exhausted. The men were no longer together in platoons or as a company, but were spread all over the place, making a speedy reorganisation of the battalion all but impossible. Any thoughts of pressing on further quickly disappeared. It would have been folly to have tried to go on. Faced with no other option for now, the men dug in to make their new position as strong as possible.

The 2nd Wiltshires had reached a trench line, later to become known as Gun Trench, crossing the Vermelles–Hulluch road at right angles. Major Shepherd later described the scene:

> Looking back over the ground they had covered, it could be seen what this advance had cost the Battalion. Our poor fellows were scattered all over the slope. Many of the figures were but wounded, and as soon as it was possible the stretcher-bearers carried them

> to the aid post. But the regimental allowance of stretcher-bearers was small, and their colossal task occupied the whole of that night.

The 2nd Wiltshires had lost 200 men in a matter of minutes and had advanced little more than a thousand yards. One of those to fall whilst gallantly leading his platoon across that piece of open ground was young Charlie Hodgins. He was seen by one of his men to have been hit, then to rise to his feet in gallant defiance and to continue urging his men on, only to be hit and fall again. This time Charlie did not get up.

The 2nd Bedfords had also been devastated. The two battalions between them had suffered 450 casualties during the assault. There was some talk within the brigade of a further attempt to advance that afternoon, but the brigade commander, Brigadier Herbert Watts, decided that to try to do so without sufficient support would be a disaster. Any thoughts of continuing were abandoned for the day. It would have been madness, even madder than all that had gone before.

Although moving on was out of the question, for the time being at least, there was no desire to give up what had been achieved thus far, and so the ground gained was consolidated and defensive positions firmly established. The 2nd Wiltshires were then ordered to move a few hundred yards to the north to take up a new position in the old German communication trench known as Breslau Avenue. The final entry in the battalion's War Diary for that day reads:

> Our losses were heavy and included the following Officers casualties: Capt G.M.U. Wilson, 2/Lts C.F.B. Hodgins, J.H. Clarke, W.H.G. Durrant killed. Major R.M.T. Gillson, 2/Lt F.H. Friend wounded, the latter seriously. At dusk the Battalion was relieved by the 9th Devonshire Regiment and took up a new front at BRESLAU AVENUE, our right resting on the latter regiment.

In addition to Charlie, the other 2nd Wiltshires officers killed during the battalion's assault that day included 21-year-old Captain Geoffrey Mervyn Underhill Wilson, second-in-command of Charlie's 'B' Company, although the Commonwealth War Graves Commission records him as having died the following day. Wilson's body was never found and so he is commemorated on the Loos Memorial (Panel 102), which forms the sides and back of Dud Corner Cemetery. The cemetery is less than a mile to the west of Loos-en-Gohelle and stands on a former German strongpoint captured by the 15th (Scottish) Division on that first day at Loos. The name

'Dud Corner' is because of the large number of unexploded enemy shells found in this area at the end of the war.

The Loos Memorial commemorates 20,638 officers and men who have no known grave who fell in this area from the first day of the Battle of Loos to the end of the war. It includes the names of 116 officers and men of the Wiltshire Regiment. Also listed on the memorial and killed on that opening day of the battle is 24-year-old 2nd Lieutenant John Harold Clark (incorrectly spelt Clarke in the War Diary) an only son from Salisbury in Wiltshire who had been in France for just a couple of weeks having been sent to the front to bolster the battalion's numbers for the battle.

Also listed in the battalion's War Diary as killed on that opening day was 2nd Lieutenant William Heinz Gilbert Durrant of the 6th Battalion Dorset Regiment who was attached to the 2nd Wiltshires for the battle. Durrant was aged thirty-five and is also recorded by the Commonwealth War Graves Commission to have died the following day. Durrant is buried in the Vermelles British Cemetery (Plot I.H.39). The cemetery contains 1,948 burials, including many who died at the château dressing station, situated next to the cemetery. The fact that Durrant is buried in Plot I, which was the cemetery's first burial plot for those who died at the dressing station, suggests he was wounded on the battlefield and then taken to the château, where he presumably died. The cemetery's later plots generally include burials from after the Armistice, when more bodies were brought in from the battlefields to the east.

One of the two officers listed in the War Diary as wounded on that opening day at Loos was 37-year-old Major Robert Moore Thacker Gillson. Married with two young children, Gillson had managed to reach the German gun emplacements but was ordered by Leatham to withdraw at nightfall. Gillson soon recovered from his wounds and two months later returned to the 2nd Wiltshires to assume command of the battalion. The other officer wounded that day was 2nd Lieutenant Frank Haward Friend. He was listed as seriously wounded having been shot in the chest. Friend died of his wounds four days later. He was just twenty-two years old and is now buried at Lillers Communal Cemetery (Plot II.D.7), Lillers being where the casualty clearing station was located. The cemetery can be found ten miles to the west-northwest of Béthune.

Elsewhere on that opening day, the British had managed to force a breakthrough of the enemy lines and had captured Loos, mainly because of superior numbers and a weakened line of German defences. But re-supply and communications issues, combined with the late arrival of the reserve forces, which had been under the command of Sir John French at the start

Amongst the 116 officers and men of the Wiltshire Regiment commemorated on the Loos Memorial are two officers who served with Charlie in 'B' Company. Captain Wilson was killed on the opening day, while 25-year-old 2nd Lieutenant Schultz was killed on the third day of the battle.

of the battle and had been held too far to the rear and not released early enough, meant the breakthrough could neither be exploited nor sustained. A further advance on that opening day would almost certainly have been possible had the reserves arrived on time, but they did not arrive on the battlefield until later in the day. Even then they had arrived tired, having been held too far behind the advance and not fully aware of the evolving tactical situation at the time. Furthermore, a combination of the weather conditions on the day and the fact that much of the battlefield had been covered by clouds of gas and smoke, made it difficult for the Royal Flying Corps to observe much of what was happening on the ground.

And so, the opening day of the Battle of Loos ended with much for the generals to think about, although Haig clearly believed things were going well. In his War Diaries and Letters, he would later describe the day as having been a 'very satisfactory one on the whole' and that it had been 'the largest advance made on the Western Front since this kind of warfare started'.

Haig's diary entry seems rather simplistic and typically optimistic given all that had happened on that first day of the Battle of Loos. Immediately to the south of the La Bassée Canal no ground had been gained at all, while further south, between Haisnes and Loos, some ground had been gained but the initial British successes had not been followed up beyond the La Bassée–Lens road, and so none of the German second line was seriously under threat. And all this, of course, had come at a cost. It was only the end of the first day, but British casualties were already high, particularly among the officers, with more than 15,000 killed, wounded, and missing. In his book *Loos 1915*, Nick Lloyd states that the total number of recorded deaths for the opening day of the battle was 6,350, of which 1,565 were from the 7th Division. Of the six attacking divisions that day, only the 15th (Scottish) Division recorded a higher figure (1,595).

Yet, despite these appallingly high casualty figures, a complete breakthrough of the German defences had not been achieved.

Chapter Sixteen

'Of course there will always be losses'

The night following the opening day of the Battle of Loos was a particularly dark one, but it was still possible to see in the distance the silhouette of moving figures against the glow of the burning village of Hulluch. The moving figures were Germans looking to recapture their guns, but they were repelled by the British who were now well dug in.

Inevitably, there were counter-attacks. In the 7th Division's area these were focused on the Quarries where a successful advance was launched by the Germans from the Hulluch area during the early hours of the 26th, causing elements of the 20th Brigade to fall back to Gun Trench. The Quarries had been hard fought for, now they were lost.

The battalion commanders had already received their orders for that day. I Corps was to commence an attack against Cité St Elie at 11 a.m., while simultaneously IV Corps would attack Hulluch and XI Corps was to attack the German second line of defence between Hulluch and Cité St Auguste to its south, and to punch through what was thought to be a thin line of defence.

As soon as dawn broke on the morning of 26 September, Leatham observed the ground around him through his binoculars, but while studying the scene he was shot in the chest. He died almost instantly. Lieutenant-Colonel Bertram Henry Leatham, DSO, of the 2nd Battalion, Yorkshire Regiment, attached 2nd Battalion, Wiltshire Regiment, is buried in the Vermelles British Cemetery (Plot VI.D.13). He was thirty-four years old.

The loss of their CO was a massive blow for the 2nd Wiltshires, and it now fell on Major Cusack Forsyth to take command of the battalion. The shelling continued relentlessly, and it rained for long periods, but there was no further fighting in that sector during the day.

That evening the 2nd Wiltshires were ordered to move once again and after being relieved by the 4th Cameron Highlanders the battalion took up a new position in reserve trenches in what was the rear of Gun Trench. It was another long, dark night, and it rained, making movement painfully slow, not helped by the continuous German shelling through the night and the heavy traffic moving along the road under the cover of darkness, bringing fresh rations and ammunition to the advancing troops and then taking the wounded away.

Daylight brought a misty start to the morning of the 27th, making it difficult for Forsyth to observe what was going on. He could barely see a few yards ahead. But what he could make out, however, were figures moving towards the Cameron Highlanders the 2nd Wiltshires were supporting. Believing the figures to be Germans, Forsyth had every reason to be concerned. He thought the enemy were mounting an attack against the British front line. Climbing out of the trench, he gave the order for the battalion to dash across the open ground to reinforce the Camerons, but no sooner had he given the command than he was hit in the leg. Unable to move himself, Forsyth urged the men on, but as soon as they left the trenches, intense enemy machine-gun fire caught them full on. It might have been only a matter of yards to the British front line, but for the second time in just three days the men of the 2nd Wiltshires were mown down. Only half of them reached the Camerons' trenches unscathed.

It would later turn out that the Camerons were not being attacked at all. Their dash across the open ground was a costly one for the 2nd Wiltshires. Amongst those killed were two of the company commanders – Captain William Murray Geddes of 'B' Company, and 'D' Company's Captain Ernest Cecil Mudge. Both are buried in the Vermelles British Cemetery (Plot VI.D.14 and Plot I.G.38 respectively), although Mudge's headstone shows him to have died on the opening day of Loos, such is the confusion of war. Also killed was 2nd Lieutenant Leonard Schultz. Schultz managed to reach the Camerons' trench, but climbed out again to give directions to men coming in and was shot in the head. His gallantry would be recognised by a posthumous Mention in Despatches, although his body was never found and so Leonard Elmslie Schultz is another to be commemorated on the Loos Memorial. Also killed in the carnage that day was 2nd Lieutenant Edgar Mack, the last of the Cortis–Hodgins–Mack musketeers to fall. Four months earlier the three had gone off together to France to go to war, full of excitement and patriotic enthusiasm. Now they were all dead. Edgar Geoffrey Mack is another of the 2nd Wiltshires to be buried in the Vermelles British Cemetery (Plot I.H.41). He was twenty-two years old and is another early burial at the cemetery, suggesting he had been wounded and taken to the château where he presumably died of his wounds.

The grave of 2nd Lieutenant Edgar Geoffrey Mack, the last of Charlie's closest friends to be killed.

The 2nd Wiltshires had been reduced to little more than company strength in just three days. What was left of the battalion initially stayed in forward positions supporting the Cameron Highlanders. Forsyth was persuaded to go rearwards to the Field Ambulance for medical treatment, leaving Lieutenant Philip Legg in command. But it was impossible for the battalion to go on and on the evening of 29 September the scanty remnants of the 2nd Wiltshires were relieved by the 8th King's and withdrew to the old British front line, from where the assault had originally started. The following day what was left of the 2nd Wiltshires marched to billets in Le Preol for a well-earned rest.

The total number of casualties (killed, wounded, and missing) suffered by the 7th Division had now exceeded 5,000. Amongst the dead was its commander, Major-General Sir Thomas Capper, who died of wounds on 27 September at the casualty clearing station at Lillers, having been shot and wounded by a sniper the day before. Capper had been returning to his headquarters along a communications trench that was overlooked from enemy positions after he had observed an assault near the Quarries. Sir Thomas was one of three divisional commanders to be killed during the Battle of Loos (Major-Generals George Thesiger and Frederick Wing being the others). Capper is buried in the Lillers Communal Cemetery (in front of II.A.). He was fifty-one years old.

For the 2nd Wiltshires the following days were spent in the peaceful surroundings of Le Preol. This gave the surviving members of the battalion the chance to rest and reorganise. Their next move was to Annequin where the battalion received a draft of new arrivals. On 11 October the 2nd Wiltshires returned to the trenches, relieving the 4th Cameron Highlanders in the same sector as before and facing the small village of Auchy, which was in German hands. By now, though, everything had gone quiet. The 2nd Wiltshires' War Diary records the words of a complimentary letter received on that day from Herbert Watts as he left the 21st Brigade on promotion to assume command of the 7th Division:

The Vermelles–Hulluch road pictured two days into the battle. Charlie and the 2nd Wiltshires had advanced along the north side of the road, the road marking the battalion's southern boundary. (*IWM*)

On relinquishing command of the 21st Brigade after a year spent with it on Active Service, I wish to place on record my deep appreciation of the splendid fighting and soldierly qualities of the Officers, NCOs and men of the Battalions in the Brigade shown throughout 12 strenuous months and proved by acts of bravery and

> devotion to duty too numerous to mention. I am quite aware that I owe my promotion to the splendid work done by those under my command and am glad to think that I shall still have my old Brigade with me.

The Battle of Loos had dragged on well into October, with there being no significant breakthrough of the German lines. More than two weeks of hard fighting had followed that fateful opening day. But although the British front line had not advanced at all in the area immediately to the south of the La Bassée Canal, in the sector to the south of the Hohenzollern Redoubt, where the ground gained ranged from 800 to 2,500 yards, the British now occupied some better positions than they had before the battle, although Cité St Elie and Hulluch were still in German hands. However, a further abortive attempt to take the Hohenzollern Redoubt on 13 October achieved little other than to add to the mounting list of casualties and effectively marked the end of the battle. The French had abandoned their offensive further south, their grand plan over, and there was no point in the British continuing an offensive at Loos. Besides, the weather would soon deteriorate as winter set in. Heavy rain would turn the already torn-up battlefield into a muddy mess, making it all but impossible to cross.

The Battle of Loos was over. It had been the British Army's largest offensive of the war so far, its first use of gas, and the first deployment of the New Army. A serious attempt had been made to break the stalemate that had existed on the Western Front, but the small advance had come at an enormous cost. The total number of British casualties suffered during the battle – killed, wounded, and missing – exceeded 50,000. One of them, just one of them, was young Charlie Hodgins. As for German losses, estimates put them around half of those suffered by the British.

Sir John French's Despatch of 15 October 1915 summarised his perspective of the Battle of Loos. It included a paragraph relating to the part played by the 7th Division on its opening day:

> In the attack of the 1st Corps the 7th Division was directed on the Quarries . . . The assault of the 7th Division succeeded at once, and in a very short time they had reached the western edge of the Quarries, Cité St. Elie and even the village of Haisnes, the tendency of the action having been to draw the troops northward.

It was Sir John's last despatch as Commander-in-Chief. Even before the Battle of Loos he had come under criticism for his handling of the BEF and had lost much of his support within the government. Now he came under further criticism for his poor tactical planning, a lack of understanding of the conditions in which his men were to fight and his poor use of the reserve divisions during the battle. French was blamed for the debacle (whether this was justified or not), and he was replaced by General Sir Douglas Haig, while the other senior British commanders at Loos, Haig included, escaped relatively unscathed.

Meanwhile, the 2nd Wiltshires' return to the trenches in October had been a brief one. By the middle of the month the men were back in billets, this time at St Hilaire. During the afternoon of 20 October, the battalion paraded in front of the new General Officer Commanding 7th Division, Major-General Herbert Watts, who had replaced Capper. At 2.30 p.m., Watts stood in front of the 2nd Wiltshires and addressed the battalion on its recent good work. He said:

> I should like to say a few words to you. I came down today because I wanted specially to see you after your very fine performance during the recent fighting and especially on account of your very fine attack on the 25th. You were ordered to attack and you advanced in a very well organised formation in a straight line. There was no hesitation, there was no holding back, to see whether others were coming on or not. Every man went straight on, and were evidently determined to get there. That was the result of very good training, of very good discipline combined with a strong sense of duty and the right spirit. You must always remember that the only way to win is for every man to be absolutely determined to go on quite irrespective of casualties , once you begin to hesitate or look to the right and left and behind to see if others are coming on it is very unlikely that the attack will be a success. On the other hand as you know if you go straight on nine times out of ten when you get up to the Bosches they surrender or if they don't surrender you have got the satisfaction of putting your bayonet into them or shooting them when they go away. Of course there will always be losses. You cannot get there without and in the recent fighting you had your full share and that added to the credit of what you did. I deplore the loss of many brave commanders not the least amongst whom was that gallant soldier your late Commanding Officer Major Leatham. I know, and you know, how hard he worked to get the Battalion into the splendid position in which it now is. Well I congratulate you and you must keep up that spirit. The Wiltshires, I know will go home with a reputation second to none.

French post card showing the devastation at Loos at the end of the war.
(*A. Richard, 84 Faub du Temple, Paris*)

Only those who were stood on the parade square at St Hilaire that afternoon of 20 October 1915 would ever know how well Watts's address went down amongst the men. It was fighting talk, of course. Besides, what else was a general meant to say to his men after such a devastating battle? As Watts had said 'there will always be losses' and there had certainly been plenty of those. The Battle of Loos had cost the 2nd Wiltshires heavily – nine officers had been killed and five wounded, and around 400 other ranks were listed as killed, wounded, or missing.

History has shown that harsh lessons had to be learned during the early battles of the First World War, such as at Loos, for victory finally to be achieved in 1918. But that explanation would likely have seemed very unconvincing to Aimée Hodgins in 1915 when she found out that her 20-year-old son was dead.

Chapter Seventeen

'He Died Like a True Briton'

So young Charlie Hodgins was dead, killed on the opening day of the Battle of Loos. For the Hodgins family their pain began four days later when his parents received the most dreaded of telegrams from the War Office. Addressed to Lieutenant-Colonel Charles Hodgins, and dated 29 September 1915, it simply reads:

> Deeply regret to inform you that 2/Lt C F B Hodgins 2/Wiltshire Regt is reported killed Sept 25/26. Lord Kitchener desires to express his sympathy. Secretary War Office

It was the worst news any parent could ever receive. But thousands of parents were going through the same thing at that time, and many more thousands would go through it before the war's end. Four days later, Charles received a further telegram:

> The King and Queen deeply regret the loss you and the army have sustained by the death of your son in the service of his country. Their majesties truly sympathise with you in your sorrow. Keeper of the Privy Purse.

At the time he received the devastating news, Charles was staying at Seaview near Ryde on the Isle of Wight. The first telegram was forwarded to him from his address in Birmingham, as was the second, from Buckingham Palace. The sight of the second telegram arriving within a few days of receiving the tragic news might have temporarily raised hope. Perhaps there had been a mistake. Perhaps Charlie had been found alive after all, amongst the wounded even, or he might have been reported as a prisoner of war. Could there possibly have been a mistake? Sadly not.

Then, on 5 October, six days after receiving the news that his son had been killed, Charles received a further telegram, which read:

> Private Mills states he saw Lieut Hodgins fall wounded in the advance on Saturday morning. Knows no further information.

This latest piece of news might have raised hope in many households, but in the Hodgins family it appears not. Charles even tried to use his position of authority to go out to France to take back the body of his son. In the early months of the war there had been cases of private exhumations to retrieve bodies of loved ones buried in France, for private burial at home at the family's expense. But the practice had been opposed for several reasons and by mid-1915 had been banned, and so Charles's request was denied. On 12 October he received a further telegram from the War Office, which read:

> Much regret sanction cannot be given for you to proceed to France. All bodies of fallen officers cannot be brought home. Seemliness.

There was nothing Charles could do. He knew his son was dead, but he must have been proud to learn that Charlie's courage had not gone unnoticed. Charles received a letter from the CO of the 2nd Wiltshires, which was almost certainly written by Major Cusack Forsyth, then the most senior officer in the battalion, and a second letter from another officer of the battalion. Parts of both of these are also found in the *Daily Graphic* article quoted below.

By now, word of the Battle of Loos, and the losses, had spread across the country. It was not long before the newspapers were reporting lists of those killed, including Charlie. Friends sent letters of condolences to the Hodgins family. One, dated 10 October 1915, came from an army colleague of Charles who was living at Windsor Castle. It reads:

> My Dear Hodgins,
>
> I hope this will reach you but I am sending to the last address I had of yours some months ago and you may have moved on. I am writing because I am terribly afraid that the boy mentioned in the casualty list a day or two ago must be your son Charlie. I am almost sure you said he was in the Wiltshire Regiment. I hope I am wrong but if not we both send our sincere sympathy to you and his mother. These are terrible times and even good news like that of the great advance is tempered by the large sacrifice of life . . .

On 27 October 1915, with the headline 'He Died Like A True Briton', the *Daily Graphic* wrote:

> Second Lieutenant C.F.B. Hodgins, 2nd Wiltshire Regiment, whose portrait is here given, was killed in action on September 25th. He comes of a Toronto family and is one of four brothers who came from Canada at the outbreak of war to join their father, Lieutenant-Colonel C.R. Hodgins, in the Empire's need. The senior officer of the regiment left writes: – 'He was leading his men splendidly (as he always did) under an exceptionally heavy fire. He was killed in front of his men. All of us had an exceptionally high opinion of your boy. The men loved him and would follow him anywhere.' Another officer wrote: – 'He died like a true British soldier, leading his men with great gallantry, and even when wounded tried to rise and take them on. He was a great favourite with his men, and they cannot speak in more glowing terms than to say he was a hero.' He was hit twice, the last time mortally.

Another newspaper, under its Roll of Honour, simply wrote:

> Hodgins – Killed in action in France on Sept 25–26, Charles Francis Burgoyne Hodgins, Second Lieutenant the Wiltshire Regiment, age twenty, third and dearly-loved son of Lieutenant Colonel C.R. and Mrs Hodgins, and grandson of the late Judge Thomas Hodgins of Toronto, Canada.

In the Record of Officers' Effects for 1915 it is recorded that a payment of £10-8-6 was made to Lieutenant-Colonel Charles Richard Hodgins following Charlie's death.

But how does a father react to the loss of a son? Men differ. Charles clearly wanted to know more and being a senior officer serving in the army at the time he was in a privileged position, and so he went in search of information. If he could not bring his son's body home then he at least wanted to know what had happened to Charlie and where his body might be.

In November, Charles decided to write to the 21st Infantry Brigade's Chaplain. It had been seven weeks since Charlie had been killed. It was not long before Charles received a reply from that officer, Padre George Trench. In a letter dated 30 November 1915, Trench wrote:

> Dear Sir,
>
> I have delayed answering your letter of November 15th because at the time it came I had no information to give you, and even now I have I fear none.

To answer your letter adequately one must try and realise something of the situation in that Vermelles area. I am giving you a rough sketch map so that you may see it the better. In the first rush of the attack we took Foss 8 and the quarries and nearly took Hulloch. Had we been able to hold Foss 8 and the quarries the situation now would have been very different. As it is all the ground between our front line and the railway is in view of the enemy. The road from Vermelles to Hulloch cannot be used during daylight and is not a very nice place even at night as it is swept by a certain number of stray bullets. To get up to our fire trench you have to take to a communication trench at the railway and it is then almost 3 miles walk up trenches to the firing line. The whole of this ground is overlooked by Foss 8, which is a huge slag heap. As you get nearer to our front line care has to be exercised as there may be a sniper on the lookout.

"HE DIED LIKE A TRUE BRITON."

Second-Lieutenant C. F. B. Hodgins, 2nd Wiltshire Regiment, whose portrait is here given, was killed in action on September 25th. He comes of a Toronto family and is one of four brothers who came from Canada at the outbreak of war to join their father, Lieutenant-Colonel C. R. Hodgins, in the Empire's need.

The senior officer of the regiment left writes:—"He was leading his men splendidly (as he always did) under an exceptionally heavy fire. He was killed . . . in front of his men. All of us had an exceptionally high opinion of your boy. The men loved him and would follow him anywhere."

Another officer writes:—"He died like a true British soldier, leading his men with great gallantry, and even when wounded tried to rise and take them on. He was a great favourite with his men, and they cannot speak in more glowing terms than to say he was a hero."

He was hit twice, the last time mortally.

Newspaper cutting from the *Daily Graphic* reporting the death of Charlie Hodgins. (*Daily Graphic*)

Today I got a pass from our Brigadier as we are not on the Vermelles bit of line. Rode over to Vermelles, left my horse there, got a guide from a Battalion who were up in that area and went right up along communication trench near the north side of Hulloch Road. I went the whole way up to within about 100 yards of our front line and as I got up near and past where I believe your son is buried I looked over the top of the parapet at frequent points to try and find the mark. I had my field glasses ready so that if I could have found the mark I could have read any inscription which might be on it. Right up at the end of my time near the front line I met an officer who knew that bit of line well and he

THE WAR *Illustrated*

No. 61. Vol. 3. 16th October, 1915. | A PICTURE-RECORD OF EVENTS BY LAND, SEA AND AIR | Edited by J. A. Hammerton

JUBILANT BRITONS IN THE HELMETS OF THE BROKEN FOE.—In a vivid letter from the front a British officer describes an amusing incident which took place after the recent advance. In the wake of a band of disconsolate German prisoners rattled a battery of enemy guns. British soldiers passing along the road were startled to see them still in charge of men wearing "pickelhauben." A closer examination revealed the jubilant, though none the less incongruous, faces of the "Khaki boys," framed in the Huns' peculiar headgear. They had captured these trophies on the field of victory.

At first the Battle of Loos was reported at home as a success, as shown on the front cover of *The War Illustrated* on 16 October 1915, with its lead paragraph titled 'Jubilant Britons in the Helmets of the Broken Foe'. (*War Illustrated*)

The War Illustrated, 16th October, 1915. Page 194

Cheering Changes in the Western Battle Front

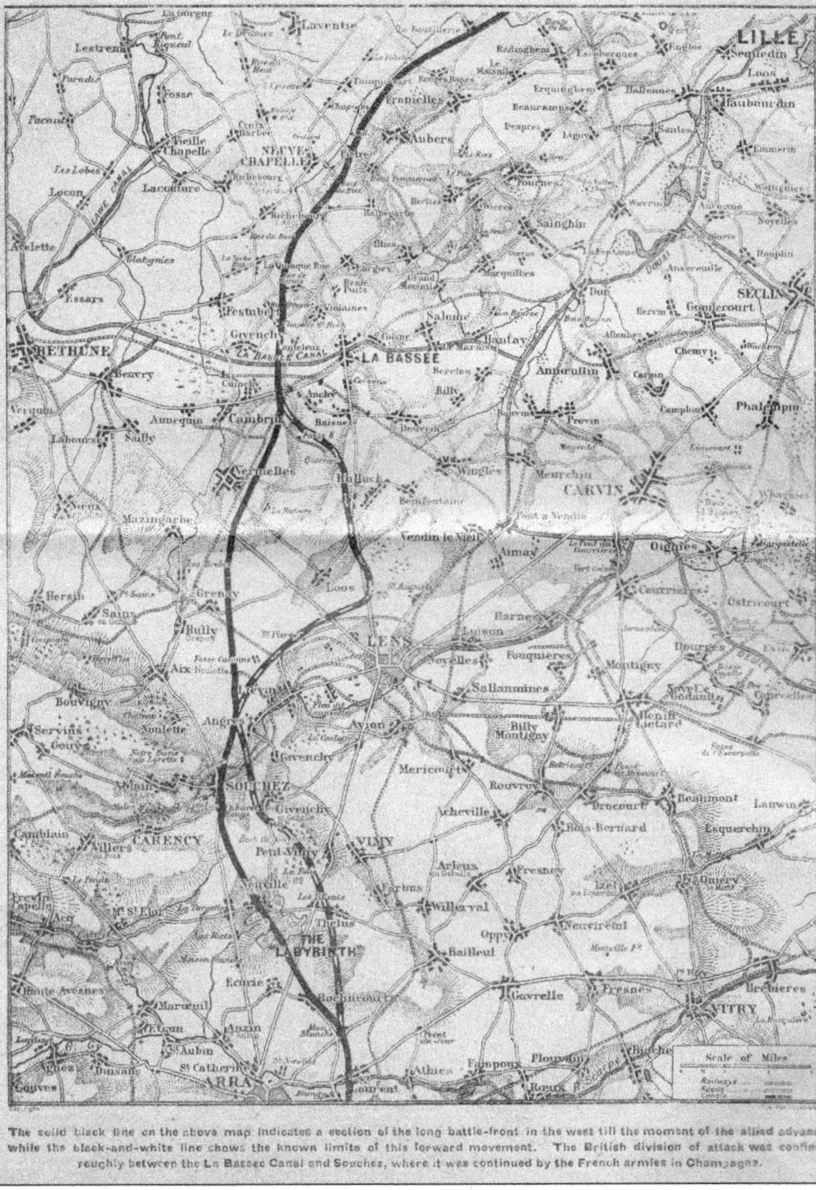

The solid black line on the above map indicates a section of the long battle-front in the west till the moment of the allied advance, while the black-and-white line shows the known limits of this forward movement. The British division of attack was confined roughly between the La Bassee Canal and Souchez, where it was continued by the French armies in Champagne.

Inside the same edition of *The War Illustrated* there is 'Cheering Changes in the Western Battle Front', with the solid black line showing the front prior to the battles and the dotted line marking the ground gained. (*War Illustrated*)

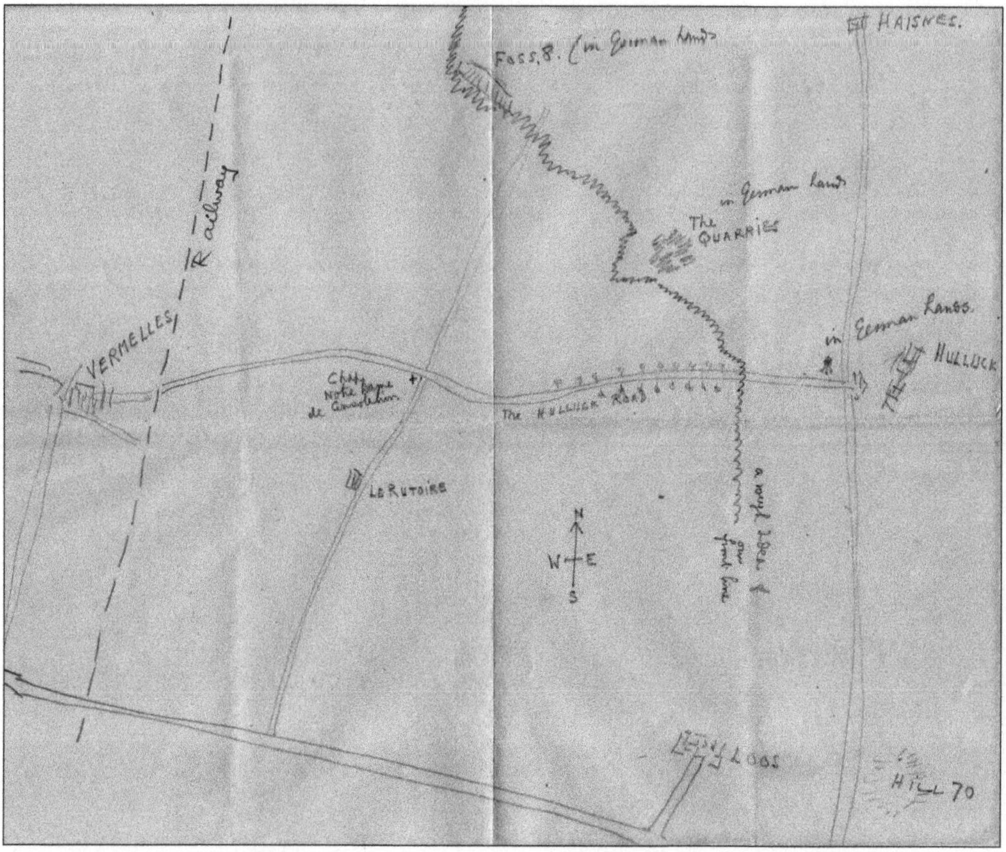

Pencil sketch by Padre George Trench, which accompanied his letter to Charlie's parents giving more details about the opening day of the battle. Trench went to extraordinary lengths to try and find out what had happened to Charlie and where his body might be.

---

pointed out to me a tower which I had not noticed from which he said some of our men had been sniped. To look over the parapet one had to come in view of this tower but fortunately apparently the sniper was away for his lunch. It would be quite impossible in my judgement to have the body removed at present even if I had found the spot. Careful search by daylight is impossible at present and search at night would be of no use and could not really be done unless our own brigade were occupying that bit of line, and only then at a certain risk.

To my knowledge only six officers killed in that fight from the 21st Infantry Brigade were brought back for burial at Vermelles.

The whole battle was such a huge and awful affair – it was more than we could do to get the wounded away. One stretcher bearer of the 2nd Wiltshire Regiment did manage to get back five bodies, four of them officers. One of the regiments of the Brigade got one body back. The Hulloch Road which we were using during the fight was shelled by day and swept by stray bullets at night and I am still surprised how they managed to get the five back. I am quite sure when Captain Geddes buried your son's body he did it because he thought it better to bury it rather than leave it. All those days our men were in very great peril and I think one can hardly realise at a distance the seeming confusion and overwork of everyone in a huge and desperate fight. Even where there are odd graves away behind the lines we have no authority for moving those bodies into regular cemeteries. I hear numbers of cases where there are single graves within a hundred yards or less of a cemetery but this is not the time for moving them. I believe that will be done after the war is over.

I felt I could not write to you until I had made a visit to the particular part of the ground where your son's body lies and I was very lucky in going up today and not yesterday as yesterday all the part I was in was subject to very heavy shell fire indeed – of which I saw the marks today – and I do not think I should have been allowed to go up yesterday had I made the attempt.

I know well from the large number of letters which I have had the great consolation it is to relatives of our brave men killed in action when they are laid in regular cemeteries and I am deeply sorry that it was not the case in regard to your son's body, but I am quite sure that at the time he was killed the best possible arrangement was made. All our Brigade knew they had desperate work before them and had to do the quickest and best they could. Even men who fell far behind that – right in the first advance Saturday morning were not buried until Tuesday or Wednesday night and three burying parties worked I know from personal experience in some danger and under very difficult circumstances as we were collecting the dead from in and around the old German front line barbed wire in the dark trying to get identification of bodies and dig a huge burying pit all in a hurry. In fact I never saw that work completed as I came away carrying a man of the party who was wounded on a stretcher.

I have written fully and plainly but I hope not unsympathetically. One could not be out here as I have been since May without realising the aching of definite news in the hearts of those at home. Thank God we know your son's body was buried, so many we do not know anything about it at all. Even today in giving me a permit to go up into the Vermelles line my Brigadier reminded me that one had to remember that as it was not of military necessity one had to exercise some care in issuing such permits. However, I am very glad I was able to go but very sorry that I was able to do nothing really satisfactory in helping you except to report that I feel any further action at present is impossible. I still believe that whenever we drive the Germans right back and Hulloch road is clear the spot may be found, as I consider it a much more likely grave to find than many.

Yours sincerely,
George F. Trench, Chaplain of Forces,
21st Infantry Brigade, attached 2nd Yorkshire Regiment,
B.E.F.

This is a remarkable letter, full of detail, and clearly shows the lengths George Trench had gone in search of as much information as he could gather so that he could reply to Charles's letter. Army chaplains so often did, knowing how important such news could be to a grieving family, or they would remain alongside someone during the final moments of their life.. They were incredibly brave men. Take, for example, the Reverend Theodore Hardy of the Army's Chaplain's Department. While attached to the 8th Lincolnshires, Hardy was awarded the Distinguished Service Order, the Military Cross, and the Victoria Cross in just nine months. His citations state numerous examples of courage, such as remaining with wounded men when under heavy fire out in no-man's land in the worst possible weather conditions, tending to the wounded when under fire, and extricating men buried during enemy shell fire, all regardless of his personal safety. Sadly, though, Hardy's luck eventually ran out just days before the end of the war when he died of wounds two days short of his fifty-fifth birthday. For someone who had been turned away for being too old to fight at the outbreak of war, Hardy went on to become one of the most highly decorated non-combatants of the First World War. Such was the courage of those who served with the Chaplain's Department – men like Theodore Hardy and George Trench who so often risked their own lives to help others.

The following week, Charles received a letter from the Privy Purse Office, Buckingham Palace, addressed to him at the Ordnance Office, York. Dated 7 December 1915, it reads:

> Sir,
>
> I am commanded by the King to convey to you an expression of His Majesty's appreciation of the patriotic spirit which has prompted your four sons to give their services to the Army.
>
> The King was much gratified to hear of the manner in which they have so readily responded to the call of their Sovereign and their country, and I am to express to you His Majesty's congratulations on their having contributed in so full a measure to the great cause for which all people of the British Empire are so bravely fighting.
>
> I have the honour to be, Sir, your obedient Servant,
>
> Signed F M Ponsonby,
> Keeper of the Privy Purse.

Then came news that Charlie's bravery at Loos had been formally recognised. He was posthumously Mentioned in Despatches. Sir John French's despatch of 15 October 1915 had concluded:

> I have many names to bring to your Lordship's notice for valuable, gallant and distinguished service during the period under review, and these will form the subject of a separate report at an early date.

It would take a while for those names to be approved and publicly announced, but on Saturday 1 January 1916, the names referred to by Sir John French in his despatch appeared in a *Supplement* to the *London Gazette*. Under the heading 'War Office', it reads:

> The following despatch has been received by the Secretary of State for War from the Field-Marshal Commanding-in-Chief the British Army in France: –
>
> General Headquarters, 30th November 1915
>
> Sir,
>
> In accordance with the last paragraph of my Despatch of the 15th October 1915, I have the honour to bring to notice the names of those whom I recommend for gallant and distinguished service in the field.

I have the honour to be, Sir, your obedient servant
J. D. P. French
Field-Marshal, Commanding-in-Chief
The British Army in France'

Included in the list of names that followed are sixteen officers and eight other ranks of the Wiltshire Regiment, including 2nd Lieutenant C. F. B. Hodgins (killed). Two other officers of the Wiltshires were also posthumously mentioned for the Battle of Loos – 2nd Lieutenant J. H. Clark and Temporary 2nd Lieutenant L. E. Schultz.

The mention in despatches of subordinates by commanders in the field is a long-standing tradition. Originally, it was a way of bringing the services of deserving officers to the attention of higher authority and often included descriptions of the services performed. During the First World War, however, there were large numbers of 'Mentions' and so the names were simply listed in the *London Gazette* without a citation. After the war it was decided that a multiple-leaved bronze oak leaf was to be worn on the Victory Medal to show such recognition. But the fact there were large numbers of 'Mentions' during the First World War should not in any way undermine the award, far from it. According to *British Gallantry Awards* by P. E. Abbot and J. M. A. Tamplin, there were 141,082 military 'Mentions' gazetted between 1914 and 1920: this figure being taken from official statistics. To put this figure into context, it means that only around 2.3% of the total number of troops under arms received such recognition.

It is also worth bearing in mind that only the Victoria Cross, the nation's highest award for gallantry, could then be awarded posthumously, and so Charlie would not have been considered for, say, the Military Cross, which could be awarded to junior officers for their bravery when under fire.

The following month, Charles received a letter from the Assistant Military Secretary. Dated 17 February 1916, it reads:

> I have it in command from His Majesty the King to inform you, as next-of-kin of the late SECOND LIEUTENANT CHARLES FRANCIS BURGOYNE HODGINS of the Wiltshire Regiment, that this officer was mentioned in a Despatch from Field Marshal Sir John French dated 30th November 1915, and published in the London Gazette dated 1st January 1916, for gallant and distinguished service in the field.

I am to express to you the King's high appreciation of these services and to add that His Majesty trusts that their public acknowledgement may be of some consolation in your bereavement.

I have the honour to be, Sir, your obedient Servant.

Signed

Colonel, Assistant Military Secretary.

Charlie's courage and leadership during that opening day of the Battle of Loos had, indeed, not gone unnoticed.

Chapter Eighteen

In Search of Charlie

There are so many sad parts to this story, one being the death of Bernard Cave-Brown-Cave, Charlie's first company commander in France and a friend of the Hodgins family, who tragically took his own life nearly two years after he was severely wounded at Givenchy. It appears that Cave-Brown-Cave had struggled to come to terms with his disability and chose to end his suffering on 4 April 1917. The following week, on 9 April, under the heading 'Captain's Suicide', the *Birmingham Daily Post* reported:

> A Bournemouth coroner's jury found on Saturday [7 April] that Captain Bernard Cave Browne Cave [*sic*], Wiltshire Regiment, aged 50, died from a bullet wound in the head, self-inflicted during temporary insanity. He lost his left leg in the war and his right was shattered. The pain he suffered caused him much depression.

And so, Givenchy had claimed another life, albeit nearly two years after the battle had taken place. Cave-Brown-Cave is commemorated in the UK Book of Remembrance, which records those who died in the two world wars and were not formally recorded by the Commonwealth War Graves Commission.

It is also simply awful to think that, of the nine officers who graduated from Sandhurst on 16 March 1915 and went straight to the Wiltshire Regiment, seven, including Charlie Hodgins, were dead within eighteen months. John Cortis and Gerald Stamford were both killed on 15 June 1915, followed by Charlie and Oliver Emanuel at Loos on 25 September. All four were killed serving with the 2nd Battalion in France. The following year, Guy Holman died of wounds on 6 July 1916 while serving with the 1st Battalion during the Battle of the Somme, and another to die of his wounds while serving with the same battalion on the Somme was Reginald Palmer; he died on 22 July 1916. Frank Verran was killed later that year, on 18 October 1916, also during the Battle of the Somme. He was serving

Former Headmaster Thomas Fry unveiled tablets listing the names of the fallen in the cloisters at Berkhamsted School on Founder's Day 1922. (*Courtesy of Berkhamsted School*)

with the 2nd Battalion. Of the other two officers to have initially gone to the Wiltshires after graduating from Sandhurst, Captain E. H. Hill died in April 1918 while serving with the Duke of Wellington's (West Riding) Regiment, which leaves only George Bryer-Ash to have survived the war. He is last mentioned in the Wiltshires' War Diary in February 1916 when temporarily in command of 'D' Company and later became an observer with the newly formed Royal Air Force. He was injured in July 1918 when his aircraft crashed on take-off and, after being invalided home, he relinquished his commission the following year on account of ill-health. As for the rest of Sandhurst's one hundred graduating officers that day in March 1915, who knows? But given the appalling loss rate amongst the nine who so valiantly went off to the Wiltshires, it can only be assumed there are many, many more sad tales to tell.

At Berkhamsted School, meanwhile, things had moved on since Charlie's days. Thomas Fry had left, having been appointed Dean of Lincoln, to be replaced by Charles Greene who would remain at Berkhamsted for thirty-eight years. Greene steered the school through the First World War.

Charlie's death was amongst the early losses of Old Berkhamstedians, but there was worse to come. In 1916 there was the Battle of the Somme, and the following year came Passchendaele. The number of former boys and masters killed in action or died of wounds continued to rise. On 22 July 1918, the school marked Founder's Day. The annual service was held in the Parish Church. Greene addressed the assembled audience and read out a proud but tragic record. There were, he said, 1,145 Old Boys who had served or were serving their country; 184 had been killed and 177 wounded, as far as was known up to that date. But, Greene added, the school could take great pride from the courage shown by Old Boys and masters alike, evinced by the long list of gallantry awards: 121 had been mentioned in despatches; seventy-eight awarded the Military Cross; seventeen the Distinguished Service Order; and twenty-eight had received foreign and other honours. One, George Pearkes, then a lieutenant-colonel serving with the Canadian Mounted Rifles, had been awarded the Victoria Cross.

When Greene addressed the audience on Founder's Day 1918 there were still more than three months of the war to go. By the time the guns fell silent the number of Old Boys killed had risen to 233, according to modern research. They had laid down their lives in Flanders, France, Gallipoli, Salonika, Mesopotamia, Palestine, and at sea and in the air. The final tally of honours and awards to Old Berkhamstedians reached 256, including a Victoria Cross to another Old Berkhamstedian, Major Brett Cloutman of the Royal Engineers. One of those listed amongst the dead and noted for his gallantry was Charlie Hodgins.

After the war Greene and the school's governors decided that a memorial to the Old Berkhamstedians who had fallen, and a thank-offering on behalf of those who had been spared, should take the form of a library and museum, and a stained-glass window in the chapel, together with a record of the names of the dead. The bronze tablets listing the names of the fallen were unveiled in the cloisters by Thomas Fry on Founder's Day 1922, and the window by Canon Glossop the next year. The new building containing the library and museum was erected in the quadrangle in line with the Chapel. It was officially opened on Founder's Day 1924. The school takes great pride in remembering all the Old Boys who fell during the First World War. The name of Charlie Hodgins is still there for all to see.

* * *

After the death of his son, Charles Hodgins raised the 120th Siege Battery Royal Artillery and went with them to France in June 1916. But during the Somme campaign of that year, he suffered shell shock and was invalided back to England. Charles then commanded the Siege Training Brigade at Bordon until he was placed on the Reserve of Officers in the Army Ordnance Department at the age of fifty-four. In May 1918 he sailed home to Canada with Aimée and Patrick on board the SS *Mauretania*. They were back at the family home at Granville Ferry in Nova Scotia once more.

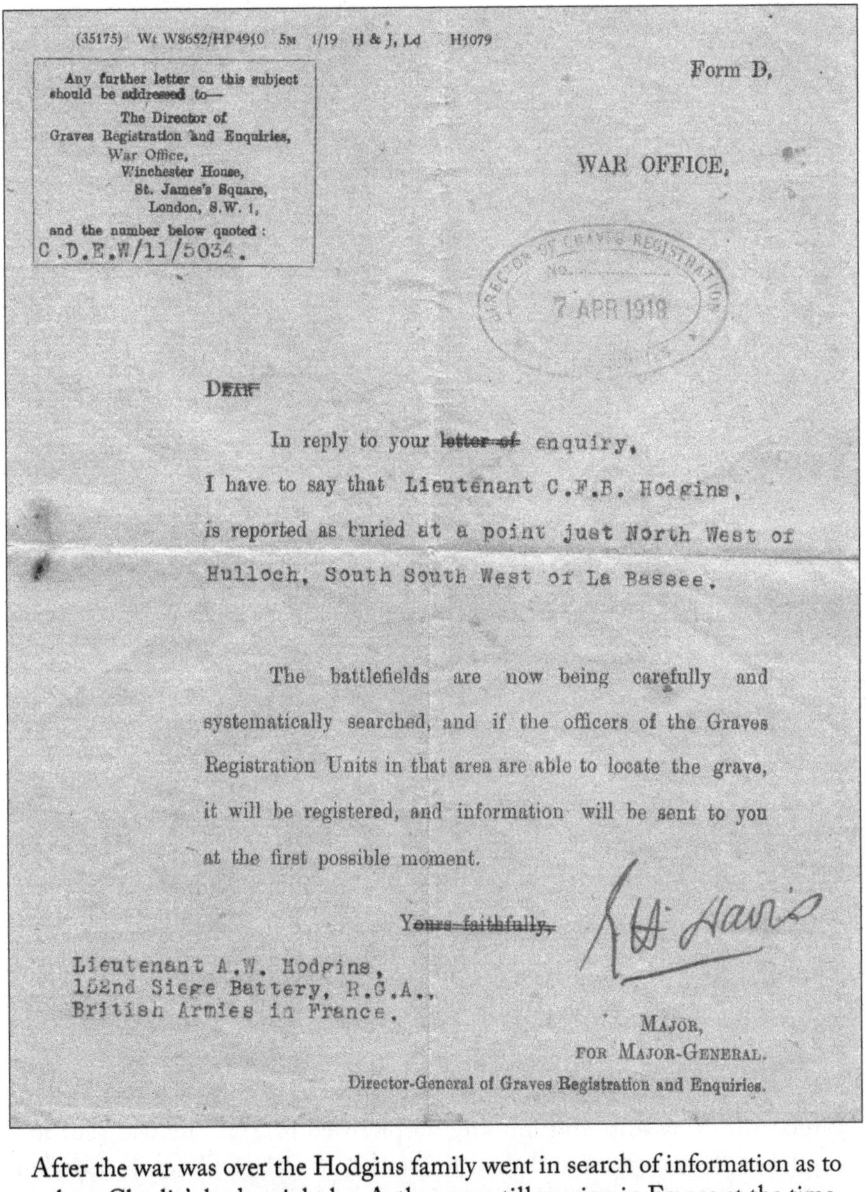

(35175) Wt W8652/HP4910 5M 1/19 H & J, Ld H1079

Form D.

Any further letter on this subject should be addressed to—
The Director of
Graves Registration and Enquiries,
War Office,
Winchester House,
St. James's Square,
London, S.W. 1,
and the number below quoted:
C.D.E.W/11/5034.

WAR OFFICE,

DIRECTOR OF GRAVES REGISTRATION
No.
7 APR 1919

D~~EAR~~

In reply to your ~~letter of~~ enquiry,

I have to say that Lieutenant C.F.B. Hodgins, is reported as buried at a point just North West of Hulloch, South South West of La Bassee.

The battlefields are now being carefully and systematically searched, and if the officers of the Graves Registration Units in that area are able to locate the grave, it will be registered, and information will be sent to you at the first possible moment.

Y~~ours faithfully,~~

Lieutenant A.W. Hodgins,
152nd Siege Battery, R.G.A.,
British Armies in France.

Major,
for Major-General.
Director-General of Graves Registration and Enquiries.

After the war was over the Hodgins family went in search of information as to where Charlie's body might be. Arthur was still serving in France at the time and was the first to approach the authorities.

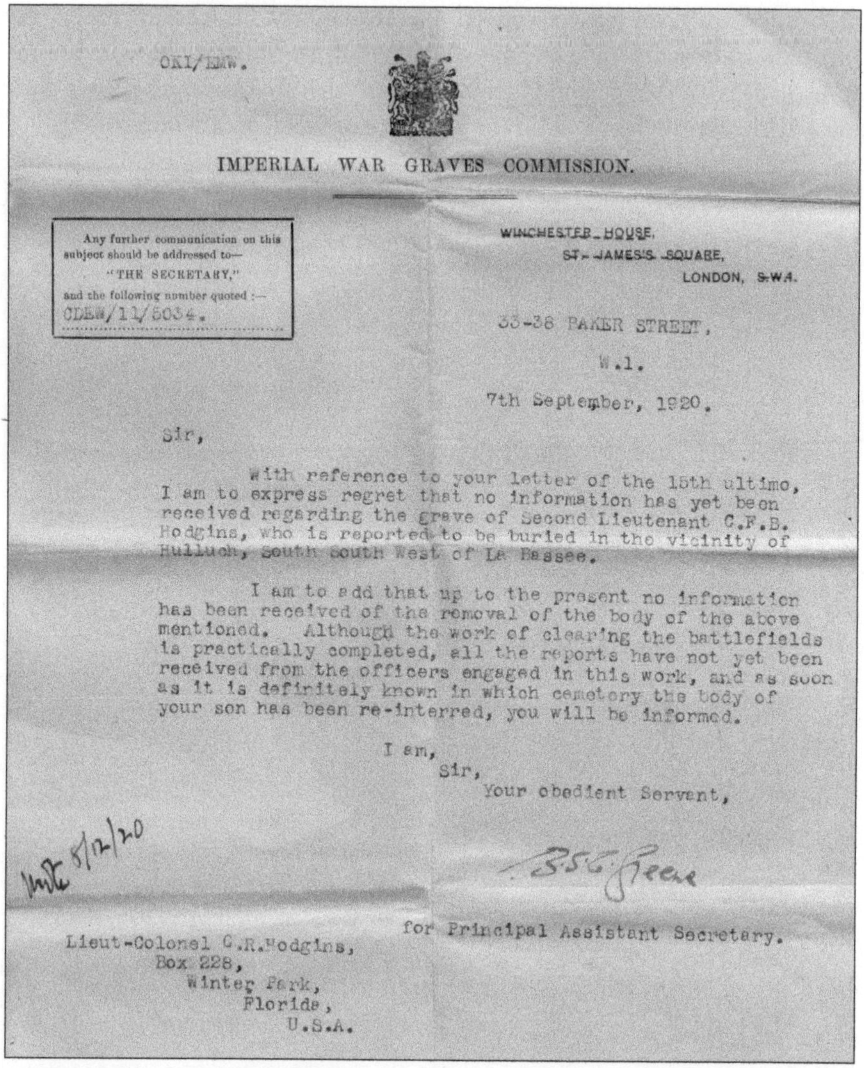
OKI/EMW.

IMPERIAL WAR GRAVES COMMISSION.

Any further communication on this subject should be addressed to—
"THE SECRETARY,"
and the following number quoted :—
CDEW/11/5034.

WINCHESTER HOUSE,
ST. JAMES'S SQUARE,
LONDON, S.W.1.

33-38 BAKER STREET,
W.1.

7th September, 1920.

Sir,

With reference to your letter of the 15th ultimo, I am to express regret that no information has yet been received regarding the grave of Second Lieutenant C.F.B. Hodgins, who is reported to be buried in the vicinity of Hulluch, South South West of La Bassee.

I am to add that up to the present no information has been received of the removal of the body of the above mentioned. Although the work of clearing the battlefields is practically completed, all the reports have not yet been received from the officers engaged in this work, and as soon as it is definitely known in which cemetery the body of your son has been re-interred, you will be informed.

I am,
Sir,
Your obedient Servant,

B.S.C. Green

for Principal Assistant Secretary.

Lieut-Colonel C.R.Hodgins,
Box 228,
Winter Park,
Florida,
U.S.A.

The wait for information went on. After more than a year of no further news, Charles twice wrote to what was then the Imperial War Graves Commission. The replies received offered no further information. This is the second reply, dated 7 September 1920, which is almost identical to the first.

As for Charlie's oldest brother, Dick, who had been wounded at Festubert in May 1915, and initially hospitalised in York, he was sent to a hospital in Birmingham and then to another at Palace Green in London. But he continued to suffer from tiredness and black-outs and after several months in hospital, he went to stay with his uncle, Sir Andrew Scoble,

Then & Now: The French town of Béthune, *top*, as it was when Charles and Richard explored the former Loos battlefield in search of Charlie. The Beffroi (belfry) de Béthune is badly scarred, but still stands. Béthune's Grand Place today, *above*. The restored Beffroi is as splendid as ever. (*Rebecca Jacobs*)

in Wimbledon, before moving to Brighton to convalesce. In 1916, Dick married Gladys Chambers in Hollingbourne in Kent, but he continued to struggle with the effects of his wounds and was eventually invalided out of the army in 1917 'for ill health following wounds' to work in food

This blurred photo from the archive shows Richard overlooking the former battlefield.

production and given retired pay. Dick then settled in Kent, taking up horticulture to help his condition improve.

John, the youngest of the four Hodgins brothers to go to war, had been just seventeen when he sailed to Britain with his family in November 1914. The following year he obtained a commission in India with the Royal Garrison Artillery, but then transferred to the 1st Queen Victoria's Own Corps of Guides and served with them as a captain on the North-West Frontier of India. He then served in Palestine and Mesopotamia but was badly wounded in 1918. He retired from military life in 1922 and returned to Canada the following year.

Arthur, meanwhile, the second oldest boy, was commissioned into the Royal Garrison Artillery in 1915. He served in the Anti-Aircraft Corps and whilst in action with a unit of heavy artillery at Purfleet in Essex on the night of 31 March 1916, hit and brought down Zeppelin *L15* attacking London, for which Arthur was later presented with a gold watch by the mayor of London. By the time the war came to an end he was serving in France as a lieutenant with the 152nd Siege Battery.

With the war over, Arthur decided to take advantage of still serving and approached the War Office for information about where Charlie's body was

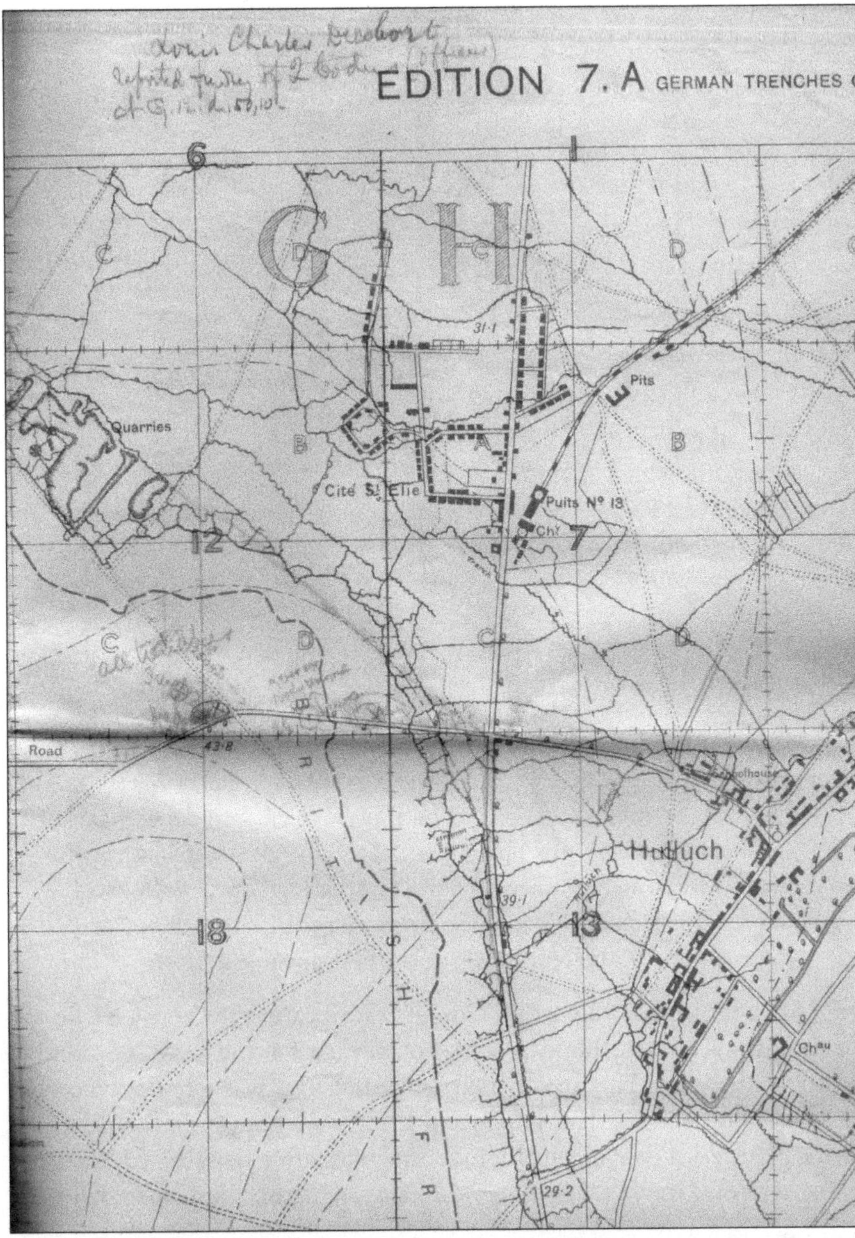

With information received from the Imperial War Graves Commission and equipped with this old British trench map showing the front line at the end of the Battle of Loos, Charles and Richard drove along the Vermelles–Hulluch road. They marked the map in pencil with places where they thought Charlie's body might possibly be found.

Charles and Richard stopped at various cemeteries around the former Loos battlefield in the vague hope there might be a grave marker somewhere marking the location of Charlie's body.

buried. The reply he received from the Director of Graves Registration, dated 7 April 1919, reads:

> In reply to your enquiry, I have to say that Lieutenant C. F. B. Hodgins, is reported as buried at a point just North-West of Hulluch, South-South-West of La Bassée.
>
> The battlefields are now being carefully and systematically searched and if the officers of the Graves Registration Units in that area are able to locate the grave, it will be registered, and information will be sent to you at the first possible moment.

Although the reply did not provide an exact location of where Charlie was buried, it was a start. But after a year of waiting for any more information to arrive there had been no further news and so it was Charles who next tried to find out what had happened to his son's body. Charles was then visiting America, staying in Florida, and the letter he received from the Imperial War Graves Commission in London, dated 4 June 1920, reads:

> Sir,
>
> In reply to your letter of the 18th ultimo with enclosures, I regret that no further information has yet been received in this office concerning the location of the grave of Second Lieutenant C. F. B. Hodgins, who is reported to be buried in the vicinity of Hulluch, South-South-West of La Bassée. All reports showing the

A line of trenches running northwards from the Vermelles–Hulluch road. From Richard's markings on the map this is possibly the line of trenches Charlie was attacking on the day he died.

names of those officers whose graves have been found in the work of exhumation have not yet been received, and should the name of your son appear in any of these you will at once be informed.

I am, Sir, your obedient servant
[signature]
for Principal Assistant Secretary.

Three months later there was still no further news, and so Charles decided to try again. The letter he received, dated 7 September 1920, reads:

Sir,

With reference to your letter of the 15th ultimo, I am to express regret that no information has yet been received regarding the grave of 2nd Lieutenant C. F. B. Hodgins, who is reported to be buried in the vicinity of Hulluch, South-South-West of La Bassée.

I am to add that up to the present no information has been received of the removal of the body of the above mentioned. Although the work of clearing the battlefields is practically completed, all the reports have not yet been received from the officers engaged in this work, and as soon as it is definitely known in which cemetery the body of your son has been re-interred, you will be informed.

I am, Sir, your obedient servant
[signature]
for Principal Assistant Secretary.

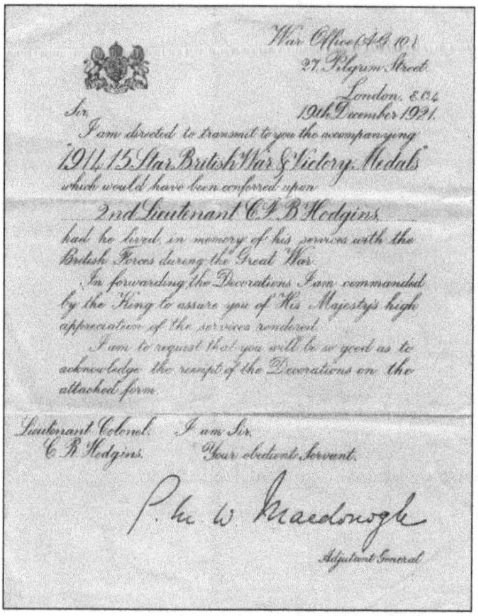

War Office (A.G. 10)
27 Pilgrim Street
London. E.C.4
19th December 1921.

Sir,

I am directed to transmit to you the accompanying
1914-15 Star, British War & Victory Medals
which would have been conferred upon
2nd Lieutenant C.F.B. Hodgins
had he lived, in memory of his services with the British Forces during the Great War.

In forwarding the Decorations I am commanded by the King to assure you of His Majesty's high appreciation of the services rendered.

I am to request that you will be so good as to acknowledge the receipt of the Decorations on the attached form.

Lieutenant Colonel
C.R. Hodgins.

I am, Sir,
Your obedient Servant.

P. h. W. Macdonogh
Adjutant General

The transmittal slip from the Record Office for Charlie's medals, which were issued to his father in 1921.

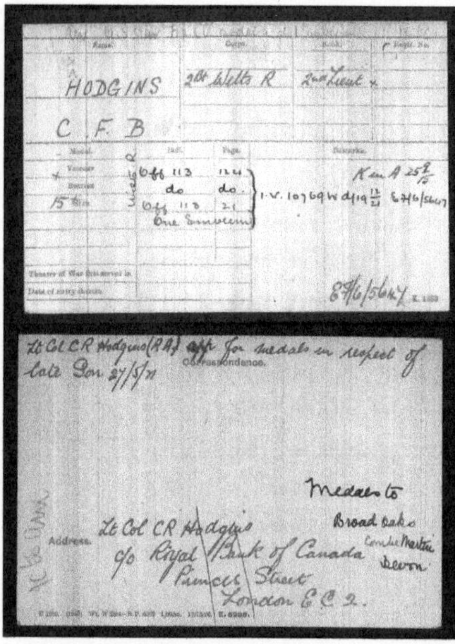

Charlie's Medal Index Card showing his entitlement. (*National Archives*)

With no further news of where his son's body might be, Charles decided to return across the Atlantic. He would go to France and visit the battlefield for himself.

Sailing from New York in October 1920, Charles joined his wife in England. She had sailed ahead of him from Montreal. The couple moved into a Georgian house called Broad Oaks, just outside Combe Martin on the north coast of Devon. From there Charles went to France with Dick to visit the battlefield where Charlie had been killed in the hope they might find where he had been laid to rest. Dick's condition had by then improved sufficiently for him to join the Territorial Army and he was now serving with the Kent Yeomanry, commanding the 386th Field Battery, Royal Artillery, with the rank of major.

Basing themselves in the French town of Béthune, Charles and Dick went in search of Charlie. With the information they had received from the Imperial War Graves Commission and equipped with an old British trench map showing the front line as it had been at the end of the Battle of Loos, they drove along the Vermelles to Hulluch road, stopping at various points. The British line in 1915 had settled to the north-west of Hulluch, still on the western side of the Lens to La Bassée road, in what had been the old German support trenches, just a hundred yards or so from where Charlie had been killed. They found the land still badly scarred and former trench lines still there. Dick marked the map with possible areas where Charlie's body might be. One note written in pencil reads 'Louis Charles Decobort reported finding of 2 bodies (officers) at G.12.d.50.10.' Dick had marked the map with an 'X' at the corresponding spot with another note 'a year ago 1 body removed'. There are other notes written on the map as well. They also visited cemeteries in the vague hope there might be a grave marker somewhere to identify Charlie's body. But although they knew approximately where Charlie might be, nothing could be found.

Charles and Dick had clearly gone to great lengths to find out what they could during their time in France, and more than a century later it is sad to think just how close they had been to where Charlie had fallen. They had been within yards of where Charlie had been killed, but they were never going to find where he was buried because what they could not have known then was that Charlie's body would remain undiscovered for several more years. The trawl of the battlefield was still going on.

Charles and Dick returned to England. Perhaps they found some comfort from visiting the battlefield. But the wait for any further news went on. When the opportunity came, Charles applied for his own war medals and for Charlie's. Both sets of medals are recorded as having been issued to Lieutenant-Colonel C. R. Hodgins (RA) at Broad Oaks, Combe Martin, Devon. The transmittal slip from the Record Office, dated 19 December 1921, which accompanied Charlie's medals, reads:

> Sir,
>
> I am directed to transmit to you the accompanying
>
> **1914–15 Star, British War and Victory Medals**
>
> which would have been conferred upon
>
> **2nd Lieutenant C. F. B. Hodgins**
>
> had he lived, in memory of his services with the British Forces during the Great War.
>
> In forwarding the Decorations I am commanded by the King to assure you of His Majesty's high appreciation of the services rendered. I am to request that you will be so good as to acknowledge the receipt of the Decorations on the attached form.
>
> I am Sir, Your obedient Servant
>
> *G. M. W. Macdonough*
>
> Adjutant General

There followed a personalised bronze memorial plaque, the idea being that some form of individual memorial should be given by the government

Bronze memorial plaque named to Charles Francis Burgoyne Hodgins, with its four-cornered card envelope.

to the next of kin of those who had lost their lives. The plaque was contained in a four-cornered card envelope, which also included an embossed inner envelope containing a condolence slip from Buckingham Palace, which reads:

> I join with my grateful people in sending you this memorial of a brave life given for others in the Great War.

G v R I

Dieu et mon Droit

HE whom this scroll commemorates was numbered among those who, at the call of King and Country, left all that was dear to them, endured hardness, faced danger, and finally passed out of the sight of men by the path of duty and self-sacrifice, giving up their own lives that others might live in freedom.

Let those who come after see to it that his name be not forgotten.

2/Lieut. Charles Francis Burgoyne Hodgins

Wiltshire Regiment

Great War Memorial Scroll to 2nd Lieutenant Charles Francis Burgoyne Hodgins, Wiltshire Regiment. The bronze plaque and scroll were intended to help families in the grieving process.

After that came a cardboard tube containing the Great War Memorial Scroll, which was connected to the award of the bronze plaque. The scroll reads:

> He whom this scroll commemorates was numbered among those who, at the call of King and Country, left all that was dear to them, endured hardness, faced danger, and finally passed out of the sight of men by the path of duty and self-sacrifice, giving up their own lives that others might live in freedom. Let those who come after see to it that his name be not forgotten.
>
> *2/Lieut Charles Francis Burgoyne Hodgins,*
> *Wiltshire Regiment*

In September 1923, Charles and Aimée returned to Canada on the new British ocean liner, SS *Doric.* They eventually settled on Vancouver Island at Colwood, a suburb of Victoria. Charles died in February 1940, aged seventy-seven, Aimée having predeceased him in 1938 at the age of seventy-two. Three of their sons had also settled on Vancouver Island. After leaving the army soon after the end of the First World War, Arthur briefly returned to Canada before moving to America as a mining engineer, where he worked for the Colorado Fuel and Iron Company. He later worked in Hong Kong and Peru before he finally returned to Canada to settle on Vancouver Island at Qualicum Beach. Arthur never married and spent much of his time playing golf, fishing, hunting, and as a member of the Church of England. He died in Saanich, British Columbia, in 1945, aged fifty-one. Patrick also settled on Vancouver Island and died in 1965 at the age of sixty-two. John, meanwhile, having retired from military life in 1922, returned to Canada the following year, moving to Vancouver Island, but in 1928 went to South Africa where he married Dorothy Williams, the youngest daughter of Gardner

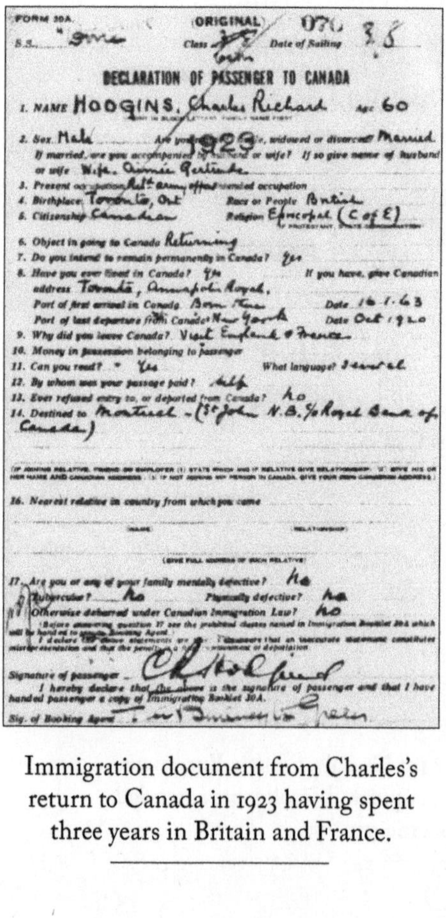
FORM 30A. (ORIGINAL) 070

S.S. "Doric" Class Date of Sailing

DECLARATION OF PASSENGER TO CANADA

1. NAME HODGINS, Charles Richard Age 60
2. Sex Male ... widowed or divorced? Married
   If married, are you accompanied by husband or wife? If so give name of husband or wife Wife, Aimée Gertrude
3. Present occupation Ret^d army officer ... occupation
4. Birthplace Toronto, Ont Race or People British
5. Citizenship Canadian Religion Episcopal (C of E)
6. Object in going to Canada Returning
7. Do you intend to remain permanently in Canada? Yes
8. Have you ever lived in Canada? Yes If you have, give Canadian address Toronto, Annapolis Royal.
   Port of first arrival in Canada Born there Date 16.1.63
   Port of last departure from Canada New York Date Oct 1920
9. Why did you leave Canada? Visit England & France
10. Money in possession belonging to passenger
11. Can you read? Yes What language?
12. By whom was your passage paid? Self
13. Ever refused entry to, or deported from Canada? no
14. Destined to Montreal – (St John N.B. c/o Royal Bank of Canada)

16. Nearest relative in country from which you came

NAME RELATIONSHIP

(GIVE FULL ADDRESS OF SUCH RELATIVE)

17. Are you or any of your family mentally defective? no
    Tubercular? no Physically defective? no
    Otherwise debarred under Canadian Immigration Law? no

Signature of passenger C R Hodgins

I hereby declare that the above is the signature of passenger and that I have handed passenger a copy of Immigration Booklet 30A.

Sig. of Booking Agent

Immigration document from Charles's return to Canada in 1923 having spent three years in Britain and France.

Williams, the Managing Director of De Beers Consolidated, South Africa. The couple had a son and then moved to Canada, settling on Vancouver Island at Qualicum Beach, where John took up golf, fishing, big-game hunting, and attended the Anglican Church. He died in June 1972, aged seventy-five.

When Charles died in 1940 the Hodgins archive passed to his eldest son, Dick, then a major in the Royal Artillery. Dick is pictured wearing a black armband following his father's death.

Dick, meanwhile, did not return to Canada to live. He settled in Kent with his wife, Gladys. They had three children; two daughters and then a son called Charles Wilfred Julius Scoble-Hodgins, who would go on to be granted a voluntary commission in the Royal Artillery, Territorial Army, and would also serve with the Kent Yeomanry. It was in the family blood.

During the Second World War, Dick was called up from the Reserve of Officers as a major and for a while commanded a coastal battery in the south-east of England. But he again suffered ill-health and was posted to a records office in the north-east before eventually being appointed an Assistant Inspector of Armaments at the Ministry of Supply. After the war Dick remained in Kent, where he died in 1973 aged eighty-one. He was the last of the five Hodgins brothers.

* * *

Charlie's remains were finally discovered in 1926, more than ten years after he had been killed. In the Imperial War Graves Commission's Burial Return, dated 27 May 1926, he was initially listed as:

> Unknown British Officer, Wiltshire Regiment, probably 2/Lieut. C. F. B. Hodgins, 2/Wiltshire Regiment, 25.9.15

But 'Unknown British Officer, Wiltshire Regiment, probably' was then crossed out when the remains were identified as Charlie's. The 'Means of Identification' column reads:

Officers Clothing, Boots and Buttons, Leather Jerkin and Putties. Skull badly smashed and all teeth missing. Body disturbed by shell fire. Height about 5' 10".

The burial return also states that there was no cross on the grave at the time his body was discovered and that none of Charlie's personal effects had been forwarded to base.

And so, Charlie's remains had finally been found more than ten years after the Battle of Loos had been fought. When plotting the map reference given on the burial return (44a. G. 12. d. 15. 20.), it places the point at where Charlie's body had been found as just a few yards to the north of the Vermelles–Hulluch Road – now the D39 – and immediately on the eastern side of what was then a track leading northward to the Quarries – now the Route de Vermelles.

When plotting this same point onto the original trench map of September 1915, it can be seen that Charlie had advanced a long way – some 800 yards or more – from where the 2nd Wiltshires had set off late in the morning of the opening day for their advance against the German

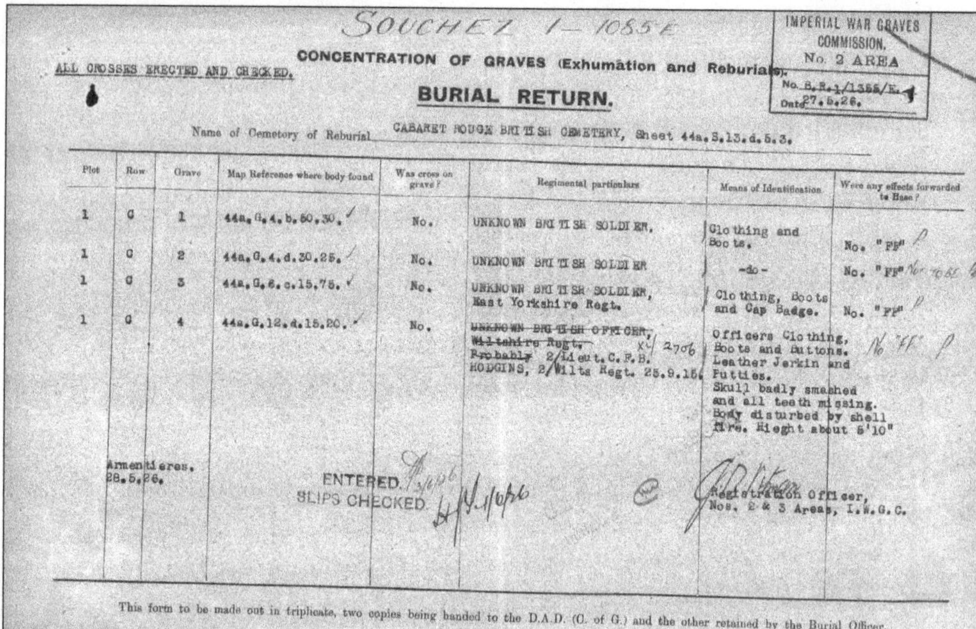

SOUCHEZ 1–1085E

IMPERIAL WAR GRAVES COMMISSION. No. 2 AREA
No. B.R.1/1355/E. Date 27.5.26.

ALL CROSSES ERECTED AND CHECKED.

CONCENTRATION OF GRAVES (Exhumation and Reburials).

BURIAL RETURN.

Name of Cemetery of Reburial CABARET ROUGE BRITISH CEMETERY, Sheet 44a.S.13.d.5.3.

Plot	Row	Grave	Map Reference where body found	Was cross on grave?	Regimental particulars	Means of Identification	Were any effects forwarded to Base?
1	C	1	44a.G.4.b.60.30.	No.	UNKNOWN BRITISH SOLDIER.	Clothing and Boots.	No. "FF"
1	C	2	44a.G.4.d.30.25.	No.	UNKNOWN BRITISH SOLDIER	-do-	No. "FF"
1	C	3	44a.G.6.c.15.75.	No.	UNKNOWN BRITISH SOLDIER, East Yorkshire Regt.	Clothing, Boots and Cap Badge.	No. "FF"
1	C	4	44a.G.12.d.15.20.	No.	UNKNOWN BRITISH OFFICER, Wiltshire Regt. Probably 2/Lieut.C.F.B. HODGINS, 2/Wilts Regt. 25.9.15.	Officers Clothing, Boots and Buttons. Leather Jerkin and Putties. Skull badly smashed and all teeth missing. Body disturbed by shell fire. Hieght about 5'10"	No "FF"

Armentieres, 28.5.26.

ENTERED.
SLIPS CHECKED.

Registration Officer, Nos. 2 & 3 Areas, I.W.G.C.

This form to be made out in triplicate, two copies being handed to the D.A.D. (C. of G.) and the other retained by the Burial Officer.

In 1926, more than ten years after he had been killed, Charlie's remains were found and he was finally laid to rest at the Cabaret Rouge British Cemetery, in Souchez. (*Commonwealth War Graves Commission*)

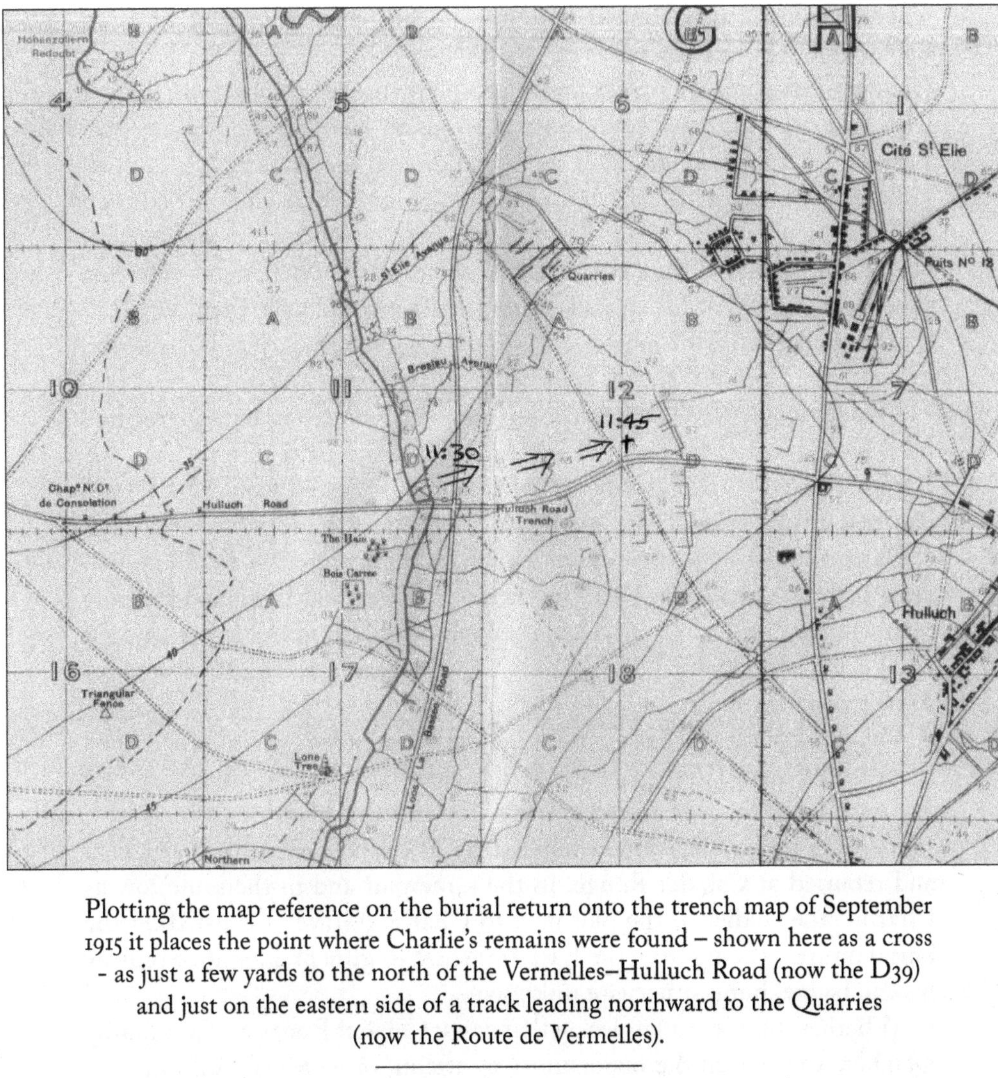

Plotting the map reference on the burial return onto the trench map of September 1915 it places the point where Charlie's remains were found – shown here as a cross - as just a few yards to the north of the Vermelles–Hulluch Road (now the D39) and just on the eastern side of a track leading northward to the Quarries (now the Route de Vermelles).

---

positions. Charlie had been moving parallel to a German communication trench, called the Hulluch Road trench, when he fell, having been caught in what must have been murderous enemy fire. Charlie would have seen the trench he was trying to reach (later to become known as Gun Trench) no more than a hundred yards or so away. It was probably the last thing he saw. The time would have been shortly before midday, the best estimate being somewhere around 11.45 a.m.

It is reasonable to assume that Charlie's company commander, Captain William Geddes, had Charlie buried at, or extremely close to, the spot where he was killed, almost certainly during that first night of 25/26 September 1915, as described by Padre George Trench in his letter to Charlie's father. There would have been many bodies to deal with at that time and it would have been too dangerous to have done anything else. Besides, by the following night the battalion had moved, and Geddes was killed early on the 27th, and so the man who knew where Charlie had been buried was also dead. And, had Charlie been wounded, he would have been taken to the dressing station at the château at Vermelles, and if he had subsequently died of his wounds there then he would have been buried in the Vermelles British Cemetery alongside his colleagues. No, Charlie was buried at, or very near to, the spot where he had been killed.

Geddes would have marked the burial spot in some way, but Charlie had been buried just yards from what then became the British front line. The countless enemy artillery bombardments that followed would have soon churned up the ground, the landscape changing with every bursting shell, and any wooden marker would quickly have disappeared. It would be two years before the Imperial War Graves Commission was born, and the only man who knew where Charlie had been buried was dead. As sad as it might be, it is understandable how Charlie's body had remained undiscovered for so many years.

On 28 May 1926, Charlie's body was exhumed from where it had been found and reburied in the Cabaret Rouge British Cemetery, Souchez – Plot I, Row C, Grave 4. At the same time, the remains of three other British soldiers, all unknown, were exhumed from the same part of the battlefield and reburied at Cabaret Rouge, in the same plot and in the same row as Charlie. The soldier in the plot next to Charlie (Grave 3) is listed on the burial return as being from the East Yorkshire Regiment, identified only by his cap badge, but is otherwise unknown.

Whether there was a service on that day at Cabaret Rouge or if any family members were given the opportunity to attend, or were even informed, is not known. It would be nice to think that someone from Charlie's family was there, but there is nothing in the family archive to suggest there was. Charles seemingly kept all correspondence relating to his son's death, and so it is reasonable to assume that had he have been informed that Charlie's remains had been found and reburied at Cabaret Rouge then there would be a letter in the archive saying just that. There are photographs in the archive showing Charles's visit to France some years before in search of his son, but there are none of Cabaret Rouge. Again, as sad as it may sound, there is nothing in the archive to confirm, or even suggest that the family ever knew.

Looking back across the ground where Charlie and the 2nd Wiltshires had gallantly advanced on that fateful morning of the opening day of the Battle of Loos. The Vermelles–Hulluch road is on the left and in the foreground is the Route de Vermelles.

This story started with a Commonwealth War Graves Commission headstone at the Cabaret Rouge British Cemetery at Souchez in France, marking the burial plot of 2nd Lieutenant C. F B. Hodgins of the Wiltshire Regiment who was killed on 25 September 1915. To understand more about the person buried there, there were so many questions that needed answering. It has taken a while to answer them, but Charlie's story has now been told. For, as it turned out, Charlie Hodgins was one of a lost generation who died for King and Country at Loos.

Bibliography & References

Published Sources

Abbott, P. E., & Tamplin, J. M. A., *British Gallantry Awards*, Enfield: Guinness Superlatives, 1971

Chasseaud, Peter, *Rats Alley: Trench Names of the Western Front, 1914–1918*, Stroud: History Press, 2006

Cherry, Niall, *Most Unfavourable Ground: The Battle of Loos 1915*, Solihull: Helion, 2005

Corrigan, Gordon, *Loos 1915: The Unwanted Battle*, Stroud: Spellmount, 2006

Doyle, Peter, *Loos 1915*, Stroud: History Press, 2012

Garnons Williams, B. H., *A History of Berkhamsted School 1541–1972*, Berkhamsted: Printed for the School, 1980

Gibson, Tom, *The Wiltshire Regiment*, London: Leo Cooper, 1969

Grehan, John, & Mace, Martin, *Despatches From the Front: Western Front 1914–1916*, Barnsley: Pen & Sword, 2013

Haig, Douglas (ed. Gary Sheffield and John Bourne), *War Diaries and Letters 1914–1918*, London: Weidenfeld & Nicolson, 2005

Hammerton, Sir J. A., *A Popular History of the Great War*, Vol II: *Extension of the Struggle: 1915*, London: Fleetway House, 1933

Lewis-Stempel, John, *Six Weeks: The Short and Gallant Life of the British Officer in the First World War*, London: Orion Books, 2011

Lloyd, Nick, *Loos 1915*, Stroud: History Press, 2008

Shepherd, Walter Scott, *The 2nd Battalion Wiltshire Regiment (99th): A Record of Their Fighting in the Great War, 1914–18*, Salisbury: The Rifles Wardrobe & Museum Trust, 2011

The National Archives

WO 95/1659/3	War Diary, 2nd Battalion, Wiltshire Regiment, 1 Aug. 1914–31 Dec. 1915
WO 95/2329/1	War Diary, 2nd Battalion, Wiltshire Regiment, 1 Jan. 1916–30 Apr. 1918
WO 372/5/32862	Medal Index Card, John Halsted Cortis
WO 372/9/224295	Medal Index Card, Charles Francis Burgoyne Hodgins
WO 372/13/14493	Medal Index Card, Edgar Geoffrey Mack
WO 372/24/30286	Mention in Despatches, C. F. B. Hodgins

Index

Key names, units, and establishments included in the book. Ranks shown are the highest mentioned for the individual in the book.